THE NAVAJO MOUNTAIN COMMUNITY

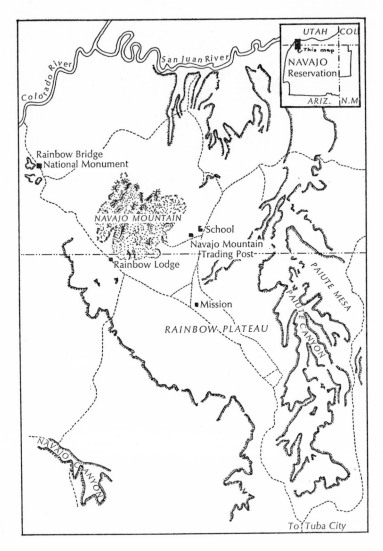

Map of the Navajo Mountain Region. Inset (upper right) shows location of this region within the four-state Navajo Reservation.

THE NAVAJO
MOUNTAIN
COMMUNITY

SOCIAL ORGANIZATION AND KINSHIP TERMINOLOGY

MARY SHEPARDSON
and BLODWEN HAMMOND

UNIVERSITY OF CALIFORNIA PRESS/1970
BERKELEY AND LOS ANGELES

UNIVERSITY OF CALIFORNIA PRESS
BERKELEY AND LOS ANGELES, CALIFORNIA

UNIVERSITY OF CALIFORNIA PRESS, LTD.
LONDON, ENGLAND

COPYRIGHT © 1970, BY
THE REGENTS OF THE UNIVERSITY OF CALIFORNIA

SBN 520–01570–3

LIBRARY OF CONGRESS CATALOG CARD NUMBER: 70–97233
PRINTED IN THE UNITED STATES OF AMERICA

ACKNOWLEDGMENTS

The field work for this study was financed in part by a number of organizations: a postdoctoral fellowship from the National Science Foundation under the auspices of the University of California; a grant from the Department of Anthropology of the University of Chicago; research grants from the National Institute of Mental Health under the auspices of the University of Chicago; the Phillips Fund of the American Philosophical Society.

The authors are particularly grateful to the missionaries, Glen and Louise Hurd, for their hospitality, many kindnesses, and friendly support. Among Navajo Mountain and Inscription House residents to whom we are indebted are Mr. and Mrs. Stokes Carson, Madeline Cameron, Mr. and Mrs. Myles Headrick, traders; Mr. and Mrs. Everett Flint, missionaries; and Lisbeth Eubank, long-time teacher.

We would like to thank the personnel of the Navajo Land Claims Division, David Brugge, Lee Correll, David de Harport, and Editha L. Watson for invaluable assistance.

Among the anthropologists who were helpful were David Aberle, Harry Hoijer, Jerrold E. Levy, Alexander J. Lindsay, Jr., and Morris Opler. Don Lyngholm and Robert Young of the Bureau of Indian Affairs aided with range-management and linguistic information. Navajo informants on kin terminology from other parts of the Reservation included Mae Angel, Maggie Platero, Mary Sells, Irene and Greyeyes Stewart, and John D. Wallace.

Our interpreters were Allen Bedoni, Victoria Bedoni, Morris Burns, Gladys Carr, Cecil Danziłikai, Gilmore Greymountain, Katherine Greymountain, Tom Greymountain, Catherine Nelson, Lucy Nelson, Isabel Onesalt, Josephine Smallcanyon, Teddy Smallcanyon, and Judy Holgate Taylor.

We would like to express our thanks to the many other people, not mentioned by name, who were generous with their time and help toward our understanding of the people and lifeways of the Navajo Mountain community.

Words cannot express our obligation to Malcolm Carr Collier for her outstanding generosity and professional cooperation. David M. Schneider and Fred Eggan merit our special gratitude for indispensable encouragement and advice.

CONTENTS

TABLES

CHARTS

APPENDIX: TABLES AND CHARTS

Table

Chart

INTRODUCTION

The Problem and Methods

The scenic area of Navajo Mountain was selected for study for a number of reasons besides its stunning beauty. Our preliminary assumption was that because of isolation, since it could be reached only by traveling a long distance on a very poor, dead-end road, this little community would retain more of the traditional way of life than could be found in other districts of the Navajo Reservation. It is a bounded region, with natural barriers of canyons, mesas, mountain and rivers. The recency of settlement by Navajos (within little more than a hundred years) would enable us to trace patterns of land preemption and historical interaction with other peoples and places. Finally it was here, in 1938, that Malcolm Carr Collier had made one of the few detailed studies of Navajo social organization to be found in the anthropological literature. Her specific data could be used for comparison with the specific data we would accumulate for a study of persistence and change after a span of twenty-

five years. All of these reasons for selecting Navajo Mountain as our unit of study proved to be justified.

Our original field work involved detailed investigation
of particular problems: a comparative political study with
Shiprock, New Mexico, as the other end of the isolation-
acculturation continuum; an inquiry into informal methods
of handling disputes; and the social effects of witchcraft beliefs and practices. The traditional bent of the community
led us quite naturally to an intensive investigation of social
structure for comparison with Malcolm Collier's data, and
for comparison also with other Navajo communities, particularly because almost the whole of traditional Navajo
social interaction is structured along kinship lines. Even
today in modernized Navajo society, kinship continues to
be the most important principle of organization.

For convenience we have divided the book into three
parts, with an introduction and a conclusion. The first part
describes the little community, its geography and climate,
its people, and demographic and other changes over a
twenty-five year period, and provides a detailed history.
The second part analyzes Navajo Mountain social organization, the types of membership groups, residence patterns,
social roles, and modes of cooperation. A third part deals
with Navajo kin terminology and its relationship to actual
behavior within the kinship-role system.

During the time of our field work, we were attentive to
problems of change. Detailed comparison with Malcolm
Collier's data on Rainbow Plateau (one section of the Navajo Mountain community) has been embodied in an article
entitled "Change and Persistence in an Isolated Navajo
Community" (Shepardson and Hammond 1964). Since this
book is focused on the greater Navajo Mountain community as a whole, and since nothing in our present analysis con-
troverts the earlier study, we have been content with a very

brief summary of only a few of the main points in the section on Persistence and Pressure for Change.

For the purposes of this study we shall consider the Navajo Mountain community as a "society," that is, a group of people whose interaction forms a social system, or "a group of human beings sharing a self-sufficient system of action which is capable of existing longer than the life span of an individual, the group being recruited at least in part by the sexual reproduction of the members" (Aberle *et al.* 1950: 101). In answer to the question of whether or not a community that is part of a tribe, and that tribe organized as a "domestic dependent nation," embedded in a national state, which in turn participates in a world community, can be called a "society," we propose to quote ourselves:

> Aberle, *et al.* (1950) and M. Levy, Jr. (1952:121) emphasize that their defined *society* is an ideal type and there is bound to be some strain for goodness of fit between abstract model and empirical system. We might do well to examine definitions of *community* before we type our concrete membership unit. Murdock defines a *community* as the 'maximal group of persons who reside together in face-to-face association . . . the most typical social group to support a total culture (1949:79, 84). Redfield lists four features of a *little community*: distinctiveness; homogeneity; smallness (so small that either it itself is the unit of personal observation or else . . . in some part . . . fully representative of the whole); self-sufficiency (providing for all or most of the activities and needs of the people in it) (1955:4). Either of these definitions might apply to [Navajo Mountain]. Firth distinguishes between the integral small community, which is self-contained, and the sectional small community which is structurally part of a wider entity (1954:49). In the recent past [Navajo Mountain] has been able to exist as an integral small

community and could conceivably so exist again if the alien structures in which it now participates were withdrawn (1964:1030).

Throughout the writing of this book we have tried to avoid the pitfall of presenting a static analysis of social structure by considering also "process," recently become so popular as to be almost a catchword. An obvious area of social process is social change, but there is more to social process than this. There are, of course, the large processes that qualify types of social action such as cooperation, competition, and conflict, but classification in these terms is extremely broad and therefore of limited usefulness for our purpose. Any active verb referring to man's behavior in society on which an "-ing" can be tacked is social process. Thus "interacting," "communicating," "sharing," "educating," "warring," "loving," and so on and on and on. It seemed to us, therefore, that the best way to capture the most meaningful kinds of processes was to fall back upon the method of structural-functional analysis, to depict the members of the little community, how they group and regroup, meeting, or failing to meet, their role expectations, and how within this social structure they interact to fulfill the fundamental requisites of a viable society.

Again, since we are primarily concerned with analysis, we have quoted freely the actual words of the people who live in this little community so that the reader will have some sense and some flavor of real life lived by real people in a real place.

FIELD METHODS

Methods of obtaining our data included three trips of two months each to Navajo Mountain in 1960, 1961 and 1962 respectively. A two-weeks' stay in the adjacent community of Inscription House in 1963 and a two-months'

stay in Oljeto in 1966 added more relevant facts from two
communities having historical connections with Navajo
Mountain. We decided, however, arbitrarily to freeze our
population, residence, and economic data as of 1961. That
part of the historical, genealogical, and dispute-handling
material that concerned the 1961 population, although collected at a later date, has been incorporated. Subsequent
work served to confirm our earlier generalizations.

We obtained interviews with as many residents of the
community, of both sexes and ages, as possible. As participant observers we attended curing rites, Chapter meetings,
and Mission services. We helped bathe the children on the
first day of school. We studied the Bible in Navajo along
with the congregation. We observed the distribution of
surplus commodities by Navajo Tribal welfare officials, the
monthly medical and dental clinics, sheep dustings, and a
Mormon Fun Day. We attended movies at the Mission and
a Christian Camp meeting, went through the steps of an
Enemy Way ceremony, and were present at a Night Chant
at Tuba City, held to ordain an old Singer who had recently
married into the Navajo Mountain community. At a girl's
puberty rite (Kinaaldá) we helped to mix and eat the cake.
We spent a weekend in Navajo Canyon with a Navajo family, gave innumerable rides to and from the trading post
and the school, and finally were present at the community
dinner and meeting for the Indian Commissioner, Philleo
Nash, and top officials of the Indian Agency from Window
Rock and Tuba City.

We have consulted documents made available to us by
the Navajo Land Claims Division and the Resources Divi-
sion of the Navajo Tribal Council; case records from the
Navajo Tribal Courts; census records and maps from the
Branch of Education; grazing records from the Branch of
Resources and case records from the Branch of Law and
Order of the Bureau of Indian Affairs; employment records

of the Museum of Northern Arizona; statistics from the welfare departments of the States of Arizona and Utah; documents and case records from the federal district courts of Arizona, Utah, and New Mexico; historical documents from the files of Indian Commissioners and Navajo Agents in the National Archives; and maps, genealogies, and field notes collected in 1938 by Malcolm Carr Collier. We have searched the anthropological literature for references by travelers, traders, and archeologists to the people and land of Navajo Mountain.

We interviewed 138 individuals, of whom 103 were Navajos and 35 non-Indians. We also met and interacted with scores of Navajos, men, women, and children whom we did not formally interview during our residence in the community. Among our informants were 48 Navajo men and 55 Navajo women; 28 non-Indian men and 7 non-Indian women. Most of the Navajos were sheepherders and small farmers; the numbers of our informants, by specialized occupations, are listed in the following table:

Table 1.—*Informants*, by *Specialized Occupations*

Navajos

OCCUPATION	MEN	WOMEN
Delegate	1	0
Former delegate	2	0
Chapter officer	4	0
Judge	1	0
Navajo Tribal employee	2	1
Trading-post employee	1	0
Medicine man	4	0
Hand trembler	2	2
Grazing-committee head	1	0
Arizona State Employment Service employee	1	0

Bureau of Indian Affairs employee 1   1
School employee 1   5
U.S. Public Health Service employee 2   1
Navajo Ordinance employee 2   o
Radio broadcaster 1   o

Non-Navajos

Anthropologist 8   1
Bureau of Indian Affairs employee 9   o
Missionary 2   2
Teacher . . . . o   1
Lawyer 1   o
Navajo Tribal employee 1   o
    (Police Captain)
Trader 6   3
Trading-post employee 1   o

This work is a complete collaboration between the two authors, not only in the collection of data in the field but in planning the research, in the analysis, and in the writing. It would be impossible at this point to identify the separate parts by authorship, and all of the final formulations have been agreed upon by both of us. The virtues, therefore, as well as the faults, are a shared responsibility.

We have decided to abandon the use of "h" in the spelling of *Navaho* in favor of the "j" or *Navajo*. The use of "h" was adopted by anthropologists to show that the word was not of Spanish orgin. However, since the Tribal Council uses *Navajo* to describe the People, we prefer to follow their usage. The spelling of Navajo words follows the Young-Morgan orthography.

PART ONE

THE NAVAJO MOUNTAIN COMMUNITY

Description

Naatsis'aan, sacred mountain of the Navajo people, is a dome-shaped mass which rises to an altitude of 10,416 feet. Seen from afar it stands out as a landmark, a blue shadow against a blue sky, majestic in its aloneness as it rises some 5,000 feet above the plateau at its base. The mountain, known in English as Navajo Mountain, is in the far northwest corner of the Navajo Reservation. It lies mostly in Utah with only a small sector of the southern part extending over into Arizona.

There is no public transportation into the community,

which is known by the same name; to reach it, one must go by private conveyance. A traveler bound for Navajo Mountain (in the early 1960's) leaves the small community of Inscription House knowing that some 35 miles further on the road will reach a dead-end at each of the two trading posts serving the area. He will find that the road ahead is tortuous. At times it follows a saddle-back ridge where he can look off in either direction for vast distances. At other times the road snakes down through narrow openings between rocky cliffs that tower hundreds of feet above; at still another section he will course across solid rock, losing sight of anything that resembles a road.

If the traveler is making the trip soon after a rain has packed solidly the many deep sand pockets in the road, he will wonder why people advised him to carry water for himself and his car and to be prepared to be stuck for a matter of hours, or perhaps overnight. Heavy winter snows sometimes close the road to all traffic for days at a time. If the roads are dry and the sand shifting, the traveler will have to dig his car out of more than one sand trap. He may have to cut boughs of juniper trees to lay in a rip-rap pattern, and overlapping of the boughs, for many feet in advance of his car in order to give the wheels better purchase.

Just as the anxiety-ridden stranger is beginning to despair of ever reaching his destination, he finds himself coming out into a relatively flat plateau where he can drive along the washboarded gravel road at the dizzying speed of 25 or 30 miles per hour.

Now and then a wagon trail branches off from the main road. It may disappear around a rocky hill, or the sharp-eyed observer may notice that it leads to a cluster of structures easy to overlook because the low earth-covered hogans and the brush lean-to's, or shelters, which make up the typical Navajo dwelling place blend almost perfectly into the countryside.

At the base of the mountain, three modern, nontraditional community centers are disposed triangle-wise. At the "Y" formed where the main road forks, leading to the two trading posts, is the Navajo Mountain Mission, a compound made up of a little hogan church, an all-purpose building, and residences for the small Mission staff.

One center, to the northeast in Cottonwood Canyon, includes the stone building of the Navajo Mountain Trading Post and the residence of the traders. A few hundred yards to the east in the same canyon, the Navajo Tribal Council has built a Chapter House for the use of the local political arm of the Tribal government. Still further east is the Indian Bureau School for beginners and first-grade students. Built in 1936, it follows the hogan-type of structure which was preferred by the "native-oriented" John Collier administration.

On the southwest side of Navajo Mountain is the complex called Rainbow Lodge, a series of small wooden buildings which includes a store, a trader's residence, and several cabins originally built for tourists but used by the trader for storage.

The community of Navajo Mountain is physically delimited by the San Juan River to the north, the Colorado River to the west, Navajo Canyon to the south, and Nakai Canyon to the east. The some 600 people of this sheep-herding and subsistence-farming community live in residence groups scattered around the 440,000 acres (about 688 square miles) that make up the total area. Steep canyons form natural barriers which tend to divide the community into four sections, Rainbow Plateau, the northern and eastern sides of the mountain, Paiute Mesa, and Navajo Canyon. To the north and the west, the land drops off rapidly into the barren red rocks of the river borders. The area is rich in scenery, but only slightly more than half of the total surface is grazing land. Scrubby juniper and piñon trees, sagebrush, and other browse stud most of the area; conifers and aspen grow at a higher level on the mountain.

A report on the geography, soil, climate, and vegetation of the Navajo Reservation was made by Paul Phillips of the Navajo Agency in 1941 (Young, 1961:358–366). There are three distinct climate zones—cold humid, steppe, and desert—to be found in the Reservation, all of which are present in the Navajo Mountain area.

The humid area of the mountain top has a rainfall which averages 16 to 27 inches a year. Winter snowfall accounts for 41 per cent of the total precipitation. Temperatures here average annually from 43 to 50 degrees, with a range from 4 to 15 in winter and from 70 to 80 in summer. The growing season averages 95 days.

The steppe zone includes Paiute Mesa and Rainbow Plateau, with an average rainfall of 12 to 16 inches annually and snow amounting to one-fourth of the total precipitation. Temperatures there average annually 45 to 50 degrees, the minimum in winter ranging from 10 to 25 and the maximum in summer from 80 to 88. In this zone the growing season is approximately 147 days per year.

The desert area includes the canyon bottoms, which descend 1,500 feet below the plateau, and the barren river borders. Here the rainfall averages from 7 to 11 inches annually. Snowfall accounts for a comparatively small portion of the total moisture supply. The average annual temperature is from 50 to 60 degrees, with a maximum in summer of 110 and a minimum in winter of 11 to 30. The growing season averages 173 days per year.

Because of excessive drainage, it is impossible to develop sufficient water by drilling wells. The best water is obtained from springs found at the base of the mountain. Mesa and plateau tops are suitable for grazing and small dry farming, and there is enough permanent water in the canyons to permit small-scale garden-plot irrigation.

Communications with the outside world are scanty. Twenty miles of poor dirt road south of Inscription House lead to a paved highway near the natural stone formation called Elephant Feet. Five miles beyond is the settlement, Tonalea. Navajo Mountain is 85 miles from the Subagency of the Bureau of Indian Affairs at Tuba City, 240 miles from Tribal headquarters at Window Rock, 95 miles from Kayenta, where Grazing Headquarters is located, and 175 miles from Flagstaff, the nearest point served by railroad.

Mail is delivered three times a week to Tonalea and is brought on to Navajo Mountain and left at one or the other of the trading posts by whichever local resident chances to be passing by and finds it convenient to perform this friendly act. There is erratic telephone service to one trading post and to the school.

The best contact for Navajos with the outside world is a battery-powered radio, considered a necessity in almost every hogan group. A Navajo hour is broadcast from Flagstaff daily, and the Navajo Tribal Council sponsors a weekly program from Gallup. Other radio stations on the periphery of the Reservation also broadcast some programs in Navajo.

Pick-ups, wagons, and saddle horses are utilized for frequent trips to a trading post, and for infrequent trips outside. One trader owns a small airplane, and a flat area has been cleared for use as a landing field.

Visitors to Navajo Mountain include the "dudes" who go on foot or on horseback to Rainbow Bridge; archeologists for the Glen Canyon Archeological Survey; Tribal and government employees who report at Chapter meetings, and who supervise activities such as sheep-dusting and well-digging; a dozen or so former residents who sometimes return on weekends or on vacations to visit relatives; and friends and kinsmen who come to the area to participate in the Enemy Way ceremonies (popularly known as "Squaw Dances") which are given each summer. Finally, the 1960, 1961, and 1962 visitors included the authors of this monograph.

The population of the community numbers 581 individuals, that is, 116 men, 126 women, and 339 children (154 boys, 185 girls) under the age of eighteen. This count includes all Indians, Navajo and Paiute, maintaining residence at Navajo Mountain during 1960 and 1961. Paiute residents number 18—5 men, 5 women, and 8 children. Population density of the area is 0.84 persons per square mile as compared to 1.6 for the Western Navajo region and 3.2 for the Reservation as a whole.

Navajo men and boys wear typical western ranch-hand clothing, that is, Levis, colored shirts or T-shirts, cowboy boots or heavy work shoes, and "5-gallon" hats. Women and girls wear long, full satin skirts topped by plush blouses, usually in vivid colors, and flat-heeled shoes. The majority of young men and boys have their hair close-cropped, but most of the older men, with a sprinkling of the younger men, continue to wear their hair long, tied in a knot behind their heads. Moccasins are frequently seen on both men and women.

The Navajo dwelling, or hogan, is most commonly a one-room, roughly circular building constructed of rough-hewn logs laid horizontally. The one doorway faces east; windows are lacking, but light and air are admitted through a smoke hole in the center of the roof. Cribbed logs form the hemispherical roof, and both top and sides are covered with a thick layer of mud, resulting in a structure which is cool in summer and warm in winter.

Not uncommon at Navajo Mountain is the old-style forked-stick conical hogan that is rapidly disappearing in other parts of the Reservation. Welfare houses, which are single-walled frame structures, are also seen, as are tents and stone houses. The last-mentioned are not a recent innovation since there is a stone house that was built by Mr. Endischee before 1910. However, a Navajo stonemason, sent by the Tribal Council to train local men in the building of the Chapter House, inspired many residents to plan stone houses for their own occupancy. Of at least ten which had been started, only two had been brought to completion 24 months later.

A hogan may vary in diameter from 15 to 25 feet. Within this one room the typical Navajo Mountain family eats together, sleeps on sheepskins laid on the dirt floor, and stores most of their personal possessions and household effects. Chairs, tables, and chests of drawers are only rarely part of the furnishings. Tin trunks, or cardboard boxes, are used to contain clothing and bedding.

A stew made of mutton, potatoes, and onions is the standard main dish, eaten three times a day. Fry-bread and coffee round out the typical meal. At harvest time fresh corn, melons, and "kneel-down bread" offer variety to the diet. The ribs of a freshly killed lamb are broiled over open coals as a change from the usual boiled meat.

No household at Navajo Mountain has piped-in water, nor does any have its own well. Barrels of water for drinking and household use are hauled from developed springs or community-owned shallow wells frequently located several miles away. Electricity is not available; Coleman lanterns, or candles, provide the necessary light when night falls. During cold weather, heat is furnished by the wood-burning cook stove, which is frequently a converted oil drum. No kind of refrigeration is used.

Neither do any households at Navajo Mountain boast of modern toilet facilities. An enamel basin is used by all members of the family for washing hands and face and for an occasional sponge bath. Males, and less frequently females, use a sweat bath, a small conical structure covered with earth, which is heated by placing hot stones within the narrow confines. Defecation and urination take place outdoors, behind any handy shrub or hillock affording a measure of privacy, a practice which, in the considered opinion of some health officials, is more sanitary in a dry climate than the "Chic Sale" found so often in rural settings.

Navajo Mountain settlement follows the traditional pattern of widely scattered residence groups, each such group occupying a camp made up of a hogan, or a cluster of hogans, and assorted outbuildings. There are 46 such camps, each having 1 to 8 hogans for a total of 112 households. Each hogan typically houses a single nuclear, or biological, family, or remnants of such, with from 1 to 18 persons dwelling in each hogan. Some camps may be no more than half a mile from the nearest neighboring residence group, whereas others may be separated by several miles.

Our census counts a residence group only once, but each of these families has at least a winter and a summer dwelling place, and some extended families have as many as six. A family, or parts of families, will move from campsite to campsite depending on grazing needs. There is also in reality frequent shifting of households within camps, that is, some married sons and married daughters move back and forth between their own and their spouse's extended family as they see fit or as circumstances demand. Widows and widowers may live with different married children in turn.

There are 21 camps on Rainbow Plateau, 13 north and east of the mountain, 9 on Paiute Mesa, and 3 in the part of Navajo Canyon that is included in the Navajo Mountain census area. Many of these families also have farming plots and summer hogans in Paiute Canyon. Table A of the appendix shows the number of camps, the number of persons in each camp, the number of households in each camp, and the number of persons in each household as of 1961. Table B of the appendix gives the composition of each camp.

The non-Indian community comprises two trading couples, a trading-post employee, a teacher who has been in Navajo Mountain for more than 20 years, and two missionary couples, one of which left before the completion of our field work. This small population is at times augmented by a wrangler, a houseworker, and a trader's son.

Relationships between resident whites and Navajos are more harmonious than those that obtain among the white people themselves. Traders are competing for a far-from-wealthy clientele. The long-time residents tend to resent newcomers. The teacher, a "John Collier traditionalist," as a sophisticated Navajo from outside described her, deplores the cultural disruption that she fears may come in the wake of missionary activity. Each non-Navajo gives valuable aid to the Indians far beyond the call of duty, provides services such as transportation and emergency flights to the hospital in Tuba City, makes telephone calls, writes letters, and at the Mission, freely gives meals and lodging to many Navajo travelers. The wife of one of the traders was born and brought up on the Reservation, speaks fluent Navajo, and serves as interpreter in many situations. The teacher, who calls herself "Old Lady Navajo Mountain," or "Grandmother," is a licensed midwife. She has delivered, named, and taught most of the younger generation, and has won the affection of the whole community of Indians.

Persistence and Pressure for Change

The community in general is "Old Navajo." Forked-stick hogans, wagons, Navajo style exclusively in women's dress,

long hair for at least half the men, inability of the majority of the adult population to speak English and to read
and write are the outward signs of traditionalism. Customs
that are tending to disappear in less isolated parts of the
Reservation, such as mother-in-law avoidance, witchcraft
accusations, arranged marriages, sororal polygyny, fear of
the dead, and belief in werewolves or "skinwalkers" flourish
at Navajo Mountain. Both Navajo ceremonies and the
Tuba City hospital are relied upon for the cure of illness.

Navajo practices and beliefs that constitute the traditional religious system continue to be all-pervasive in the
lives of the residents of Navajo Mountain. All the people
share, either wholly or to a large extent, beliefs in the causes
of disease and death, in witchcraft, and in the efficacy of
Navajo ceremonials in dispelling illness, in countering
witchcraft, in securing good crops and plentiful rainfall,
and in ensuring survival and well-being. Every ceremony
is conducted for the purpose of attracting good or of ex-
orcising evil.

Navajo Mountain does not hold the big ceremonies such
as Night Way and Mountain Top Way, of which the
Yeibichai and the Fire Dance respectively are the public
exhibitions. The largest Sing given here is Enemy Way
(Squaw Dance) which is held three or four times each
year. Many of the smaller Chants such as Navajo Wind Way,
Shooting Way, Life Way, Evil Way and Blessing Way are
frequently conducted. The Enemy Way ceremonies are the
big social events of the community, combining as they do
features of a curing ceremony, beneficial to all who attend; a convivial gathering which will draw relatives and
friends from as far away as Shonto, Kayenta, or Tuba City;
a drinking bout for some; and a courting party for others.
Some two or three hundred people customarily attend.

In 1962 a Rain Chant was held at Navajo Mountain,
following a prolonged drought. Ritual objects were car-

ried for deposit on the top of the mountain, with most of the leading "medicine men" of the region cooperating. This particular Chant is seldom heard now at Navajo Mountain; a Singer explained:

> There used to be rain-makers long ago. There were four men who were very good; when they were alive there was plenty of rain, but then they died. No more rain. Now, there is no one who knows the proper way.

Other minor rituals, such as treating a horse after he has thrown a rider—in order to avoid repetition of the mishap—are conducted on the spot by any individual who knows the rites.

Christianity has been introduced into Navajo Mountain. Since 1946, Episcopalians from Saint Christopher's Mission to the Navajo, with headquarters at Bluff, Utah, have carried on missionary activity in the community. In the summer of 1962, the Vicar from Saint Christopher's made the 500-mile round trip once a month to hold mass in the hogan of a communicant.

In 1955, the Christian and Missionary Alliance established a permanent mission on the plateau. Members of the congregation, about 25 Navajo Christians, are learning to read the Bible and sing hymns in the Navajo language. In addition to church and Sunday-school services the Mission compound and its facilities are open to all of the residents of Navajo Mountain. Many Indians who rarely if ever attend sacred services will call upon the missionaries in time of emergency, asking them to furnish transportation, to bury the dead, to help repair a broken down car, or to extend overnight hospitality. Women enjoy the weekly sewing sessions. Holiday meals, as well as the occasional movie or other entertainment program, are well attended by men, women, and children.

The Church of the Latter Day Saints stations Elders

(missionaries) on the Reservation who visit hogans to talk to the Navajos. In the summer of 1962, a Mormon team of two young men set up headquarters in a trailer parked at one of the trading posts. However, since their church had no plan at that time to construct a permanent installation or offer services to the residents other than purely religious ones, the local delegate to the Tribal Council obtained a ruling from the Tribe that prohibited them from remaining.

The Native American Church, more commonly known as "Peyotism," is not active at Navajo Mountain. This pan-Indian cult with its Christian elements spread to the Navajo Reservation from the Utes. It was outlawed, as of the early 1960's, by the Navajo Tribal Council and has erupted as a political issue in some parts of the Reservation, but has had no impact so far on the people of Navajo Mountain.

In the area of political activity, of decision-making, and of dealing with the surrounding society, Navajo Mountain shows both persistence and change. Decisions in the traditional system were made within and among the kin groups on the basis of consensus of the adult members. Leaders were accorded temporary authority; a warrior during a raid, a hunt leader during the hunt, a Singer during a Chant, and a headman or influential person would be consulted on occasion. This informal "political" system, except for acts of warfare, still persists in the community. However, there are in addition three "modern" authority systems that make rules and administer services to Navajo Mountain. They are the Navajo Tribal Council, the Federal government, and the States of Arizona and Utah. (This network of interlocking political groups will be explored in more detail in the section on Decision-making and Dealing with the Surrounding Society.)

The Navajo Tribal Council is a body of elected councilmen (delegates) each representing an election precinct, and a chairman and vice-chairman who run for office in all precincts of the Reservation. Navajo Mountain chooses a councilman every 4 years. The local arm of modern government is the Chapter. Every Indian resident of Navajo Mountain belongs to and participates in Chapter activities. The president, vice-president, and secretary and the grazing-committee chairman are the local political officials.

The federal government makes decisions and provides services for the community through the Bureau of Indian Affairs and the United States Public Health Service. The Tuba City subagency, a division of the Navajo Agency, deals directly with Navajo Mountain. It administers the 2-year boarding school of the Branch of Education, B.I.A., advises and gives aid on grazing matters and water development, and, at least until 1963 when major improvements were made, performed the function of what can laughingly be called "maintaining" the Navajo Mountain road. The United States Public Health Service, through its Tuba City and Kayenta hospitals, provides free medical and dental care.

The states of Arizona and Utah have no jurisdiction over the Reservation as such. Since 1950 the states have shared with the federal government the expense of welfare for the aged, dependent children, and the blind. They rule on the eligibility of state residents to vote in general elections. As of 1961 and 1962, no resident of Navajo Mountain was registered to vote in these elections, whether because of illiteracy, lack of interest, or the 60-mile distance to the polls at Tonalea.

Thus it can be seen from this brief sketch that even the most isolated Navajo community, although clinging to its old traditions, is being inescapably drawn into modern political life.

There are at least four systems of "law" or methods of

handling disputes, in addition to self-help, concurrently operating in Navajo Mountain. All except one, the informal traditional method of meetings between kin groups, or members of kin groups, are modern and "intrusive." The grazing committees, the transitional system of the Navajo Tribal Courts, and finally the Federal legal system are derived from the outside.

Navajo Mountain people still resort to meetings among kin which are called by the interested parties to mediate disputes that have arisen within the community. Traditionally the mediator is a local headman, a wise Singer, or the respected leader of a large and important extended family or matrilineage. Today the mediator is often the Chapter president or the councilman who has been asked to serve in this role. Sometimes the case is aired at a Chapter meeting before the assembled community. These methods save the litigants long and costly trips to the Navajo Court at Tuba City.

The courts of the Navajo tribe have jurisdiction over misdemeanors and domestic issues. The Tuba City court has a resident judge, a courthouse and a jail, a police captain, and a police force.

The federal district courts in Arizona and Utah (New Mexico for the eastern side) handle felonies. (These systems of "law and order" will be discussed in more detail and analyzed under Social Control.)

Acculturation pressures are less significant in Navajo Mountain than in most of the other areas of the Reservation. Although the missionaries stationed there deplore Navajo superstition as "devil worship" and aim to save souls by the creation of true Christians of a fundamentalist bent, their emphasis is on building a Navajo Christian church. As they said, "We are trying to establish an indigenous, not a white man's, church. We want some form of Christian worship to remain when we are gone." The little church is in the form of a hogan; the woman missionary wears Navajo clothes and the missionary, like the Navajo communicants, comes to church in blue jeans.

With the teacher manifesting respect for Navajo Way, and the traders observing a hands-off policy toward Navajo customs, most of the acculturative pressures come from the Bureau of Indian Affairs, the U.S. Public Health Service, and the Navajo Tribal Council. These organizations are advocates of soil conservation, modern farming methods, education, modern medicine, sanitary domestic water, and such non-Navajo customs as representative government, birth certificates, marriage licenses, monogamy, and welfare payments. However, since the enforced stock-reduction program of the 1930's, the policy of the Indian Bureau has been increasingly geared to persuasion rather than coercion, to providing advice and services rather than to imposing an overall political scheme, and the Navajo Tribal Council acts in Navajo Mountain chiefly as a new supplier of services.

The community has successfully ignored rulings that threaten the old order: herds have been allowed to increase to the point where the area is seriously overgrazed, compulsory education is evaded, resolutions against polygyny are circumvented, and modern court decisions are overruled if the community judgment is a variance with them.

Even young people who have been educated in the modern school system appear to enjoy life in the old way. A graduate of a Colorado high school, working outside, wrote us after a vacation spent in Navajo Mountain that she "sure had fun at home, herding the sheep and riding the horses." Another high-school graduate, a young man receiving training as an electronics technician in Cleveland, wrote to his sister expressing his longing to return to Navajo Mountain, "just to be away from all of these people and the noise of the city." Every native of Navajo Mountain who leaves the locality does so with apparent reluctance.

Returning veterans of the armed forces have exerted a strong pressure for change in some communities on the Reservation. Six men living in Navajo Mountain are veterans, two of them nonlocal men who have married into the community. All of these men are married to conservative women, live in an extended-family camp, and have had little influence as a force for change. One man who fought in the South Pacific theatre owns the only passenger-type car in the community and has built a small stone house for himself and his wife and children. No one else in Navajo Mountain has been moved to follow his example. This same veteran is secretary of the local Chapter. In this official capacity he instigated a series of Saturday-night movies which were shown at the Mission. The first several pictures he selected for viewing were all war movies, "Guadalcanal," "Iwo Jima," and the like. A motion picture dramatizing the sinking of the Titanic, "A Night to Remember," was shown as a change of pace, but was judged by the veteran to have been unsatisfactory. "I like true movies, about things that really happened," he said. "I don't like those about something that someone just made up in their heads." The rest of the shows were war movies with a South Pacific setting.

Another veteran, shivering in the cold and without money to buy a warm garment, was offered a World War II field jacket. He gently, but firmly, refused the gift. "I wore a coat like that for four years; I couldn't bear to wear it again."

The most significant changes on Rainbow Plateau, which Malcolm Collier studied in 1938, are population growth, lessening of the isolation, and higher and more secure standards of living. The population of Rainbow Plateau had increased by 1962 from 135 to 323 individuals. Automobiles and radios have reduced the isolation. In 1938 Collier was able to report the number and purpose of all visits by Navajos into the area. In 1962 this would have been difficult because of increased mobility, but perhaps not impossible. Collier estimated per capita income at $108.23; in 1962 we estimated it at $522.00. Even taking into consideration the decline of the purchasing power of the dollar, the per capita income had more than doubled. The family residential pattern showed remarkable stability. We easily identified Collier's nine camps (1966:25), which had increased to 21 through growth and division of the same nine extended families. Matrilocality as a preferred residence pattern for married couples was reinforced. The number of couples residing matrilocally increased from 56% to 63%; patrilocal residence decreased from 33% to 24%; neolocal residence increased from 11% to 13%.

It appears that the structure of action of the self-sufficient society is largely intact. Even so, the little community is increasingly subject to stress and strain. The sharp increase in population, together with overutilization of all available land, endangers the pastoral base. Young couples find it more and more difficult to set up households because of economic problems and rules of clan exogamy that limit the number of eligible spouses in this much intermarried community. In 1961, 30 men and 22 women in Navajo Mountain had never been married—a disproportionately large number of celibates in a society given to early marriage.

Ever-increasing dependence on subsidization by the Tribe and the federal government to augment income from traditional sources makes the value of modern educated leadership apparent to all. The desire to follow the ways of the People is losing ground in face of the need for cash to buy batteries for the radio, gasoline for the pick-up, soft drinks, coffee, and candy bars, which young and old have come to enjoy. In order to attain and maintain the present standard of living, a sizable number of the young adult

generation have had to leave their beloved homes and kinfolk to seek wage work in the alien, lonely, and confusing
outer world.

History of the Community

The first residents of the Navajo Mountian area were the
Ancient Ones or "Anasazi," as the Navajos call them. They
left hundreds of ruins to dot the plateaus, mesa tops, and
canyons. Open masonry sites, pueblos, cliff dwellings,
granaries, petroglyphs, lithic sites where stone implements
were prepared, irrigation complexes consisting of stone-
lined ditches, cisterns, and terraces, and prehistoric foot-
holds and trails give evidence of their occupation.

Early investigations were carried out by a number of
archeologists and amateur explorers. The most recent survey and exacavations were made for the Glen Canyon Archeological Project, in which the University of Utah directed work north of the San Juan and the Museum of
Northern Arizona that south of the river.

Alexander J. Lindsay, Jr. of the Museum of Northern
Arizona furnished the data on which the following summary is based:

In the area bounded by Navajo Canyon on the west,
Paiute Farms on the east, the San Juan River on the north,
and the Arizona-Utah State line on the south, over 1,000
sites were noted. An estimated 100 more sites lie on Rainbow Plateau below the Arizona line. Artifacts of a chopper-
core-scraper complex were found in Pleistocene gravels
along the Colorado and San Juan Rivers. The earliest
period represented (following the Pecos classification) is
Basketmaker II (A.D. 1 to 600), with sites found on the
river and on the highlands. There is little evidence of Bas-

ketmaker III period (A.D. 600 to 800), what there is being found only in Navajo Canyon. Pueblo I (A.D. 800 to 1000) is represented particularly south of the Arizona line, mostly in Navajo Canyon and on upper Paiute Mesa. Pueblo II (A.D. 1000 to 1150) yields sites over the whole area. The most dynamic period, Pueblo II to III (A.D. 1100 to 1250), saw the spread of the Kayenta culture across the river. This was a time of rapid expansion of the Anasazi lifeway. Evidence of trade goods indicates contact with Mesa Verde. This period yields agricultural sites, irrigation complexes, architectural development and incipient communalization. Pueblo III period (A.D. 1150 to 1300) can be divided into three parts. From 1150 to 1200, the Kayenta culture was moving outward. From 1200 to 1250, it showed maximum stability, but from 1250 to 1300 the culture began to withdraw into the nuclear Kayenta area, and the alluvial terraces along the river were abandoned at this time. The large pueblos, Kiet Siel, Betatakin, and Inscription House, were deserted and never reoccupied. The Anasazi era never reopened in the Glen Canyon region after 1300. Between 1300 and 1850, the finds show layers of Hopi sherds, then sterile layers, and finally evidence of Navajo occupation (personal communication, 1965).

In this area, earliest reliable tree-ring dates for Navajo hogans, sweathouses, and corrals taken from wood samples are 1815 and 1829, according to Lee Correll and David Brugge of the Navajo Land Claims Division. Other tree-ring dates range from 1775 to 1895 on samples from abandoned structures (Stokes and Smiley, 1964:15,16).

The region south of Rainbow Plateau was known to the Spaniards at least by the 17th century. The date 1661 was found in Navajo Canyon on ruins, now called Inscription House, by children accompanying the Cummings-Wetherill expedition in 1909 (Gillmor and Wetherill, 1934:162). William Y. Adams quotes a European, Guillaume de l'Isle, as stating that in 1700 "Apaches de Navaio" were living north-west of the Hopi, possibly even beyond the Colorado River (1963:37). Later in the 18th century, the Spanish explorers, Francisco Anastasio Dominguez and Francisco Silvestre Velez de Escalante, of the Order of Friars Minor, met only Paiutes when they forded the Colorado River on November 7, 1776, about 40 miles from the present site of Lee's Ferry, at a place now called the Crossing of the Fathers. On the rim of the canyon of Navajo Creek they halted on a mesa.

> Near this mesa we found some ranchos of the Yutas Payuchis, neighbors and friends of the Cosninas. We made great efforts through the Laguna and other companions to induce them to come to where we were, but either because they suspected that we were friends of the Moquinos [Hopi], toward whom they are very hostile, or because they had never seen Spaniards and greatly feared us, we were unable to induce them to come (Bolton, 1950:228).

In 1823, a Mexican military expedition under Jose Antonio Vizcarra pursued Navajos north of the Hopi mesas, where their leader, Juanico, had taken his flocks. According to David Brugge's identification of the sites in the diary, the military detachment went up Narrow Canyon as far as Paiute Canyon. Twice troops attacked "rancherias" of Paiutes, thinking they were Navajos. Although the Paiutes failed to reveal the whereabouts of the Navajos, the Spaniards were convinced that they had this information because goats were in their possession, "which only Navajos have." On Skeleton Mesa, Vizcarra sighted Juanico, his party, and their horses and cattle (Brugge, 1964:237,242,243). Colonel Don Francisco Salazar, with another detachment of troops, marched to the junction of the San Juan and Colorado Rivers. He also attacked a group of Paiutes, "four little ranches of Paiutes hiding in a small canyon in rough terrain," believing them to be Navajos. He followed the trail of sheep and goats, cattle and horses (Brugge, 1964:243).

The documentary evidence, then, indicates that Navajos were herding in the general area of Navajo Mountain and were associating with the San Juan band of Paiutes in the early 1800's.

Jacob Hamblin, the Mormon pioneer, made his first trip south of the Colorado by way of the Crossing of the Fathers to the Hopi mesas in 1858. By the time of his second trip in 1859, he had become friendly with a Navajo "chief" named Spaneshanks who was living south of Navajo Mountain. In the fall of 1860, Hamblin was directed to establish a mission among the Hopis. The second day's journey from the Colorado River, he and his party met four Navajos who warned them that if they continued to the next watering place they would be killed by hostile Navajos. "They invited us to go with them to Spaneshanks' camp, where they assured us we would find protection." Unfortunately Hamblin feared that his animals would not reach Spaneshanks' camp without water. At the waterhole, they fell in with some Navajos who "made a treaty with us that if we would trade them the goods we had brought along, and especially our ammunition, we might go home." Despite this agreement, one of the party, young George Smith, was killed by some of these Indians while hunting for his straying horse. The remaining members of the Mormon party took refuge with the friendly Spaneshanks (Little, 1881:267–271). Maurice Kildare, in an article based on information he received from old traders who knew Spaneshanks in his declining years, said he had been given his nickname because he owned a Spanish horse. Another name for him was Todachene Nez [Tall Bitter Water Clansman]. Until his death, in May, 1910, he lived in the Navajo Canyon–Kaibito area (Kildare, 1965:21, 54).

Narratives of older Navajo Mountain informants refer to

the Fearing Time or *Naahondzond* in the late 1850's when Utes were raiding Navajos. The policy of the United States at that time was to encourage other tribes to prey upon Navajos (Bailey, 1964:120). In the early part of 1863, the United States Army assigned Kit Carson, the famous scout, the task of rounding up all Navajo Indians and removing them to Fort Sumner beyond the Pecos River in New Mexico. Many Navajos living already in the west, and others who joined them because of the disturbances, hid out in the rough country north and west of the Hopi villages and escaped capture (Bartlett, 1954:4). These hostilities stimulated migrations of Navajos from the Carrizo Mountains and Chinle into the more remote sections of Black Mesa, Monument Valley and the canyons near Navajo Mountain.

Hoskinini [Hashké neiní] was the most famous Navajo to take refuge near Navajo Mountain. He, his wife, his wife's two sisters whom he later married, his five-year-old son, Hoskinini Begay, two uncles, a brother, two Ute slave women, the grandfather and grandmother of Man Who Swears, Yellow Hair's wife, her sister and daughter, Laughing Boy, and two infants accompanied him. A few stragglers and 20 sheep completed the party. For six years, during the time of the Conquest, they remained near Navajo Mountain (Kelly, 1941 and 1953).

The period of the Conquest coincided with hostilities between Utes and Mormons which caused the abandonment of many of the Mormon frontier settlements. The disturbances stimulated the Navajos to raid across the Colorado River. Jacob Hamblin reports that in 1861 and 1863 "the Navajo and other Indians east of the Colorado River were raiding the Mormon settlements and driving off hundreds of cattle, valuable horses and mules" (Cleland and Brooks, 1955). In 1865 Hamblin crossed the Colorado to recover some horses stolen from Kanab, but "We did not succeed in recovering the stolen horses. We were informed by the

Moquis that the old Navajo chief, the friendly Spaneshanks, had been discarded by his band, that his son had succeeded him as chief and that he was disposed to raid at any favorable opportunity" (Little, 1881:292, 293). Maurice Kildare says that Spaneshanks turned against Hamblin when his son and a companion were killed in ambush by a group of Mormons (Kildare, 1965:22).

The Treaty of 1868 between the Navajos and the United States Government ended the Fort Sumner "experiment" and permitted the conquered Navajos to return to a portion of their old territory that had been set up as a reservation. In 1872, Jacob Hamblin attended a gathering of some 6,000 Navajos assembled at Fort Defiance to receive government rations. Here he made a peace agreement between the Indians and the Mormons which was reaffirmed in a meeting with some western Navajo "chiefs" who did not consider themselves bound by the 1868 treaty or any Fort Defiance treaty since they had never been rounded up. Hamblin describes how 80 Navajos were in Kanab on his return. They had come on foot for the most part, bringing their blankets to trade. "Some of their women accompanied them, which is their custom when going on a peaceable expedition" (Little, 1881:304–313). The diaries of John D. Lee, another Mormon pioneer, well known as a participant in the Mountain Meadow Massacre of "Gentile" pioneers, are filled with references to Navajo trading parties (Cleland and Brooks, 1955).

The Navajo Mountain area was prospected in the 1880's. Navajo Agent Galen Eastman wrote on March 13, 1882, referring to Dargar Sikie [Dugai Sikaad], one of the first Navajo residents of Navajo Canyon according to our own informants:

> A headman among the Navajos residing in the far west complains that white men prospectors disturb their

> stock. . . . They say they have no objection to the white
> men finding and working mines in their vicinity if they
> do not interfere with their stock and range. They de-
> sire to live at Peace and on good terms with white men
> . . . but they have always lived there and their fathers
> before them, and when the lands are surveyed expect
> to homestead their homes the same as white men do
> (Letter Books of the Navajo Agents).

There is an inscription on a rock near the Navajo Mountain Trading Post bearing the date "1882" and the name
"G. Miller" which confirms the statement that prospectors
were in the area in the 1800's (Crampton, 1965:125).

At this time, Galen Eastman mentions Paiutes in his Letter Book entries. He reports in 1881 that forty starving
Paiutes came into Fort Defiance asking for food. There
were bonds of friendship, he said, between the Paiutes and
Navajos north and west of the reservation boundaries. In
1883, a United States Army scouting party found both Navajos and Paiutes south of the San Juan River. In 1884 a
heliograph station was placed on Navajo Mountain by
United States troops under a Captain Thomas (Beals *et al*,
1945:1). Gladwell and Cecil Richardson, sons of the early
trader, S. I. Richardson, confirm this story and say they have
seen evidences of the station on top of Navajo Mountain.

The first description of the Navajo Mountain area from
the Navajo point of view appears in the autobiography of
Left Handed, the son of Old Man Hat, as recorded by
Walter Dyk. Left Handed describes how his family when to
Paiute Canyon *circa* 1884 to herd their sheep. Here they
met a Paiute leader, Nabhadzin [Nabotsin], who ordered
them out of the canyon. Old Man Hat refused to obey.

> You're just a Paiute, that's all. I'm not a bit scared of
> you. You think you scare me, but you can't scare
> me at all. All around here, all over around Navajo

Mountain belongs to me. It doesn't really belong to me, it belongs to all the Navaho; so you've got no business riding up like this (Dyk, 1938:111, 112).

Other Navajos are mentioned as herding in and out of Paiute Canyon and on Paiute Mesa, such as Hoskinini's herder, His Horse Is Slow, and Old Man Won't Do As He's Told. Ancestors of present-day Navajo Mountain residents, according to our genealogies, appear in this narrative. They are Giving Out Anger [Hashké neiní], Big Chancres [Chach'osh or Whiteman Killer], Whiskers [Dugai Sikaad], Wounded Smith [Atsidii K'aa' Kehe] and Hairy Face [Ni ditł'oi]. At a Squaw Dance, Left Handed is proposed to by a Navajo Mountain girl (if we can judge by her clan affiliations, this girl was the daughter of Whiteman Killer) (Dyk, 1938:360–364).

A second life story recorded by Walter Dyk in "A Navaho Autobiography" describes the herding trips that Big Mexican's family made into the Navajo Mountain area between 1871 and 1882 (1947:17, 18).

On May 17, 1884, by executive order of the President of the United States, Chester A. Arthur, certain lands lying between 109° longitude west and 111° 30', south of the San Juan River and north of 36° 30' latitude, were added to the Navajo Reservation. This includes the whole of the Navajo Mountain community area. On November 19, 1892, President Benjamin Harrison restored 431,160 acres north of the southern boundary of Utah and west of 110° longitude to the public domain. This Paiute Strip remained in uncertain status for 50 years and was later returned to the Reservation. From 1908 to 1922 it was subject to Indian use and was administered by the Western Navajo Agency (Young, 1961:256–257).

The dramatic incident that brought a settler to Rainbow

Plateau was a murder. This killing took place near Tuba City, where Mormons had been living since 1875 while Hopis, Paiutes and Navajos farmed nearby in Moencopi Wash. In 1892, Lot Smith, a Mormon, shot some sheep belonging to relatives of Chach'osh when they wandered into his pasture. In retaliation, or to protect himself and the herder, Chach'osh shot and killed Lot Smith. The hand-written record of the coroner's inquest, preserved in the Court House in Flagstaff, states that Lot Smith met his death at the hands of an unknown Indian. The killer was later identified as "Chactos." Navajo Agent David Shipley was convinced that the Indian had shot in self-defense. This was also the opinion of Lt. R.E.L. Michie of the United States Cavalry who was sent by the Army to investigate the affair. Three Navajo Agents in succession worked on the case. Chach'osh surrendered to Agent Shipley, but by September 23, 1895, he had not been brought to trial, although he had been indicted in July of that year. He was evidently exonerated of murder, and came to live in Navajo Mountain with his wife and their children, including three daughters and the man who was to become their mutual husband. Chach'osh was known by this time as Whiteman Killer or Killer of Red Moustache. Substantially this same story was told us by his youngest daughter in 1960.

Mormon title to land around Tuba City (which the Mormons had named for a Hopi chief) was not clear, and in 1903 the United States Government purchased the Morman improvements for $48,000 and established the Western Navajo School and Agency (Young, 1961:258).

In 1906 it was reported that Navajos were taking farms from the "Pah Ute" band in Paiute Canyon because the farms lay within the Navajo Reservation. About 100 Paiutes were living north of the Arizona line and south of the San Juan. "It is said that they learned from the Navajos the art of weaving blankets and understand the care of sheep," Indian Commissioner Francis Leupp wrote to the Secretary of the Interior on September 14, 1906. The report of Agent John Hunter on August 26, 1908, estimated that 60 Paiutes were living in Paiute Canyon, and they had sheep, goats, ponies, cattle, corn, pumpkins, and melons. "Nasja is the head Pahute in Pahute Canyon; they recognize the authority of the United States and trade at Bluff and Oljatoh, Utah, and Red Lake, Arizona."

The discovery of Rainbow Bridge by white men occurred in 1909. They were guided to the great rock arch by an Indian. An amusing description of the controversy as to whether John Wetherill, Byron Cummings, or W.B. Douglass saw it first, or reached it first, is given in Mrs. Louisa Wade Wetherill's story (Gillmor and Wetherill, 1952:161– 171). A controversy still rages between the relatives of One Eyed Salt and the kin of the Paiute, Nasja Begay, as to the identity of the Indian guide. Mrs. Wetherill gives the credit to Nasja Begay. In 1910 the United States Government established the Navajo National Monument, including Rainbow Bridge, Betatakin and Inscription House. John Wetherill, the Oljeto trader, had begun amateur explorations in the Navajo Mountain area as early as 1900, and in the years that followed, a number of archeologists surveyed the region. Among them were Earl Morris, Ralph Beals, Neil Judd, J. Walker Fewkes, Harold S. Gladwin, A. V. Kidder, Byron Cummings, for whom Cummings Mesa was named, and the amateur Charles L. Bernheimer.

In 1923, S. I. Richardson, a trader, built a road into Navajo Mountain, hoping to attract tourist trade to Rainbow Bridge. The move was bitterly opposed by rival traders and their Navajo allies. Cecil Richardson describes how he and his father were met by a "delegation" of 23 Navajos, who forbade them to go further. After some show of violence and some parley, and particularly because of the bravery and foresight of a Navajo policeman, John Daw, who was accompanying the Richardsons, the Navajos allowed them to proceed. This incident is dramatically recounted by Maurice Kildare (1966:14). Cecil Richardson described to us the isolation of the Navajo Mountain community:

> The people in that area had very little white contact. They didn't want other Indians to come in. They had lots of sheep, cattle, and horses, 1,000 head of horses. There were only two ways to get into the valley. Otherwise you had to come through the canyons from Kayenta.

Rainbow Lodge and a trading post were built in 1924, and S. I. Richardson and his son, Cecil, managed the business for 2 years; the next managers were Stanton and Ida Mae Borum. In 1928, William and Katherine Wilson took it over, and in 1942, Barry Goldwater bought a partnership in the enterprise, which operated until a fire in 1951 burned down the Lodge and nearly took the lives of the Wilsons. The trading post was reestablished in 1958 by Myles and Doris Headrick.

A second trading post on the other side of the mountain was pioneered by Ben and Myrl Wetherill as a "tent operation." It is described by Clyde Kluckhohn, the anthropologist, who visited the area with a group of college mates in 1928 (Kluckhohn, 1933:67). A permanent post was established by the Dunn family from Chilchinbito on April 11, 1932. In the 1940's it was run by Madelene Dunn Owen and her husband, Jack Owen, and in 1944 was sold to Elvin and Phyllis Kerley. Jack Owen died in 1948. From 1944 until some time in the 1950's, the Navajo Mountain Trading Post was managed by Lloyd Bowles. Madelene

Owen, later Mrs. Ralph Cameron, bought back the Navajo Mountain store on July 1, 1952. The Camerons continue to operate the trading business and conduct guided trips to Rainbow Bridge.

On June 4, 1934, the Paiute Strip was restored to the Navajo Reservation by an Act of Congress (Young, 1961: 257).

In 1936 a two-grade day school was constructed for beginners and the first grade. The first teacher was Ann Franks, who was succeeded by Lewis Durant after two years. In the early 1940's, Lisbeth Eubank took over the position of teacher-principal, a post that she held for 20 years, to become one of the most famous schoolteachers on the Navajo Reservation. In 1946 the day school was enlarged into a boarding school.

The Christianizing of Navajo Mountain Indians began in 1942 when the Reverend Baxter Liebler, known as the "Missionary with Long Hair," established Saint Christopher's Mission (Episcopal) at Bluff, Utah. Navajo Mountain was one of his visitation areas. Harold Drake, a Navajo born on the northeastern side of the mountain, was a Presbyterian evangelist at Tuba City and Kayenta. He made it a practice to hold Christian camp meetings near his birthplace. In 1955, Glen and Louise Hurd, after more than a decade of work at Hard Rocks Mission near Oraibi, came to live in Navajo Mountain. Licensed for missionary work by the Navajo Tribe, they have built a group of religious structures and hold regular Sunday School and church services. The Mission is nondenominational, affiliated with the Christian and Missionary Alliance, a fundamentalist group. Everett and Ruth Flint assisted the Hurds for five years and were succeeded, briefly, by Mr. and Mrs. Wesley Glass, Mr. and Mrs. David Ekstedt, and Fred and Sarah Bedoni. Delbert and Pauline Smallcanyon are among the most active Christian Navajos.

Navajo Mountain has elected a delegate to the Navajo Tribal Council since its establishment in 1923. Among the residents who are said by informants to have served as councilmen are John Fat, Charley Drake, Kay Bedoni, Alfred Miles, Slim Eltsosie, Segony Yazhi Begay, Leslie Tomasyo, Bert Tallsalt, Joe Fuller and Harold Drake.

In 1927, Agent John Hunter set up the first local political organization, called the Chapter, in the Leupp Agency. Other communities followed suit, including Navajo Mountain. The Chapter continued to operate as long as it was sponsored by the Bureau of Indian Affairs, but when the Bureau withdrew support during the stock-reduction crisis, the Navajo Mountain Chapter, like so many others on the Reservation, languished and died. It was revived in 1955 when the Navajo Tribal Council reactivated this form of local organization, and certified Chapters as part of the formal political system.

In the 1940's the teacher, Lisbeth Eubank, set up an Advisory Board for the school in an effort to interest the adults in education for their children. Heads of large extended families were chosen for the School Board as the best representatives of the traditional social structure. As the only operating community organization, the Board soon took on the activities that had been previously handled by the Chapter. Disputes were settled informally through discussion and compromise. One of the sharpest problems was the status of Navajo Mountain Paiutes now that the Paiute Strip was officially part of the Navajo Reservation. Although all of the resident Paiutes were Navajoized on the surface, and some had intermarried with Navajos and gone into the clan system, others retained their clanless Paiute identity. As a result of community demands, Paiutes in the area were given census numbers in the Navajo Tribe and were empowered to exercise full political rights. The School Board was instrumental in dealing with this problem.

SETTLEMENT PATTERNS

There is some scholarly controversy regarding the date of Navajo occupation of the Navajo Mountain area. Jerrold Levy contends that the first permanent settlement on Kaibito Plateau (a community that is contiguous to Navajo Canyon) took place in the 1880's, paralleling the settlement of Navajo Mountain as described by Collier (Levy, 1962:790). Malcolm Collier dates the first arrival of Whiteman Killer as 1890 and permanent settlement of Rainbow Plateau as of the 1920's (1966:18). Evidences of early occupation, according to Levy, simply bear witness to the fact that Navajos herded in and out of this far-western area.

However, tree-ring dates from hogans, documents we have cited, affidavits obtained from aged informants by the Navajo Land Claims Division, and our own field interviews have convinced us of earlier Navajo settlement. For example, a number of the ancestors of present-day Navajo Mountain residents are said by their direct descendants to have been born on Rainbow Plateau, in Paiute Canyon and in Navajo Canyon. Possibly they were born in the course of herding expeditions, but it is our contention that transhumance, moving about with the flocks over wide areas, constituted the typical residence pattern of Navajos both before and after Fort Sumner. This is the picture, certainly, that emerges from the autobiographies recorded by Walter Dyk. Year-round settlement as we see it today is of more recent date, the "permanency" increasing with the increasing scarcity of land.

William Y. Adams postulates three major groupings of Navajo settlers in his reconstruction of the history of the Shonto community. One came from the Black Mesa band; a second spread into the Inscription House–Navajo Canyon area; a third was derived from Hoskinini's band near Ol-jeto. These are substantially the same groups and lineages to whom the residents of Navajo Mountain can trace their descent and their claims to the use of land. Most of the Paiute lines are of long-time residence, probably having originated north of the San Juan River.

The concept of localized lineage is useful in the reconstruction of settlement patterns of Navajo Mountain. Localized matrilineages are descent lines headed by women who were born or settled in Navajo Mountain and whose descendants continue to reside there. Consideration of clan affiliation alone obscures the actual genealogical connections that can still be traced to the pioneer or founding ancestress. In some cases, several sisters, or a sister and a brother, or a maternal uncle and his niece are among the first residents of their lineage in Navajo Mountain. Data showing the specific localized matrilineages and their clans, their provenience, and the date of settlement will be given in the appendix by geographical sections: Navajo Canyon; Rainbow Plateau; northeast of the mountain and Paiute Canyon; and Paiute Mesa.

The founding matrilineages in Navajo Canyon, *Tábąąhá*, *Tł'ízí łání*, and *Tsi'naajinii*, are from Adams' basic Inscription House–Navajo Canyon population group with admixtures from the Black Mesa Band.

Rainbow Plateau's first settlers were from a *Tł'ízí łání* lineage from Navajo Canyon; an *Ashįįhí* lineage and a *Tó dich'ii'nii* lineage from the Black Mesa Band.

Northeast of the Mountain and in Paiute Canyon we find clear evidence of early Paiute occupancy. The connections of this San Juan Band are with Southern Paiutes from across the river. There are possibly three original descent lines of Paiutes living here but these cannot properly be called lineages in this bilateral society. The principal founding population elements in addition to Paiutes are the indigenous Paiute *Áshįįhí* lineage and one *Biťahnii* lineage from the Oljeto-Kayenta area.

Paiute Mesa had three founding lineages of three different clans. The basic population elements in this area were from the indigenous Paiute *Áshįįhí* lineage, a *Tábąąhá* matrilineage from the Kaibito-Inscription House area, and a *Lók'aa' dine' é* matrilineage from Oljeto.

Altogether, in Navajo Mountain today, there are 24 matrilineages representing 10 different clans and 3 lines of Paiutes. The longest generation span as measured from the youngest living generation to the settler generation is seven, that of the *Ťizí łání* matrilineage from Navajo Canyon and Rainbow Plateau. Two matrilineages are of six generations: *Áshįįhí* and Paiute *Áshįįhí*. Lines of five traceable generation spans consist of two Paiute lines, a *Tó dích'iinii* matrilineage, and a *Biťahnii* matrilineage. Of four-generation span are one Paiute line, a *Tó dích'iinii (Bįįh Bitoodnii)* lineage, one *Tábąąhá* and one *Kiyaa'áanii* lineage. Of three-generation span: one *Tábąąhá* lineage, three *Táchii'nii* lineages, one *Tó dích'ii'nii* and one *Lók'aa' dine' é* lineage. Of two-generation span: one *Ťizí łání* and four *Tó dích'ii'nii* lineages, two *Lók'aa' dine'é* lineages, one *Táchii'nii* and one *Tábąąhá* lineage, and one *Honágháahnii* lineage.

Specific areas of provenience include, on the east, Kayenta, Chinle, Narrow Canyon, Rock Point, Carrizo Mountains, and Mexican Hat; on the south, Oraibi Wash, Black Mesa, Piñon, Shonto, and Tuba City; on the west, Gap and Kaibito; and on the north, Bear's Ears. According to statements of our informants, 15 of the ancestors and oldest settlers were born at Navajo Mountain, 12 in Navajo Canyon, and 1 on Paiute Mesa.

There follow some of the statements obtained in the course of our field work, or by the Navajo Land Claims investigators, from the living descendants of the Navajo pioneers:

Paul Begay of Inscription House said, "The land around here belongs to Navajos. About five families hid out here and never went to Fort Sumner."

Eighty-seven year old Paul Tallman (Ayóó ń Nezí or Yellow Grass) said:

> My mother's grandmother, a *Tábąąhá*, Asdzáán Bitł'ízí (Goat Woman) told me that Navajo Canyon was occupied by Navajos during the time of the Navajo-Ute wars. She was a young grown woman during that time. My father's grandmother, Abé Saní (Old Milk) of the *Tsi'naajinii* clan lived in the canyon before and during Fort Sumner.

Bahe Ketchum traces his ancestry to two early residents of the Canyon. He told us, "My old Grandpop escaped going to Fort Sumner by living in Navajo Canyon."

Becky Smallcanyon of the *Tł'ízí łání* clan said:

> What clans were here first? *Tł'ízí łání, Tó dich'ii'nii* and *Tábąąhá*. They were in these canyons. My great grandfather, Dugai Sikaad, was born and lived in the canyon. After Fort Sumner, sheep were given to the Navajos at Fort Defiance, but the *Tł'ízí łání* around here didn't get any. That's because they were hiding out. They had many sheep before. My grandmother's husband, a *Tó dich'ii'nii*, used to trade blankets way into Utah. Trade with the Mormons. There wasn't much water on Rainbow Plateau. People from the canyon used to come here with their sheep.

Mabel Onesalt, the youngest of the three wives of Endishchee and a daughter of Whiteman Killer, told us the following story:

> My father's brother lived near Tuba City. My father went to visit his brother to make belts. A white man

was living at Tuba on the east side of the canyon. The white man had cows, fenced in place, grass. My father's brother was living up above that white man. He didn't know his sheep went down there. My father's brother's younger wife ran to take the sheep out of the field. The white man came along the road on a horse. The horse jumped over the fence. The white man killed the sheep, lots of them, and then shot at the girl to scare her. My father's brother chased him on horseback. My father came along and chased him too. My father shot the white man. Lots of white people were around and they were dangerous. My sisters and I went between Shonto and in Navajo Canyon. I wasn't married then. My two sisters were married to the same man, Mr. Pinetree or Endishchee.

The general consensus among informants is that the *Ashįįhí*, now the largest clan in Navajo Mountain, arrived with the advent of Whiteman Killer and his family in 1892.

Dick's Old Sister, an aged Paiute, told the Navajo Land Claims Division that she was born about 1880. She said that her mother was born in Paiute Canyon and that her father's father had come from Bear's Ears across the San Juan River. "Paiute Canyon was named for my father's father," she said proudly.

We have presented sufficient evidence in this section on the history of the far-western Navajo area and Navajo Mountain in particular, we believe, to substantiate the fact that Navajos have occupied this territory for more than a hundred years, both before and after the incarceration of the majority of the tribe in Bosque Redondo.

PART TWO

SOCIAL
STRUCTURE

This part of the book will be devoted to an analysis of the descriptive and specific data presented in the community study. An attempt will be made to show how the residents of Navajo Mountain are organized into subgroups and roles, including those based on age, sex, kinship, occupation, residence, property, authority, and status, and how the social functions of these subgroups make possible the cohesiveness and continuity of their way of life.

A society may be defined as the group of people whose interaction forms a social system; social structure may be conceived as the established pattern of internal organization of a society. It involves the recurring interactive processes, the behavior patterns operating through a structure of role relations, all of which at some point interrelate to form an on-going, self-maintaining, self-reproducing, and bounded system of shared values and beliefs.

A study of social organization includes an analysis of *what* must be done: the requisites of a society; *who* does it: the recognized social positions (statuses) and behavior patterns appropriate to such positions (roles); and by what *processes*: cooperation and competition, social control, conflict.

Membership Groups

Three principles of grouping that are the bases of membership units in traditional Navajo society are (1) kinship, (2) coresidence, and (3) cooperation. Each structural unit is organized on one or more of these principles. There are no supra-kin groups, occupational associations or neighborhood organizations that derive from traditional Navajo forms. The modern Tribal Council, with its local arm, the Chapter, integrates the Navajo Mountain Community on a locality basis for political decision, for the organization of local services, and for dealing with the surrounding society.

CORESIDENT KINSHIP GROUPS

Nuclear family. The nuclear family is a kinship, residence, and cooperating unit consisting of a man, his wife, and his unmarried children. It is the smallest viable economic and residence group in Navajo society. The members eat, sleep, and live together in the same hogan. As a group, the nuclear family bears the principal responsibility for the economic support and rearing of the children. Traditionally, it is attached at the outset to an extended family, preferably, but not invariably, that of the bride. Later the nuclear family may break off and establish its own camp, but this is usually not done until the couple has acquired enough livestock and enough manpower to be self-sustaining.

Extended family. The extended family is a group based on kinship, coresidence, and cooperation, that comprises typically three generations—grandparental, parental, and children. It is composed of at least two nuclear families, affiliated through the extension of the parent-child relationship, each living in its own hogan "within shouting distance of each other." Each member of the extended family is expected to contribute work, sheep, or money to common enterprises, and, conversely, expects from the group aid in paying a debt, in holding a Sing, or in providing the goods that are customarily demanded as a bride price. The extended family offers security to individuals who have left the group, but who are free to return in case of unemployment, divorce, or the death of a spouse. It may divide or it may expand through the creation of new nuclear families, or it may agglutinate through the attachment of relatives who are neither couples nor children of resident couples, according to the exigencies of the moment.

In an extended family there is a structure of authority, however flexible and informal, wherein the principal responsibility for organizing joint efforts rests upon the oldest able-bodied male. The amount and quality of authority exercised varies with the personality of the actor. An older woman may play this strong role. The head of an extended family can only plan, advise, and ask cooperation; he has no specific coercive authority that is recognized as legitimate either by the family or by the local community. The head of a household is expected to talk things over with the other adult members of the camp.

Residence Patterns at Navajo Mountain. No discussion of residence patterns can be entered into without first defining the terms that will be used. A completely satisfactory typology for residence patterning is still to be formulated, despite valiant efforts by Murdock (1949), Goodenough (1956), Fischer (1958), and Barnes (1960). The problem is complicated by the need to type the residence pattern preferred by the society; to type the residence patterns of individual households, of married couples, and of camps; and to show changes in residence pattern. Some of the suggested methods, such as that of Fischer, which try to take most of these needs into account, become too unwieldly for common use and comparative purposes. We propose to use the following residence categories.

We shall speak of a *household* as the occupants, or occupant, of one hogan. This is typically a nuclear family, that is, a man and wife (or in rare instances, a man and plural wives) with or without unmarried children. A widow, with or without children, or a widower, with or without children, may also constitute a household. Certain households at Navajo Mountain are made up of close kin related in various other ways.

A *camp* is that household, or cluster of households, that makes us a residence unit. It is always a clearly defined territorial entity.

Households will be categorized as follows: *neolocal*, when a single nuclear family constitutes the residence unit; *matrilocal*, when that household is attached to the camp of the wife's parents; *patrilocal*, when the household is attached to the camp of the husband's parents; *consanguineolocal*, when the household is attached to a camp through other kinds of kinship ties.

Head-of-camp is that senior couple (or widow/widower) around whom the other households have nucleated.

Camps will be classed as *neolocal* when a single household constitutes the camp; *matrilocal* when the camp is made up of the households of senior kinsmen and those of married daughters; *patrilocal* when the camp is made up of the household of senior kinsmen and those of married sons; *bilocal* when the camp is made up of the household of senior kinsmen and those of both married daughters and married sons; *mixed* when the camp includes households of couples or individuals who are not the children of head-of-camp.

Five hundred and seventy-eight residents of Navajo Mountain live in 112 households, and two women and a child live on the school campus. The number of occupants of each household varies from one to eighteen persons. Thirty-nine (34.5%) of the households are matrilocal; seventeen (15%) are neolocal; sixteen (14.1%) are patrilocal; fifteen (13.3%) are consanguineolocal. Twenty-six households (23.1%) are those of the senior kinsman, or kinsmen, classified as head-of-camp. The household of a man married to the daughter of his fathers present wife has necessarily been counted as both patrilocal and matrilocal.

There are 46 camps at Navajo Mountain, varying in size from one household to eight. Seventeen (37%) of the camps are neolocal; thirteen (28.3%) are matrilocal; eight (17.4%) are mixed; six (13%) are bilocal; two (4.3%) are patrilocal.

Matrilocal households outnumber any other type, but neolocal camps are the most frequent. Customarily, a newly wed couple does not establish a neolocal camp except in the case of wage workers, who are few in number in this locality.

It should be noted that in 16 camps, those that are typed as patrilocal, bilocal, or mixed, children are being brought up with paternal instead of, or in addition to, maternal kinsmen.

Unfortunately, this typology does not picture the frequency of shifts in residence, but since there is no fixed rule that governs change of residence in Navajo society, this terminology will suffice to show the distribution at any given time. Table 2 shows residence patterns by household and camp.

Table 2.—*Navajo Mountain Residence Patterns*

HOUSEHOLDS			CAMPS		
Matrilocal	39	(34.5%)	Neolocal	17	(37%)
Neolocal	17	(15%)	Matrilocal	13	(28.3%)
Patrilocal	16	(14.1%)	Mixed	8	(17.4%)
Consanguineolocal	15	(13.3%)	Bilocal	6	(13%)
Head-of-camp	26	(23.1%)	Patrilocal	2	(4.3%)

LARGER KINSHIP GROUPS

Lineage. A lineage is a consanguineal kin group, produced by a rule of descent, that can be genealogically traced from a common ancestor through males (patrilineal), or from a common ancestress through females (matrilineal). A *patrilineage* branches with each progenitor, and a *matrilineage* with each progenitrix. The concept of lineage has not been widely used in the analysis of Navajo social structure. Reichard (1928), Kimball and Provinse (1942), Kluckhohn and Leighton (1946), and Aberle (1961) do not discuss lineage. Adams uses "resident lineage" in his study of Shonto (1963). Resident lineages, he says, "are essentially historical divisions which because of the social and historical traditions of Navajo land tenure may retain a certain amount of functional significance as land-use communities." However, when he states that "Shonto's resident lineages may include the households of siblings of either sex plus their married children and grandchildren of either sex" (1963: 59), he is obviously dealing with a bilateral family rather than with a lineage, which, by definition, includes only descendants through a single line.

We have found the concept of lineage to be functionally

useful for the analysis of settlement, residence patterns, cooperation, and locus of frequent interaction in Navajo society. A Navajo matrilineage never meets as a formal decision-making group, nor does it wield authority as a unit. However, the most urgent obligations for mutual aid fall upon members of the lineage, and on close investigation, many activities ascribed to the clan will be found to be limited to actual kin rather than fictive kin groups. It is not synonymous with "outfit" nor with "land-use community," a term used by Kimball and Provinse to designate a larger residential group consisting of both related and unrelated lineages occupying a common territory.

A lineage, perhaps best referred to as a *maximal lineage*, consists of all the members alive or dead who trace actual descent unilinearly from a common ancestor. In the Navajo case this is a matrilineage, that is, the descendants of a common ancestor through females. A *lineage group*, to use Radcliffe-Brown's phrase, is composed of all members of a lineage who are alive at one time (1952:14–15). A *localized matrilineage* includes those members of a matrilineage who live in one community, and a *minimal matrilineage* embraces the children of one mother.

The basic manner of acquiring land in Navajo society is through the preemption and subsequent inheritance of land use rights within a maximal matrilineage. A nuclear or extended family will settle in a region and make use of a definite land area for grazing and farming, and if such preemption is not challenged by previous occupants, a customary use right accrues to members of the preempting lineage. Theoretically, water resources are available to everyone, but in practice use rights to springs are acquired by preemption, rest in the group, and cannot be alienated by an individual. Permission for others to use the water may be granted or withheld at the group's discretion, but should not be refused in case of emergency. Individuals who marry into the lineage will enjoy use rights to the extended family land so long as they participate as co-operating members of the group. If they leave the extended family, whose core is a lineage section, because of divorce or the death of the spouse, they will usually reactivate a claim to the land of their own matrilineage, that is, return to their mother's or their sister's camp.

If a couple withdraws from the extended family and sets up a separate camp, they will usually occupy land previously claimed by the matrilineage of the original settling family. There are variations on the procedure of claiming land-use rights through mothers and sisters. Children will acquire use rights to land preempted by their father's matrilineage in those infrequent cases where their mother is living with her husband's family.

A first inspection of residence patterns in the Navajo Mountain area appears to show a clustering of clans within a wide section of territory. On closer examination, armed with a knowledge of the genealogical relationships, we can see that the significant clan group, that is, those members of the clan who are expected to take responsibility for ceremonies and who owe each other mutual aid in crises, are members of a matrilineage of that clan. Other members of the same clan may take part in the ceremonies, but they appear to be under no greater obligation to do so than are unrelated neighbors and acquaintances.

A critical examination of the kinship and clan relationship to the patient of all individuals who participated in more than a casual manner in a particular Squaw Dance led us to the conclusion that although obligation falls upon members of the patient's matrilineage (and their spouses), upon his own affinals, and upon his own children (and their spouses), the burden of such participation rests primarily upon members of his minimal lineage. Examining patterns of cooperation, we found, for example, that men who had married into Navajo Mountain, or men who had married out, would return to their own matrilineages to ask them to hold a ceremony for them when the need arose. In no case did they appeal to the local clan members where they were residing. In one instance, a *Kiyaa'áanii*, married and working in Kayenta for several years, asked his parents and siblings in Navajo Mountain to hold a Squaw Dance for him. In another, two men, parallel cousins and members of the *Bit'ahnii* clan, went several hundred miles away to the camp of a sister of one of them to be co-patients at a Squaw Dance.

On still another occasion, an *Ashįįhí*, living in Navajo Canyon, came to Rainbow Plateau seeking help from his dead mother's sister and his own two sisters. These women and the aunt's son, his parallel cousin or "brother," agreed to hold a Squaw Dance for him. A preliminary planning session was held, which we were invited to attend. Taking a leading part in the activities were the patient and his wife, the host and his wife, the two sisters and their mutual husband, and the medicine man who would officiate. The drum and the drum stick were prepared, and there was talk about who would be asked to donate, where the first and second night's activities would take place, and the distribution of work in the building of temporary shelters that had to be constructed for members of the patient's matrilineage, of his wife's matrilineage, and for his father's matrilineage.

Members of each of the participating matrilineages were asked to contribute sheep, flour, coffee, sugar, and lard. Not all the members of any one clan in the Navajo Mountain area donated food, although most of them attended as spectators (and diners), on much the same footing as did neighbors, unrelated friends, and white people. In short, the groups on which the greatest obligation fell were the matrilineages, rather than the clans, of the close consanguineal and affinal relatives of the patient.

Interaction is more frequent within the localized lineage than within the maximal lineage, and it is greatest within the minimal lineage, that is, among the children of one mother. There are variants of this pattern because of the accepted practice of polygyny. When one man is married to sisters and all of his children live in one camp, there may be little distinction between full and half siblings. This is particularly true if one of the mothers dies. However, we were told by a young woman of a polygynous family that there was a sharp distinction in intimacy between the children of the plural wives of her father. We observed this distinction in frequency of interaction in another polygynous family where the common father, toward the end of his life, had chosen to live with one wife exclusively, in preference to the other.

The Clan and Clan Group. In Navajo society, the clan and linked clans are the largest structural units based on kinship. The clan may be defined as a "consanguineal kin-group whose members acknowledge a traditional bond of common descent in the maternal or paternal line but are unable always to trace the actual genealogical relations between individuals" (Bellah, 1952:139). Navajo clans are exogamic, named, matrilineal, and dispersed. They are not corporate groups; they own no property or rituals and they never function as units. Clan membership, ascribed by birth, serves to regulate marriage and to provide a widespread network for hospitality. A Navajo takes his mother's clan and is spoken of as "born for" his father's clan, which serves to acknowledge patrilineal as well as matrilineal relationship.

The resident population of 563 Navajos belong to 14 different clans. The largest is the *Ashįįhí* clan with 117 members. Five clans have only one member living in the community: *Hashk'ąą hadzohó, Mą'ii deeshgiizhnii, Naakaii dine'é,* and *Tł'ááshchí'i* are each represented by one in-

marrying male, and *Honágháahnii* by one in-marrying female. The remainder of the population, eighteen Paiutes,
are without clans. Navajo Mountain clan size and distribution by sex and age are shown in Table 3.

Table 3.—Navajo Mountain Clans, 1961*

CLAN NAME	MEN	WOMEN	CHILDREN	TOTAL
Ashįįhi	24	27	66	117
Tó dích'ii'nii	21	21	60	102
Tł'izí łání	15	10	43	68
Paiute *Ashįįhi*	13	14	37	64
Tábąąhá	9	7	30	46
Táchii'nii	11	10	25	46
Lók'aa' dine'é	7	16	21	44
Bit'ahnii	5	7	26	38
Kiyaa'áanii	2	8	23	33
Hashk'ąą hadzohó ...	1	—	—	1
Honágháahnii	—	1	—	1
Mą'ii deeshgiizhnii ...	1	—	—	1
Naakaii dine'é	1	—	—	1
Tł'ááshchí'i	1	—	—	1
TOTAL				563

* For English translations of clan names, see Appendix, table C, p. 258.

The rules governing clan exogamy are that marriage is
prohibited (1) into own clan, (2) into father's clan, and
(3) with a person whose father's clan is the same as own
father's clan. Marriage is, therefore, prohibited between
all cross-cousins and all parallel cousins, since a paternal
cross-cousin is a member of father's clan; a paternal parallel
cousin is born for father's clan; a maternal cross-cousin is
born for Ego's clan; a maternal parallel cousin is a member
of Ego's clan.

Failure to observe the incest taboos as defined by clan

membership, as well as by blood ties within the nuclear family, incurs the danger of an illness called *iich'ąą* or "moth madness." This punishment will be inflicted even upon couples who are unaware of the incestuous relationship. The symptoms described by Navajos indicate *grand mal* or epileptic seizures. Gladys Reichard says that Navajos believe that victims of moth madness have so little control over themselves that they become rash and insane and may jump into the fire like a moth. The Navajo explanation of moth madness is given in the Myth of the Butterfly People. The legendary hermaphrodite, Begochidi, made sexual advances to both men and women among these people, thus bringing about procreation. When he left the Butterfly People, the parents were so opposed to marriage outside of the group that they instituted brother-sister unions. Katherine Spencer says:

> The decision to try brother-sister marriage results from the barrier raised against marriage with aliens, a ban which is doubly determined. In the first place marriage has been forbidden by the berdache protector, Begochidi, who has paid sexual attentions to both the young boys and the young girls. In addition, their parents are reluctant to let the children whom they have raised with such care and love be taken from them in marriage. But the solution to this predicament by instituting brother-sister marriage results in the participants' self-destruction by rushing madly into the fire. The moth or butterfly which flies into the fire thus becomes the symbol for 'craziness' resulting from incest (1957:148).

A young man from Navajo Mountain said:

> If you go around with your clan sister this is bad. This will hurt the whole family. You will go crazy when you get old. You'll shake like Hastiin Sání. Of course I don't

think Hastiin Sání did anything bad. He probably got
the shakes from sleeping once on a bear's bed, and once
lightning hit him.

An informant from Chinle described incest as a secret
crime. He said that a ceremony could be performed over the
guilty person, a Sing called *iich'ąąjí* or Moth Way.

> That was in the olden days. Now no one knows the
> ceremony. It is forgotten. A person should supply a
> new basket which has never been used. Moth herbs are
> boiled so they can be administered by mouth. They
> cleanse the body by making a person vomit. The sick
> person should have a coyote skin with a tail attached.
> This should be worn by the person during the cere-
> mony. This Sing is not done in a hogan but in a sweat-
> house. But no one knows the ceremony now. No one
> wanted to learn it. But I know a man who had inter-
> course with two ladies of his own clan, real close rela-
> tives. He fell on the ground and had a convulsion. The
> two ladies had the same sickness and died of it, but the
> man had the Moth Way Sing and he's all right now.

Hospitality is extended to clan relatives. A Navajo visiting in an area where he is not known will seek out a member of his own clan from whom he may expect a friendly
reception, and further connections in a community can also
be made through a clan relative.

There are reports in the anthropological literature that
the clan once functioned as a corporate group, owning
property and rituals, exercising responsibility in the settlement of feuds, in payment of fines, and generally in social
control. The Franciscan Fathers write:

> Quarrels among neighbors and members of different
> clans are common. An amicable settlement is often
> reached privately and by representative members of
> the disputing clans . . . . A heavy fine of horses and
> cattle is levied upon the crime of rape, and is always

exacted by the relatives (clansmen) of the victim . . . . In
many districts land is held in severalty by members of
one or affiliated clans to the exclusion of others (1910:
439, 450, 265).

If this was once the case, it is no longer true. We are inclined to believe that this situation never obtained. Otherwise, it seems unlikely that such strong corporate powers
could be lost without a trace. Even at the time of Father
Berard Haile's investigations, around the turn of the century, it was not possible to observe the clan functioning as
a corporate group. In our field work, we found that Navajos
tend to describe genealogical connections as clan relatives.
For example, an informant referred to "my clan brother"
when he was speaking English. This relative was actually
his parallel cousin whom he addressed by the term for
"brother" in Navajo. Certain actions were described to us
as performed by "those Ashįįhi" or "those Tó dich'įį'nii."
On closer investigation we found that the reference was to
a single Ashįįhi family, never to all of the Ashįįhi in the
area nor to the whole clan. In the case of a shooting (ruled
as justifiable homicide by the Federal court) the fatal fight
was between two Ashįįhi men. Five sheep in the indemnity
were given by an Ashįįhi woman, sister of the killer, to the
Táchii'nii wife of the dead man, *not* on the insistence of her
clansmen, but in response to the demand of the dead man's
mother, an Ashįįhi. In another instance, described to us by
a non-Indian as an example of where the "Ashįįhi got together and clamped down," we were told that the Ashįįhi
decided they did not wish to be represented by nonentities
from the community. Instead they ran a young member of
their clan for councilman. However, this young "Ashįįhi"
turned out to be a Tó dich'ii'nii named "Salt" (the English
translation of Ashįįhi), and, of course, in a community-wide
election he could not have been successful on Ashįįhi votes
alone.

David Aberle has postulated the existence of a Local Clan Element, a unit of all the members of one clan residing in an area which acts as a group in decision-making and in the performance of the other corporate functions ascribed to "clan" in the literature. Obviously the widely dispersed nature of Navajo clans would preclude any joint action by all clan members (Aberle 1961:108). We were unable to find a single instance in Navajo Mountain in which all the members of one clan acted as a unit. Fellow clansmen may be asked to help in an enterprise, since clan membership is an important line for kinship extension (one's father's lineage and one's affinal connections being the other main lines of kinship extension). All large cooperative efforts that we investigated included members of more than one clan, some affinals, and both matrilineal and patrilineal relatives of the person or persons central to the joint action. This was discussed in detail under *Lineage*.

Ranking of clans presents a difficult problem. There is no formal, all-tribal rating scale; ranking frequently depends on the clan affiliations of one's informants, as does the identification of the four original clans in mythology. Clyde Kluckhohn believed that there was an informal ranking of clans. He stated:

> To some extent clans *are* ranked in prestige order across localities. In my experience, for instance, Mexican People, Ute People, and Paiute People and a few others are always sneered at a bit and the members thereof tend to be defensive and sometimes to claim that their clan is the same as, *e.g.*, one of the water clans which, I think, always have some prestige. So do *Táchii'nii, Kiyaa'áanii*, and some others. It is true that clan status depends in part on locality - but not completely (personal communication, 1960).

There is a belief that "slave" clans are looked down upon. We were unable to verify this. One version of the origin legend has it that *Ashįįhi* is a slave clan (Young and Morgan, 1954:22). However, *Ashįįhi* in Navajo Mountain consider their clan to be preeminent because their forebears were early settlers and because they outnumber all other local clans. There is a tendency on the part of long-time resident whites to develop clan preferences (unless they ignore clans altogether) and to be supercilious about certain clans that "don't count."

In our opinion, high ranking of a clan in a locality depends generally on (1) superiority in numbers, (2) superior wealth or land use rights, (3) early occupancy of the area, and (4) general prestige of the resident members based on individual behavior. Clans, no matter what their prestige may be in other areas, that are represented in Navajo Mountain by only one small lineage cannot compete in prestige there with the larger and longer established clans.

The "People" in Navajo Mountain look down upon the Paiutes as "not-Navajo." They are still the butt of mild jokes, as they were at the time of Malcolm Collier's 1938 study.

No deliberate attempt is made to preserve a clan through adoption. In the old days, slaves and members of other tribes were permitted to affiliate themselves with a Navajo clan, but that was in order to relate themselves to the kinship system rather than to conserve or expand the clan. Navajo clans may, and do, become extinct as their membership dies out. They may be absorbed into a closely related clan, or they may divide into several linked clans of varying degrees of closeness and differing exogamic prohibitions. This perhaps explains the confusion in Navajo clan linkages as compared to the clear phratry pattern of the Western Apache (Kaut, 1956:49) and of the Hopi (Eggan, 1950:64). The mechanisms by which other Indians affiliate with the Navajo tribe through the clan system are illustrated in Navajo Mountain in the case of children of Paiute

and Ute mothers by Navajo fathers, who have assumed
Navajo clans. Versions of how Paiutes became *Ashįįhí* differ
with the informant. One man explained that his grandfather had captured a Paiute woman near Chinle and
brought her to Navajo Mountain. She took her captor's clan,
Ashįįhí, and founded the Paiute *Ashįįhí* line. An aged
Navajo woman told us, "Navajos bought little Paiute children living in Paiute Canyon. They were Asdzáán *Ashįįhí*'s
slaves and helped in herding and around the hogan. The
Paiutes grew up and thought they were *Ashįįhí*." Needless
to say, this is not the explanation given by the Paiute
Ashįįhí themselves. They admit to Paiute admixture, but
not to any previous condition of servitude. One Paiute
Ashįįhí girl told us that her mother's mother's mother, an
orphan, had been raised by a light-skinned Indian, "probably a Cheyenne," from whom she had taken the clan
Ashįįhí. Most of the Ute *Táchii'niis* in the area trace connections with Hoskinini's band. Since it is known that
he had 32 Ute women slaves at the time of his death (Gillmor and Wetherill, 1953:180), it is possible that these slave
women took the clan of Hoskinini, "Chief of the Western
Side." Other informants described themselves as Zuni
Tábąąhá and *Naakaii* (Mexican) *dine'é*, but could not say
how their ancestresses became "Navajo." One of Malcolm
Collier's informants in 1938 said that about 30 years before,
there was a lot of sickness and many Paiutes died. Navajos
found their children in hogans; these children later just
called themselves *Ashįįhí* or *Táchii'nii*.

The question of *linked clans* is a complicated one. Theoretically, the rules of clan exogamy and for the extension
of kin terms by clan affiliation apply also to linked clans.
In practice, however, there are two types of linked clans,
those that are "the same," and those that are affiliated but
merely "friendly." Exogamic prohibitions apply to the
first but not to the second type of interrelated clans.

Unfortunately, no one has been able to establish a neat system of Navajo clan groups or reconstruct vanished phratries as Kaut has done for the Western Apache clans (1957: 40–42). There is no agreement on the four original clans. David Aberle says that the government survey of clans made in the 1930's, which was based on consensus among previously published sources and among the special informants used for the survey, established nine clan groups with eight unassigned clans. "It is clear," Aberle concludes, "that there is no reservation-wide, universally valid clan-group system. Nevertheless, the 'majority-rule' government system has a general validity" (1961:182–183).

Clan linkages are supposedly derived from Navajo "history" as detailed in the origin myths. Katherine Spencer, who has made an extensive analysis of these myths, writes:

> Sometimes clans are spoken of as 'friends' or 'related'. ... The relationships may be so close that intermarriage is prohibited . . . . Sometimes it is specified that two clans are friends but may not intermarry . . . . Reasons for clans becoming affiliated are often not given. It is stated merely that they 'are related,' 'are believed to be related,' or 'become special friends' (1947:64–65).

She says further that two girl captives may call each other "sister" and be the founders of two related clans, or two groups may come from the same place, or two may live as neighbors, or groups may discover that their names are similar. A clan may split but remain related to the parent clan. A captive may take the clan of her captor (1947:65).

Despite our high hopes, we were no more fortunate than our anthropological predecessors in ferreting out a consistent system of clan groups for Navajo Mountain. Most Navajos could give only with difficulty the names of clans linked to their own and to their father's clan, and no two lists were exactly alike. Four "medicine men," cited by our informants as the local residents most likely to know all about clan links, disagreed. Such an amount of variation within a numerically small, intermarrying community with frequent face-to-face contacts and extensive ceremonial cooperation indicates that the Navajo clan-group system is highly flexible. This may be a result of the great increase of population (as compared with the Western Apache), of dispersed residence over millions of acres, or of the fact that Navajo clans (unlike Western Apache clans) are not corporate, landholding groups.

Our Navajo Mountain "medicine men" told us that some clans are "the same," and their members cannot intermarry; some clans are "friendly" and "go along together." This last was illustrated by shuffling of the feet to suggest walking. Members of the "friendly" clans can marry each other, we were told.

Clans that are considered "the same," and therefore exogamous are:

> Kin łichíí'nii and Tł'izí łání
> Tó dích'íí'nii and Bįįh bitoodnii
> Lók'aa' dine'é and Bił'ahnii
> Áshįįhí and Mą'ii deeshgiizhnii

Ute Táchii'nii, Paiute Áshįįhí, and Naasht'ézhi dine'é (Zuni) Tábąąhá are "foreign" versions of the counterpart Navajo clan.

Table 4 indicates the differences of opinion among Navajo Mountain informants about clan linkages. For convenience and comparability we use Gladys Reichard's system of numbering Navajo clans (1928:11). Seven groups of linked clans were distinguished by our informants. We have included in each group all of the clans that any one informant considered to be linked. The table shows that there is general agreement about certain linkages but a difference of opinion about others.

Table 4.—Clan Linkages, According to Navajo Mountain Informants

Clans and their numbering (G. Reichard's system)	Informants								
	Tom Laughter (Singer)	Robert Sombrero (Singer)	Jackson Greymountain (Singer)	Eugene Holgate	Ephraim Crank	Aggie Smallcanyon	Mable Navajo (Diviner)	Lucy Nelson	Betsy Longsalt
(14) Tʼízí táni	(14)	(14)	(14)		(14)		(14)	(14)	(14)
(15) Kin łichiiʼnii	(15)	(15)	(15)		(15)		(15)	(15)	
(16) Tłáashchiʼi	(16)	(16)	(16)		(16)		(16)	(16)	
(17) Tsiʼnaajinii	(17)	(17)	(17)		(17)		(17)	(17)	
(19) Deeshchiiʼnii	(19)	(19)	(19)		(19)		(19)	(19)	
(1) Taʼneeszahnii				(1)					
(4) Tó ʼdháni				(4)					
(6) Hashkʼąą hadzohó	(6)	(6)	(6)	(6)		(6)	(6)	(6)	
(32) Áshįįhi	(32)	(32)	(32)	(32)		(32)	(32)	(32)	
(33) Mąʼii deeshgiizhnii	(33)		(33)	(33)		(33)	(33)	(33)	
(34) Dibé tizhini	(34)	(34)	(34)	(34)		(34)	(34)	(34)	
(36) Tábąąhá						(36)	(36)		
(38) Tsé ńjíkíní	(38)	(38)	(38)					(38)	
(1) Taʼneeszahnii		(1)							
(28) Tsin sikaadnii	(28)	(28)	(28)	(28)	(28)				(28)
(29) Tó dichʼiiʼnii	(29)	(29)	(29)	(29)	(29)				(29)

(30)	Biih bitoodnii	(30)	(30)	(30)	(30)	(30)	(30)		(30)
(35)	Tó dokozhi		(44)	(35)	(35)	(35)			
(44)	Adoo' tsosni			(44)	(44)	(44)			
(tk)	Tsé Kinaake'é			(tk)	(tk)				
(51a)	Chishi dine'é						(51a)		
(2)	Dziłt'ahnii			(2)	(2)				
(5)	Nihoobáanii			(5)	(5)				
(20d)	Naaneesht'ézhi	(20d)	(20d)	(20d)	(20d)				
(36)	Tábąąhá	(36)	(36)	(36)	(36)				
(37)	Haltsooí dine'é	(37)	(37)	(37)	(37)				
(39)	Ts'ah yisk'idnii		(39)	(39)					
(td)	T'aadii dine'é	(td)	(td)	(td)	(td)				
(3)	Honágháahnii		(3)	(3)					
(8)	Lók'aa' dine'é	(8)	(8)	(8)	(8)		(8)	(8)	
(9)	Bit'ahnii	(9)	(9)	(9)	(9)		(9)	(9)	
(10)	Tótsohnii	(10)		(10)	(10)				
(11)	Tsé deeshgizhnii	(11)		(11)	(11)				
(22)	Kiyaa'áanii	(22)		(22)	(22)		(22)	(22)	
(20)	Táchii'nii	(20)	(20)	(20)	(20)				
(20a)	Náťoh dine'é	(20a)	(20a)	(20a)	(20a)				
(20c)	Yé'ii dine'é				(20c)				
(13)	Naaneesht'ézhi			(13)					
(24)	Tó 'aheedlíinii	(24)		(24)	(24)				
(25)	Naakaii dine'é	(25)	(25)	(25)	(25)				
(26)	Tséikeehé	(26)		(26)	(26)				
(dł)	Dzaanééz łání			(dł)	(dł)				

The Navajo clan system gives a continuity to the kinship system which the dispersed and shallow lineages and the evanescent extended and nuclear families do not. Genealogical connections are not long remembered; dead relatives are soon, and it seems almost deliberately, forgotten. Navajos cannot comprehend why anyone, even an ethnographer, should be interested in such far-off kinsmen. The use of clan names, ascription to mother's clan, and incest taboos reinforce the importance of reckoning clan affiliations.

LARGER COOPERATING GROUPS

A greater number of Navajos cooperate in the giving of ceremonials, but such cooperation is *on occasion only.* Because of the extensive concerted effort required for an Enemy Way (Squaw Dance) ceremonial, information on who contributes to the affair is regarded as one key to the identification of the largest group which will engage in collective action. For this reason we made comprehensive inquiries about the organization of a Squaw Dance from many informants.

> The main problem is feeding the people. You need wood and water and food. You need someone to herd sheep while the Sing is going on. A Squaw Dance costs about $200 in food. Maybe more; up to $500 or $600, depending on how many people come. You pay the medicine man in money and gifts. Then you need presents for the people who bring the stick; presents are thrown out of the hogan twice. You need three different places to give this Sing.

A general question about who contributes to a Squaw Dance elicited general answers, "Anyone who wants to," "It's up to them," "The relatives," "Friends and neighbors." Specific questions relating to five different Squaw

Dances held at Navajo Mountain brought out a more definite pattern of cooperation, at least as to the order in which
individuals are asked to help. A man will ask his relatives
to assist; his wife will ask hers.

> A person expects his mother, his mother's sister, his
> sisters and his brothers and his children to help out in
> that order. But, it's up to them. A person does not get
> angry if they refuse; there are always enough people
> who are willing to help.

According to the ideal pattern no one is coerced into
giving assistance, but, in fact, a great deal of informal social
pressure is brought to bear. In one case we observed, a
young man fabricated an excuse to leave the area temporarily so that he would not have to help in a Sing given for
his wife's ailing grandfather. In another instance, a man
aired a complaint in a Chapter meeting that his own half-
sisters were refusing to participate in giving a Squaw Dance
for their own brother. This charge was angrily denied in
the meeting by one of the sisters. In a third case, a man told
us that he was being witched by an old "medicine man" because he had refused to contribute to a nine-night ceremony
given in another community which was in the nature of an
ordination into that rite for the old Singer.

There is no group at Navajo Mountain today that cor-
responds to the "outfit" described by Kluckhohn and
Leighton as the "group of relatives (larger than the extended family) who regularly cooperate for certain purposes" (1946:62); neither did Malcolm Carr Collier find
such an organized group in 1938. She states, "When help
beyond the resources of the camp is needed, it may be drawn
from almost any other camp with emphasis on certain kin
relationships."

Jerrold Levy has postulated a theory that where the outfit has disappeared in the western Navajo region the cause

lies in the economic leveling that stemmed from stock reduction and the permit system. At present, grazing control virtually prevents any one man from acquiring enough wealth in livestock to develop the kind of economic dominance and authority that would tend to attach other extended families, nuclear families, or individual kinsmen to him as head of an outfit (personal communication, 1962).

Kinship Roles and Kinship Behavior

A kinship system is a way of ordering a society, or segments of a society, on the principle of consanguineal or fictive kin relationships. This system can be analyzed in terms of roles and expected role behavior, as well as in terms of kin groups and expected behavior by members of those concrete units. People in social positions do not behave in a random manner, and their actions are influenced by their own expectations and those of others in the group or society in which they are the participants. A *role* is a set of expectations applied to an incumbent of a social position. Role entails attributes and obligations for expected, predictable behavior in terms of a society's norms. *Position* is the location of an actor, or class of actors, in a system of social relationships. *Role behavior* is the actual performance in this position. *Role player* is the incumbent of a position. *Status* is the sum of roles played by any one person at any one time. These definitions are based on Gross, Mason, McEachern (1958:17).

Role differentiation and assignment is a functional requisite for every society in order to ensure through the allocation of rights and responsibilities that individuals will be motivated to carry out the necessary activities for maintaining an on-going society.

Because of the simplicity and homogeneity of traditional Navajo society, one can safely say that there is a consensus on the definition of roles, that expectations for proper role behavior are shared by the society as a whole. No role except the strictly biological male role is closed to women. It is possible, though rare, for a woman to become a Singer, a political headwoman, even a hunter, or in the old days to take part in raids and reprisals. No such roles were played by Navajo Mountain women to our knowledge, but women Singers and leaders from other areas were among their acquaintances.

Some modification of traditional role behavior has been made necessary by changing conditions, such as a money economy and wage work, but for a community like Navajo Mountain, kin role behavior is only slightly altered, and this only under special circumstances.

It is well to distinguish between ideal role behavior and actual behavior when it varies from the norms. A kinship role may be a membership role, that is, what a kinship group expects of certain members. We have dealt with this to some extent in the discussion of social groups, which in traditional Navajo society were almost exclusively kinship, or fictive kinship, groups. Further discussion is reserved for the section on patterns of cooperation. There is also an interpersonal kin role which is paired, that is, called into action by its relation to another kinship role, such as husband-wife, or mother-child. The interrelation of the kinship roles forms a system, the principal role system in Navajo society. Some picture of the number of roles that a Navajo plays, and the paired roles to which he must respond, clarifies the concept of strain by highlighting the areas of conflict. We will assess these relationships and show which paired roles take precedence over others.

HUSBAND—WIFE

They form a key-role pair in Navajo society. Ideally, this is the only position in which sexual intercourse is per-

mitted. The romantic complex does not obtain in Navajo
society, where marriages are preferably arranged, as we
discuss in more detail under marriage. Also, ideally the
husband-wife relationship is one of cooperation and companionship. Essentially, it is a democratic association. Navajo women share all the rights enjoyed by men. Each
partner owns his own sheep and horses, and ownership of
land for both men and women consists of use rights to
the land held by one's extended family or matrilineage, or
use rights to land held by the extended family into which
a spouse has married. These latter rights are contractual,
activated by coresidence, and extinguished on the dissolu-
tion of the marriage. Thus, there is little possibility of the
economic domination of one partner over the other.

Despite the lack of romance, many Navajo marriages
last for a lifetime. Overt, public demonstration of mutual
physical attraction is suppressed, but outsiders are struck
by the kindness, consideration and gentleness that many
young and old couples show to each other, and the pride
that they take in each other's achievements as craft workers
or leaders. There is a paucity of words of endearment in
the language; kinship terms are used to express affection,
and the phrase 'ayói 'óosh'ni is translated sometimes as "I
love her," and sometimes as "I respect her."

Often white informants, "Old Indian Hands," will characterize Navajo husbands as irresponsible and parasitic.
The oft-repeated statement is "Navajo women own the
sheep and do most of the work." We did not find this to be
generally true. Not only was almost every adult man doing
his full share of the work of the household, and of the
extended family in which he lived, but he was expected to
return at intervals to help his family of origin.

Public roles are played by men. Nominally and actually,
the husband is head of his household and the spokesman
for it. But, as with all forms of Navajo leadership, he is

expected to make decisions and exercise authority only after consultation with the women of his family. Several times we found to our dismay that work arrangements concluded with a husband the night before were vetoed or changed the next day by his wife.

In order to assess whether or not the husband-wife relationship is an area of strain in Navajo society, we analyzed both the informal dispute cases and the cases taken to the Navajo Tribal Courts by kin categories. More than a third of 67 informal cases of disputes between relatives were in the husband-wife category. Of 35 Tribal Court cases, more than half involved husbands and wives. In 8 informal cases, a husband complained against a wife; in 14 cases, the wife complained against her husband. In 23 court cases, only one husband, as compared to 22 wives, was a plaintiff.

The bases for disputes were jealousy, adultery, excessive drinking, assault and battery, desertion and nonsupport, in-law interference, laziness (husbands so charged their wives), and arguments revolving around the question of whether a couple should live with the husband's parents or with the wife's parents.

Sanctions which restrict excessively authoritarian behavior on the part of a husband are scolding, nagging, failure to cooperate, and divorce. Drunkenness, infidelity, and other unacceptable activities may provoke physical retaliation such as scratching, biting, and kicking. For example, Asdzáán Tso pushed her philandering husband face down in the mud and sat on him. A brawl that started after a Chapter meeting was described to us as follows:

> Hooch was passed around after the meeting, outside the trading post. Tempers flared. The Kiya'áanii boys were murderous. When one young man went after his opponent with a jagged bottle, the ladies stepped in to break it up. They raised a huge viga that had been cut on top of Navajo Mountain for use in remodeling

the trading post, knocked over the men, literally mowed them down, and each wife took her Hastiin home.

Sanctions applied by a husband to a wife include those listed above, plus beatings. Navajo husbands usually suppress violent and hostile behavior, but give way under the influence of alcohol. Despite the fact that there is probably less drinking in Navajo Mountain than in other parts of the Reservation (because of the 120-mile distance between the community and the source of supply, except for homebrewed "grey water"), excessive drinking is a common source of strain between husband and wife even here. One wife, speaking of her husband—who is a heavy, though sporadic drinker—said to us, "I can forgive him because most of the time he is kind to me." The physically active life led by Navajo women stands them in good stead in altercations with intoxicated husbands. One young woman offered her opinion, "I don't want to get married. The man might get drunk and maybe kill you." It should be noted that a few women also drink to excess.

> Left Handed's wife wanted a divorce and she asked me to help out. Her husband got drunk and talked mean to her. She said he wanted to make her daughter his second wife, but she asked me not to bring this up at the meeting we were going to have.
>
> Grace and Buddy are having trouble; Buddy wants to live with his mother, and Grace wants to live with hers. He took the little baby over to see his mother and they didn't come back. We had to take our daughter over there to see what was going on. Buddy decided to come back with us, after all.

Only a few of these marital disputes end in divorce, but the conclusion must be that the husband-wife relationship in Navajo society is fraught with great strain.

MOTHER–CHILD

The mother is the chief nurturant and authority figure in the rearing of Navajo children. A child's first two or three years are spent constantly with the mother because of nursing demands. He is displaced only with the arrival of the next baby. There is much affectionate interaction between mother and growing child. The mother depends chiefly on example and verbal admonition to instill ideals of correct behavior.

> My mother usually scolded me when I didn't do what she told me to do, like herding sheep or getting wood or hauling in the water.

The affectionate relationship between mother and child persists as the child grows. We saw a mother visiting at the Navajo Mountain School shyly brush the hair from her little boy's eyes while he leaned against her and patted her knee. When a child has gone away from Navajo Mountain to a far-off boarding school, usually at the age of eight, communication becomes difficult because of the language barrier. Children writing home in English must depend on translation, thus losing much of the flavor of the feelings expressed. For example, we saw a post card, "Hello, Mom. Just to wish you a big fat Hi!", a difficult sentiment to translate.

Grown-up sons have an affectionate and respectful attitude toward their mothers. One man told us that he would ask a favor of his mother before he would ask his father. A mother contributes to a son or daughter in case of need. She gives gifts to her children, a sheep or a colt. In answer to our question, "Who gives you gifts?" the first answer was always, "My mother." Other relatives were mentioned later, but this was qualified with, "It depends on how much they love you." Likewise, in answer to the question, "To whom do you give gifts?", the first answer was always, "To my mother," and other relatives were mentioned later.

> When one of our horses had a colt I asked my mother if it could be mine. So she gave it to me. We each have some sheep; I never told my mother I wanted sheep but she told me I had some.

> I get some welfare, Old Age Assistance, about $60.00 a month. It isn't much because I have to help my sons. Howard doesn't have a job, and you know Carl lost his arm in an auto accident and can't work.

Mothers and daughters are constant companions in work and recreation. As there have been, and still are, a number of girls without schooling in Navajo Mountain, many daughters spend their whole lives in the company of their mothers and sisters. Even educated girls who have returned from school will be found working with their mothers, listening to the Navajo Hour on the radio, or just chatting about the day's events. If they live matrilocally, much of their time will be spent in their mother's hogan.

> Now that I have graduated from high school, I wish I could get a job at Navajo Mountain. I like it here; I'd like to be living here with Mom.

Children expect to inherit from their mother, their share depending on a number of circumstances that will be discussed under Patterns of Cooperation. In some instances, if their widowed mother marries again, they may share in the bride price given for her.

> I helped to arrange the marriage of my brother's widow to an old medicine man. He paid quite a lot for her; her daughters took the jewelry, and her sons divided the stock and the money.

Children feel a lasting responsibility for their mother.
They visit her frequently, and expect to help her with her
work. Duties to parents (and other kin) may take precedence over gainful employment, as we learned when we
tried to hire interpreters.

> I'm sorry. I sure would like to work for you today, but
> my mother asked me to take my brother to the hospital
> in Tuba to have his sore foot treated.

> I can't work with you this week because I have to drive
> my father and mother to their far-off sheep camp.

Sons and daughters employed away from the area send
money home, but this is not an assured pattern. A young
woman working at the Navajo Mountain School contributed to the support of an aged father and stepmother. On
some occasions, daughters and sons have given up jobs in
other areas when requested to come home to help out with
the herding and farming.

The same patterns of authority and affection are extended to a stepmother or to a father's plural wife, or to a
mother's sister if she assumes the mother role over children
who have lost their own mother.

> When my mother was dying, she asked my father's
> older wife to take good care of her children—and she
> surely did do that.

A son or a daughter can joke with his mother about his
father's clan relatives. "Not mean; just for fun. My mother
can joke me about my father's clan, say that I might be
stingy with a *Lók'aa' dine'é* girl, for example."

We heard of only one instance of a mother-daughter relationship degenerating into a bitter quarrel. The daughter
took her husband's part against her mother, who was refusing to lend any more money to her son-in-law. Husband

and wife packed up their immediate possessions, picked up their five children, and moved to the family winter camp. After a cooling-off period, ruptured relations were restored.

In another case, a mother took her daughter to court for "incest" with a parallel cousin. This was not so much a quarrel between mother and daughter but an effort on the part of the mother to protect her daughter from the physical effects of incest.

The mother-child relationship is accorded high precedence in Navajo society and overt evidences of strain are expected to be suppressed.

FATHER–CHILD

The father in Navajo Mountain wields more authority than a review of the anthropological literature would lead one to expect. This may be a function of his more constant presence at home than in the old days when he was frequently away hunting, trading, or journeying for salt. Even two decades ago many Navajo fathers, engaged in off-Reservation war-industry work or railroad maintenance, were absent from their families for long periods of time. Now wage work, welfare payments, and free services from the Federal government supplement income from traditional sources, and most married men do not seek permanent work away from home. Only one man from the entire community holds a job on the outside, and he is home every weekend with his wife and children.

Today, in Navajo Mountain, ideally and actually, the father shares responsibility with the mother for the support and training of his children. He advises, teaches manners and male skills, punishes, gives gifts, and comes to the aid of grown children in time of stress.

> I teach my children how to behave. My wife and I do.

> A woman missionary said, "I was eating with Laugh-

ing Boy and his family. Laughing Boy corrected his little boy's table manners, and instructed him to eat a barbecued rib by picking the meat off the bone with his fingers and putting it in his mouth. The little boy said, pointing to me, 'But she puts the whole rib up to her mouth and bites off pieces.' Said Laughing Boy sternly, 'You do it the Navajo way - she just doesn't know any better.' "

My father told us, 'Don't be in a rush about eating.'

Father or mother punishes a naughty child; mother's brother doesn't have anything to say when you are little. Only when you grow up.

My father is so old he has no sense about money. He spends every cent he gets hold of for jewelry which he gives to his children. He gave me this beautiful string of turquoise and coral.

My father gave me a good rope horse when I was about 15.

One of our local boys was in Los Angeles on relocation. He got drunk, got in trouble, and was thrown in jail. His father had to go and bail him out and bring him home.

One of Tall Jack's daughters married out. After several years, word filtered back that she was not being well treated by her husband and his relatives. Tall Jack went over there and brought her home.

The Navajo father is markedly affectionate and playful with younger children and companionable with older sons. If he is a Singer, he will frequently teach the legends and Chants to his sons, and to his daughters as well, if they are interested in learning. A grown son living at home will herd with his father, work with him in the fields, spend much time with him in the upkeep or repair of a car. Companionship between fathers and sons may even be carried to the point of joint drinking sprees. Father and son will fight in each other's defense during a drunken brawl.

An elderly man, particularly one whose family of origin has become dispersed, thereby relieving him of major responsibility to them, will divide his sheep permit among his children with whom he is living. The prime motive for this generous gesture is to become eligible for welfare payments, because regulations prohibit a welfare recipient from owning more than 50 sheep units.

Two teen-age girls told us to ask permission of their father rather than of their mother when we invited them to go on a picnic. They quoted their father freely, his opinions on religion, on laziness, on children's duties. "Our father is head man of our family," said a young man, referring to a long-haired, non-English-speaking older man, sire of twelve sons, several of whom are high-school educated and successful in holding good jobs away from home.

> My brothers and I turn the money we earn over to our father. We are glad to do this; we are happy that we can repay him for all of the kind things he did for us when we were growing up.

The young man who made this statement is unmarried and living at his parents' camp.

A white resident said:

> Navajo women are very placid, they do what mama and papa say, especially papa. We went to a traditional wedding ceremony recently - the girl and her mother had never seen the bridegroom.

Children owe help and respect to their fathers. Sanctions for proper behavior on the part of grown-up children are informal. The strong desire to be considered a good son or daughter, and the recurring need for help from one's family on occasion, serve to motivate children toward correct filial behavior. In public a son will play a secondary role to his father, though in private he may be his chief aide and adviser.

The womenfolk of an old man's family adorned him tenderly in preparation for picture-taking, and a young grandson held up action until he could secure an unruly grey lock with a bobby pin.

> Our father went to Washington to testify in the land claims case. His group was shown around, and at the White House they were introduced to President Kennedy. My father was confused and said, 'You are not Washington, our president. I've seen pictures of him and he is an old man with a beard; are you his son?' Later, when he got back home, he got after his children because they had not explained to him that Washington is not president now. He said to us, 'You let me go there and make a fool of myself.'

A child can joke with his or her father about his clan. "You can make a joke with him and say, 'You married into my clan'."

We have described the preferred patterns of behavior between father and children, and have noted that actual behavior generally supports the ideal. There are, however, elements of strain in the relationship. The Navajo penchant for not telling another individual what he must or must not do makes the role of headman of a camp difficult for unaggressive men.

> Dad tries to get advice from his sons and sons-in-law, instead of giving it. Now they don't respect him or pay any attention to him. We hear them calling him, the 'Old Man.'

Sometimes there are bitter clashes between father and children. A father called the police to arrest his son for being drunk and bellicose. Another man complained to the Navajo Tribal Court that his daughter was guilty of illicit cohabitation with a Paiute, that she was drinking excessively and neglecting her children and her sheep.

A young man left home, declaring that he would never return. "My father made a slave of me when I was at home. He almost worked me to death."

The most drastic quarrel between father and son resulted in a suicide attempt by the young man, who shot himself in the stomach when his father taunted him.

The traditional custom of turning over responsibility for children to the mother's relatives in case of her death or the breakup of the nuclear family has given rise to a stereotype of the irresponsible and unstable Navajo father. In view of the cooperation and affection between father and children that we observed at Navajo Mountain, and the paucity of dispute cases that were reported to us or recorded by the court, the Navajo father most often appears as responsible, respected, and much loved.

SIBLING–SIBLING

This is one of the strongest ties in Navajo society. Siblings are raised in the same household and belong to the same matrilineage. They share the same clan affiliations, and, therefore, the same network of kinship relations. There is a lifelong feeling of mutual responsibility.

We were unable to find any sharp distinctions in behavior based on relative age of siblings to correspond with the precise denotation of older and younger brother, older and younger sister, in Navajo kin terminology, and to the meticulous specification of order of birth in the listings of siblings informants always give. An older brother, or an older sister, may be delegated the task of looking after a younger sibling for short periods. In answer to our questions we were assured that no effort is made to arrange the marriage of an older sibling before that of a younger one—there is no Leah who must be worked for before Jacob can marry Rachel. Nor is there discrimination by age in the distribution of an estate, since other factors such as who was taking care of the deceased, who has the skills to use the property, who is present at the distribution, and so forth, come into play.

Even when the coresidential tie is broken, there is much visiting among siblings. Sibling exchange is a frequent form of marriage. That is, when a man or a woman marries into a family, he or she will often take the initiative in arranging a marriage between one of his or her siblings and the brother or sister of the spouse.

> After Jean married Jake, she helped arrange for me to marry his brother.

> My older brother married into that family, so he thought it would be a good idea for our other brother to marry his wife's sister. That way they could both live in Oljeto.

An elder sister will often care for young siblings when their mother dies.

> My sister was sixteen years old when our mother died. We lived with relatives, but my sister was the one who really took care of me.

> When my mother died her sister took the younger children, but the older ones went with my father way down the canyon where he had a place. Our eleven-year-old sister helped with the cooking and with the care of the children.

Siblings cannot joke with each other about clans, because they belong to the same clan and are born for the same clan. They do joke with each other, however, but there are variations in acceptable patterns by sex, that is, sister to sister, brother to brother, and brother to sister.

Half-brothers and sisters may share as close a bond as full brothers and sisters. However, this is not invariably true.

> I was surprised to see in my husband's family how all of the children of the old man seem to feel very close, even those with different mothers. In my family, where my father also had three wives at the same time, we felt much closer to our own brothers and sisters - same father, same mother.

BROTHER–BROTHER

This is a close, warm, friendly relationship of cooperation in work and play. Navajo Mountain brothers usually share the same interests because of the cultural homogeneity. Brothers herd together, go to school together, support each other in fights, leave the Reservation together to look for work, and feel a very real sense of responsibility for each other's welfare.

> My brother is in the hospital. The doctor says he was bitten by a spider. I want to go to Cow Springs [75 miles away] to get my mother and father, and a medicine man. You never know - he may have been witched.

Even when brothers no longer live in the same camp or the same community, they continue to visit each other frequently, meet at the parental camp, and give aid to each other in time of need.

> My car is out of clutch, and my brother has come from Grand Canyon to help me fix it.

> I'm sure I can stay with my brother for a few days; he
> has a job now.

> Whiteman Killer had gone to Bodoway to visit his
> brother who was sick. He never came back; he died over
> there himself. He was too old to have made such a
> long trip.

The levirate, the custom of marrying a brother's widow,
though not formalized as a rule, is considered a good practice. In this way a man assumes responsibility for his brother's children and acts as a real father.

Brothers can joke each other about girls, or tease each
other.

> You can joke your brother about an ugly girl being his
> girl friend. Or, you can challenge him to a race; you
> can jump in the snow or in cold water and dare him to
> follow. You can wrestle with him or tease him and say,
> 'Why do you sleep all the time?' or 'Why do you have to
> shave all the time?' You can make rough jokes, but you
> can't joke him about clans because your clan and the
> clan you are born for are the same as his.

Strain may arise between brothers over problems of
sharing work, over land use rights, or over inheritance, but
lasting rifts are rare. In our collection of both formal and
informal disputes, we have only one complaint made by a
brother against a brother. This case of deliberately damag-
ing a car was taken to the Navajo Tribal Court.

BROTHER–SISTER

This is a strong, affectionate relationship of mutual aid.
Brothers and sisters are brought up in the same hogan; as
children they play together and herd together. When they
approach adolescence, companionship is less constant be-

cause their work obligations have become increasingly dif-
ferentiated. We were expecting to find stronger avoidance
patterns, however, than proved to be the case. In spending
the night with a family, we noted that two teen-age sisters
slept with their 11-year-old brother between them under
one blanket. A 19-year-old girl asked us to leave the hogan
while she changed her skirt, but her 20-year-old brother
was allowed to remain inside. A brother uses a polite form
of the verb to address a grown sister, but this form is also
used for other members of the family. A man assured us
that it would be quite proper for him to drive alone with
his sister to the hospital, or to the trading post. One educated boy said he did not "bother his sisters," and, in fact,
he seemed to fraternize very little with them. However, in
seeking advice about further schooling, he consulted his
older sister, a high-school graduate.

> I talked it over with my sister because neither my
> mother nor my father went to school, and they do not
> understand these things.

Married brothers and sisters show continued interest in
each other's welfare and accept high standards of mutual
aid.

> I have to take some milk to my sister's baby in Navajo
> Mountain. She can't get this kind around there.

> When Grandpa Tsosie married that woman from In-
> scription House, it was his sister who arranged it. She
> got his children to help out with the bride price.

> I've got to get to Tuba City; there is a family over by
> Tall Mountain that is trying to witch my sister. I have
> to go to the police before they kill her.

A brother will stay with his sister's family when he is
visiting in the area. One man, working and living at the

Navajo Mountain trading post, has a second home with his sister's family.

Although brothers and sisters cannot joke about clans, they tease each other about boy friends and girl friends. They can say, "You have a dirty face." An old medicine man explained, "They tell in one of our myths about how the Children of the Sun visited their Father, that is the origin of the custom of joking with your sisters about being dirty. The Sun said to his children, "You are dirty." He combed their hair and said, "Now you are pretty." Two teenage girls said, "We joke our brother about his drinking problem." An older man said, "When you are older you don't joke so much, or tease so much. Only once in a while. I don't joke with my sister because I have only one sister left, and she is too kind-hearted."

Despite the warmth of this relationship, it is also an area fraught with very great strain. This is because one of the beliefs regarding Navajo witchcraft is that a witch must sacrifice someone near and dear to him, usually a favorite sister, in order to validate his position as a witch among witches. As a result, whenever a woman dies, her brother may fall under suspicion of having practiced witchcraft against her.

> If you want to learn witchcraft you have to kill your best-loved sister, or make some other such sacrifice.

Two of the bitterest quarrels in Navajo Mountain concern brothers and sisters. In one, a brother is suspected of having brought about the violent death of three of his sister's children. In another case, when two sisters died, suspicion fell on a brother. Both he and his son were accused of witchcraft and their sudden deaths within a few hours of each other have been ascribed to counterwitchcraft measures taken against them by a remaining sister and her family.

Tall Man had two other sisters. He loved them both, but he became a skin walker and he killed them both.

SISTER–SISTER

In Navajo society, where camaraderie is based almost exclusively on kinship, sisters are afforded the greatest possibility for the closest lifelong relationship. As children they live, work, and play together. They go to school together, and when they marry they are likely to live in adjacent hogans in their camp of origin. Living thus, only a few yards apart, they spend much time together and are constantly available to each other for mutual aid in daily household tasks, in exchanging babysitting stints, in butchering a lamb, or in entertaining with small talk a sister who is weaving.

> I had an older sister. I followed her everywhere. We herded together, did everything together. I was eight years old and she was eighteen. I was her shadow, they say. She died suddenly; I refused to believe she was dead; I couldn't believe it. I went looking for her; I looked everywhere we had been together. I wouldn't eat, and I couldn't sleep. My family decided to send me away for my own good. They took me to the nearest school, thirty-five miles away.

There are innumerable instances of a woman gladly making a very real sacrifice to help out a sister who is in need.

> Neither my mother nor my father wanted me to go to school, but I was determined to get an education. I had been in school only two years when my older sister's husband died. She had several small children and needed me to help in herding. There was nothing I

> could do except come home to help her. I never got
> any more schooling.

Sisters can joke, but not about clans. They can tease each
other about a dirty face or about boy friends, much like the
patterned joking with and between brothers.

Strong and affectionate as this relationship is, both ideally
and actually, it may break down over jealousy and interest
in the same man.

> Mary was married to Bill Johns. Then Marian wanted
> him. The sisters quarreled bitterly, even hit each other
> at the beginning. Marian went after him and got him,
> and now the three of them live together in the same
> hogan.

Other cases of sororal polygyny indicate that frequently
both sisters accept the situation without undue strain.

Two Navajo Mountain sisters quarreled over the division
of their deceased mother's sheep permit. Unable to resolve
the difference, one sister left the family camp and prevailed
upon her mother's brother to keep her flock with his.

MOTHER'S BROTHER–SISTER'S CHILD

Since in so many matrilineal societies of the world the
mother's brother plays the principal authority role, it has
become almost a truism in anthropological theory to regard
him as the leading jural figure (Radcliffe-Brown, 1952:15)
(Eggan, 1950:37) (Schneider and Gough, 1961:11). Our ob-
servations and our questioning about this role in Navajo
Mountain convince us that the authority of the mother's
brother does not supersede that of the father as male head
of the family, sharing with the mother control over the children. Our informants seemed surprised at the question,

"Did your mother's brother punish you?" One girl answered, "How could he when he wasn't around to know what I was doing?" Only one elderly man reported that his mother's brother used to spank him, but he added quickly, "That was because he was a mean man."

Frequency of interaction between a maternal uncle and his nieces and nephews will depend on coresidence. If he resides in a bilocal camp with his sister's family, the association will be constant. If he lives in a nearby camp in the same community, it will be regular, but even if he resides at a distance, he will maintain contact with his sisters through visiting. In some cases, the mother's brother may be of nearly the same age as his nephew, and if they live in the same camp they may be close companions. A young Navajo who pulled us out of the sand, where we had been stuck all night, referred to the young man who came riding up with him as "My Buddy." Later we found out that the "buddy" was his mother's brother.

The mother's brother is expected to take particular interest in his sister's children. He gives them gifts, and they can turn to him for help. If he is a "medicine man," he will teach any sister's son who is interested the Sings he knows. He is the preferred kinsman to assist in arranging marriages for his maternal nephews and nieces. He is one of the relatives who may tell the children the origin legends or coyote stories in winter time.

> The father disciplines the children, not the mother's brother, at least not any mother's brother I know.

> My mother's brother is teaching me to sing. He's getting old and he's having trouble with his throat so he's giving his knowledge and ceremonies to me. I learned another song from my other uncle. Deer Hoof. He gave me a deer hoof rattle and a buffalo hide.

> My brother and I always help out with our sisters' children, boy or girl, when there are marriage arrangements. We talk it over with the other parents and we give something for the gifts [bride price] when our nephews are going to get married.

The mother's brother may also share in the bride price given for his sister's daughter if he has taken part in the marriage arrangements.

> Emmet was on his way home from a Squaw Dance and he stayed overnight at our hogan. He saw me; then he wanted me. I was about fifteen years old and Emmet was twenty-seven. My grandmother arranged my marriage; Emmet's father's father asked for me. My grandmother turned him down, so his mother's brother came. She turned him down. So his mother's half-brother came, and he stayed all day. He wouldn't leave until my grandmother said, 'Yes.' My own mother's brother, Edward Day, said, 'This thing is foolish; let's say 'Yes' and let this man go home.' The present was a real good necklace, and a mule and two horses, and some other things. Edward Day took the necklace and the mule.

When a mother's brother dies, his sisters' children show concern. They expect to inherit something from his estate, at least some token to remember him by. In the days before sheep permits and Indian Court rules of inheritance, a sister's children might receive a substantial share of the sheep herd left by a maternal uncle.

The roughest joking with the exception of joking between male cross cousins is permissible between mother's brother and sister's son. Sexual jokes are in order. They can call each other *báshishchíin bakạ*, or, "male married to a woman of the clan for which I was born." *Bakạ* is a vulgar term for male, correctly used for animals only. Tricks can be played on a mother's brother, and vice versa.

You can steal his hat or pull his pants off. He isn't sup-
posed to get mad. Your mother's brother can call you
sha'ayéhé, 'The one who marries for me.' He can joke
you about your father's clan; ask you if you are in love
with your father's relatives. He can tease you about
having a dirty face. He can joke with his sister's daughter too, but no dirty jokes because she's a girl.

The status of mother's brother is not the strongest authority role in Navajo society, and if no mother's brother
is readily available, a substitute will serve. However, this is
a valued kin position, and the incumbent is regularly called
upon, if possible, to meet the obligations of the role.

Any strain we observed derived largely from the personalities of the role players. One 80-year-old man remembered vividly how irascible his uncle was. Another told us
in detail how he was forced to work for his mother's brother,
herd sheep, grind corn, and fetch wood. "He made a slave
out of me," we were told.

We have no record of a court case in which a mother's
brother was accused of injuring a sister's son or daughter.
In one informal case, a mother's brother lassoed a sister's
daughter who was riding horseback through his corn field,
leaving severe rope burns on her neck. In another informal
case a mother's brother was suspected of witching his sister's
son when the boy was struck by lightning and left with
impaired hearing.

MOTHER'S SISTER–SISTER'S CHILD

This perhaps is the closest collateral relationship of any
kin position in the next ascending or descending generation. Married sisters living in the same camp are presumably
best friends, and are expected to take a particular interest in
each other's children and be prepared to assume the mother
role in time of emergency. Mother's sister is called "little

mother" and she in turn addresses her sister's children by
the same terms she uses for her own children; however, she
does not assume the authority-responsibility role of mother
in the normal course of events.

> You know those two married daughters of my sister
> who died; I see them more than anyone else does. I
> think of them as my own daughters.

In cases of sororal polygyny, the maternal aunt is co-wife
of the child's father and the mother of his half-siblings. This
relationship appears to reinforce an already close tie. The
tendency toward the sororate means that in the event of the
mother's death, her sister is likely to become stepmother
as well as aunt.

A grown niece cooperates with her mother's sister in the
everyday tasks around their family camp; a nephew acknowledges an obligation to her, but the fact of living
in another camp after he marries cuts down the amount of
contact, thereby making the aunt-niece relationship more
important than the aunt-nephew dyad.

Joking is permitted with the mother's sister. She can be
called *shizhá'áád*, the term for women who have married
Ego's kin in the first ascending and first descending generations. "You can say, 'Hello, *báshishchíin be'esdzáán*,' or
'Hello, woman who married into the clan for which I was
born!' " The humor of these jokes lies in the play on affinal versus blood-kin relationships.

There appears to be little structural strain in this relationship. Although there are several instances in our genealogies
of men marrying the maternal nieces of their wives, there
is no record of hostility toward the polygynous relationship.
However, in one case, a woman quarreled bitterly with her
sister's daughter who bore a child to the aunt's husband,
and refused to allow her niece the status of co-wife. In another case a woman complained to the police when her

sister's son, a known psychopath, threatened her with bodily harm. But, in general, the strain in this relationship is no greater than can be found in all paired roles defined by rights and obligations where some individuals fail to meet the patterned expectations.

FATHER'S SIBLING—BROTHER'S CHILD

Just as the kin terms for paternal uncle and aunt differ from uncle and aunt on the maternal side, so do the expectations differ. Father's brother is not viewed as a father substitute in spite of the fact that he may be called by the father term and that there is a weak tendency toward the levirate. Father's sister is neither looked upon as a mother substitute nor called "little" mother. However, there is on both sides a very real recognition of close kinship and a sense of obligation to help out in time of need. An informant whose father died leaving a number of small children said accusingly, "With me and the rest of us, we didn't get anything from my father's relatives. I never ate any of their food or anything."

Ego's father frequently visits his camp of origin, taking his wife and children with him, especially if he intends to remain there for several days. In this way children come to know their father's sister well, if not intimately. Father's brother, on the other hand, is usually not present unless by chance he, too, is visiting his parental camp, so contact with him is apt to be less frequent.

A father's brother who is a Singer will teach his nephew the songs, and even help him to acquire a medicine bag.

Joking: "You can joke with your father's brother, but not so rough as with your mother's brother. If he is born for Manygoats, I can say, 'Tł'ízí łání bahastiin' (husband of a Manygoats), which, of course, he cannot be. I can joke him with a nickname; I can call him any name and pat him on the shoulder. You can joke your father's sister with the clan she is born for, but not mean, just for fun."

There is a record of two court cases in which a father's sister filed a complaint against her brother's sons for assault and battery. In one informal case a father's brother complained about the disorderly conduct of his brother's son.

Strain in these role relations appears to be at a minimum. Harmony exists as long as these kin show the respect and willingness to help that any good Navajo expects from a "real close relative."

MOTHER'S MOTHER–DAUGHTER'S CHILD

The relationship between maternal grandmother and grandchild is ideally close and affectionate. The grandmother usually lives in the same camp with the growing children of her daughters, and she shares in their care, training and discipline. If she does not live with them she visits frequently. In a number of cases Navajos cited their mother's mother as the person who told them the legends and instructed them in proper behavior. Many maternal grandmothers raise their dead daughters' children. Often a daughter will give a child, usually a girl, to her mother to bring up as companion and helper.

The mother's mother is always consulted about, and many times she takes an active part in, marriage arrangements for a granddaughter or grandson. If she does so for a granddaughter she will share in the bride price. She may be asked to speak at the wedding. Not only is her role one of authority, but it also calls upon her to show indulgence and affection to her grandchild. She is expected to give them gifts and come to their aid.

> Our grandmother gave Janet her sheep permit when she applied for Old Age Assistance. It was because

> Janet was the oldest girl and closest to Grandma. She helped her a lot and spent most of her time with her.

She has an important voice in the distribution of an estate within her matrilineage.

> My mother used to live around here. She lived with her granddaughter, who was my niece. When she died that girl got all her property. I did not get a thing, no land, no sheep, no jewelry.

Grandchildren are expected to help their grandmother in her old age. One hears frequent complaints by non-kin, "No one does anything for that old lady," but the burden of caring for the aged has been lightened by the institution of Old Age Assistance. Nowadays there is often rivalry between grandchildren who are eager to take care of the elderly individual and share in the benefits of a regular monthly check.

Mild joking is permitted with a maternal grandmother.

Strain in this relationship arises when the mother's mother exceeds the authority that the grandchild believes to be legitimate. If she makes too heavy demands upon a grandchild she is considered to be a slave driver.

> I couldn't refuse to marry Jeffrey once my grandmother had agreed to accept him. I couldn't go against her; I was a kind of slave to her.

Sometimes grandchildren who are interested in "going the white way" object to the old matriarch's pressure for maintaining traditions, but quarrels with maternal grandmothers seldom reach a community meeting or the court since Navajos believe that overt evidences of strain in this relationship should be suppressed. The mother's mother is a strongly conservative role in Navajo society; she is the traditionalist who serves to keep alive the old Navajo way.

MOTHER'S FATHER–DAUGHTER'S CHILD

This is a strong relationship closely resembling that of mother's mother-daughter's child. Coresidence and respect for age enhance the ties. Grandchildren with whom we talked regarded their maternal grandfathers with respect, or with tender amusement, depending on the personality of the old man. A mother's father indulges his daughter's children and enjoys giving presents to them. He is often the relative who tells the legends to young children. When he dies, his grandchildren will expect to inherit something, perhaps only the oft-mentioned "token to remember him by," but also perhaps the bulk of his estate if they have assumed the burden of caring for him in his old age.

Joking is permitted with a mother's father, but gentle or teasing jokes only. "No bad jokes; you can challenge him to a race or a wrestling match," a grandson said. Or, "you can tease about some ladies being interested in him." It was in just such terms that our interpreter teased her grandfather when she took us to interview him.

FATHER'S PARENTS–SON'S CHILD

Paternal grandparents do not tend to enjoy as close a relationship with their sons' children as do maternal grandparents with their daughters' children, if for no other reason than that they are likely to live in different camps. For the same reason, their authority is reduced. However, there is frequently much visiting back-and-forth and an acknowledged obligation to help out in time of need. One elderly widow complained to us that the lion's share of her monthly Old Age Assistance check went to help the children of a disabled son.

In one apparently aberrant case, a granddaughter told us

that her father's father was intent on killing his grandchildren one by one through witchcraft.

PARALLEL COUSINS

Parallel cousins on both maternal and paternal sides are called by the brother-sister terms. On the mother's side, they belong to the same clan as Ego but they may be born for a different clan. On the fathers side, the parallel cousin and Ego are born for the same clan but may belong to different clans. They will share both clans if their fathers have married into the same clan.

This is a friendly, helpful relationship rather like that of siblings but attenuated. Maternal parallel cousins may grow up in the same camp and will play together and share many of the same experiences.

Joking is permitted with parallel cousins mainly in the form of teasing. The favorite Navajo Mountain jokes are about Paiutes, such as "Nasja is your boy friend," and "Wochan is your girl friend." One young man jokes Laura, his maternal parallel cousin, by saying when he sees her wearing her glasses, "You look like a fly." Or, if a fat woman goes by he says, "There goes Laura." She will give the rejoinder, "There goes your wife." He may point out an ugly man and say, "That's your husband."

The built-in strain of this relationship centers upon use rights to land. Maternal parallel cousins claim their use rights to land through the original preempting couple of their matrilineage. With increasing population and consequent limitation of land, cousins may quarrel over their share of grazing and farming areas. There are instances where a man or a woman has been away from the Reservation and on his return wishes to take up the use of grazing or agricultural land, claiming his right through parent or grandparent. If the land has been used by cousins in the

meantime, they may resent the "intrusion" of new sheepherders, although they are obliged to recognize the fact that
their parallel cousins have valid claims.

CROSS COUSINS

The children of mother's brother will be born for Ego's
clan, whereas the children of father's sister will be members
of the clan for which Ego is born, resulting in the same
reciprocal relationship for both sets of cross cousins. These
kin of the same generation do not ordinarily live in the
same camp, but the relationship is a warm and friendly
one. Male cross cousins call each other *shił naa'aash*, "He
goes along with me," and as the term suggests, they are
frequently close companions.

Very vulgar behavior is permitted between male cross
cousins, including sexual references and crude jokes, tricks,
challenges, and forfeits. It is the roughest joking relationship to be permitted among Navajos, with the exception
of mother's brother to sister's son. Female cross cousins do
not tend to be companionable in the manner of male cousins, nor is the same latitude in joking permitted. Girl
cousins tease each other in a mild manner, as do boy and
girl cousins.

We did not find any specific instances to show inherent
strain in this relationship.

AFFINALS

The network of affinal relationships is a sensitive one. It
is structured through marriage negotiations, the bride price,
the customs of sororal polygyny, a tendency toward the levirate and the sororate, and sibling exchange. To unite families through strong marital ties is considered of great
importance in Navajo society, because cooperation is organized almost exclusively within a kinship framework.

The qualitative differences between affinal and genealogical or clan relationships is underlined in a number of ways. Affinal terms of reference are distinct from terms used to refer to genealogical or clan kin. There is a joking pattern in which the humor rests entirely on the misuse of affinal terms as address terms for certain categories of close blood kin. The only imperative avoidance pattern, that between son-in-law and mother-in-law, is maintained by a supernatural threat of blindness. The delicacy of the affinal relationship is emphasized in the request patterns appropriate to the planning of a large curing ceremonial. Each spouse assumes the responsibility for approaching his own kin for aid.

MOTHER-IN-LAW–SON-IN-LAW

This is an extremely sensitive paired role in Navajo society. The pattern of complete mutual avoidance is explained by Navajos as a respect relationship. The residence of a son-in-law in his mother-in-law's camp is a preferred pattern, a camp in which she is a strong authority figure while he has contractual rights only. The continuing close relationship between mother and daughter serves to reinforce her strong position and to increase the difficulties inherent in a son-in-law role. Further strain lies in the fact that a husband has obligations to three families, his family of procreation, his mother-in-law's family, and his family of origin.

WIFE'S SISTER–SISTER'S HUSBAND

The ideal pattern for this relationship is one of mild avoidance. These people, however, live in the same camp and there may be frequent interaction. Sororal polygyny being an accepted marriage pattern, the wife frequently exhibits extreme jealousy, which causes strain in this relationship.

The only case of open flirting we observed was between a man and his wife's sister. The wife was not present.

FATHER-IN-LAW—SON-IN-LAW

This is a difficult relationship since it involves the subordination of a son-in-law to a comparative stranger in the planning of joint activities. However, there are many cases of long-lasting and amicable cooperation between father-in-law and son-in-law in Navajo Mountain. The father-in-law may champion the son-in-law in the face of family and community criticism. There was a dramatic case of a man accused of practicing witchcraft whose life was saved through the intervention of his father-in-law. In another instance a father-in-law was indefatigable in helping to arrange the Sings that prepared his son-in-law for "ordination" as a Yeibichai Singer.

The informal pressure for younger men to defer to older men is so strong that many potential clashes are avoided. If the son-in-law is more efficient than his father-in-law, and if he is diplomatic, the subordination-superordination may be reversed and the son-in-law will become the *de facto* leader of the extended family. This inevitably takes place as the father-in-law becomes too old to accept his share of responsibility.

Summary

Kinship roles are defined by Navajo society in preferred patterns of mutual expectation for behavior, in rights and obligations expectably attached to positions in the kinship system. These are underlined in the classificatory terminology, in patterned joking, and in the value system that defines a good man or a good woman as a good kinsman. But this is a flexible, negotiating society which allows for the use of alternates in kinship roles and kinship terminology. Despite the matrilineal, matrilocal bias, father's lineage and clan are important, both in themselves and as substitute roles for matrilineal kinsmen. The flexibility of residence patterns means that children of couples who are living patrilocally will interact more frequently with father's rather than mother's kinsmen. The strong sibling tie means continuing interaction with brothers and sisters through visits and aid in life crises despite wide geographical separation.

There are no fixed, ranked positions that entail inalienable rights and entitle an individual incumbent to superiority regardless of the quality of his performance. Leadership roles in the community depend on personality and achieved prestige and to a lesser degree this is also true of leadership in the extended family. However, what constitutes prestige is limited to acceptable traditional behavior, allowing little room for the type of originality and aggressive individuality that in the outside society is most often associated with the achievement of success.

Patterns of Cooperation

Earning a Living

Life in Navajo Mountain is organized about a mixed pastoral and farming economy. True, herding and farming no longer suffice to support the population, which has increased many times over, and traditional sources of income must be augmented by welfare payments and wage work, but the center of economic interest still lies in the sheep. Dry farming and small irrigated plots in the canyons attract seasonal attention, but the uncertain yield from agriculture is supplementary, as is the income from singing for ceremonials, and the crafts of weaving, basketry, and leather-working.

Nontraditional ways of earning a living can be fitted into the regular cooperative pattern of a family-based pastoralism. In Navajo Mountain there are fewer than a dozen permanent wage-work positions. A few families work as migratory laborers for several weeks during the year, but the most important source of jobs is the 10-day Tribal work projects, which are rotated among the able-bodied men. Monthly welfare checks supplement the seasonal cash income from lambs and wool.

Maintenance of the household is the other activity in which there is regular cooperation. This requires the building and care of hogans, the hauling of wood and water, cooking, and the making, washing, and repairing of clothing. The division of labor is by residence group, by sex, and by age.

HERDING

Sheep are individually owned and earmarked. At the present time, the head of the household, or even the oldest man in the extended family, may be the sole person named on the Tribal-issued sheep permit, but each member of the family knows how many and which sheep are his. Children who herd are given sheep as the nucleus of a future flock.

> I was given sheep for herding when I was a little girl. If you don't herd sheep you don't get any.

Other ways of acquiring sheep are through the purchase of a permit or through inheritance. The aged, before applying for Old Age Assistance, often distribute their sheep and assign their sheep permit among the children or grandchildren with whom they are living.

Cattle are also individually owned. They are turned loose in the canyons and rounded up for sale. The few cows and bulls in Navajo Mountain are locally referred to as "brag cattle." Horses, too, are individually owned as beloved possessions that lend prestige to their owners. They are belled, allowed to wander free (a menace to planted fields), but have to be rounded up for use.

Sheep must be taken to water at least every other day, and they must be grazed for part of each day. They are herded in a common flock by the members of an extended family or camp. If an "outsider," or nonmember, of the extended family herds, he expects to be paid, whereas members of the camp are considered to be helping to take care of their own sheep. Sixty or seventy years ago, slaves were used by some families to herd and farm.

Traditionally, Navajo children were the sheepherders, and they still do most of the herding in the summer; but in wintertime when they are away at school, the task falls upon the adult men and women, even on the very old if they are able-bodied. Some families in Navajo Mountain keep a tractable child out of school to do this work, and the role of Little Herder is easily identifiable in the area today. Women with small children may be excused from their share of herding but other members of the camp who shirk their part often find themselves involved in a family dispute.

> Prudence and Genevieve had a fight last summer because Prudence wouldn't herd sheep. Genevieve told her to take her sheep and go somewhere else, so she put them in with her mother's brother's herd and went to live with her husband's family.

Women share with men in the work of lambing, castrating horses, shearing, dipping and dusting (under the supervision of an employee of the Bureau of Indian Affairs or of the Navajo Tribe), and in the butchering.

> We all herd together, my sister and I, my husband, and my brother. My older brother works so we herd his sheep with ours. My mother's too. She has her own permit.
>
> We herd our sheep together, my sons and sons-in-law and their families, all of us in the family that lives together.
>
> My mother is out on the Plateau right now with my sisters. They are herding sheep. My father herds in the wintertime when we are all in school.

Individuals, by turns, furnish a sheep to be butchered, and the meat is shared among nuclear families constituting the camp.

> We divide a sheep with my sisters and their families. We take turns killing a sheep and passing it around. My mother plans out what is to be done. She will say, 'Now, Desbah, it's your turn to kill a sheep.'

An extended family bases its claim to the use of land for grazing on preemption or on relationship to the original family that preempted the land. Every member of the camp shares in these use rights, which cannot be alienated without the agreement of the entire extended family.

FARMING

Agricultural techniques are simple, requiring only a few hand tools. Farms are not individually owned; use rights to farming land, like those governing grazing land, are based on preemption or relationship to the original preempting family. They accrue to the family that first cleared and cultivated the land. If the plots are not farmed for a long time, longer than is reasonable for letting a field lie fallow, another family may plant a crop. However, it is prudent and proper to ask permission of the family that had formerly used the land.

> No one owns the land. You don't divide it. You just talk it over. You ask if you can use the land.

> Barbara took over the Tso family field. But the Tsos didn't plant corn. The Tsos could have caused trouble for her and her husband, but they didn't because they hadn't been using the land. If they had been using it, they could have taken the matter to the Chapter. Barbara and the Tsos are kind of distantly related.

All the adult men in the camp, plus the boys, cooperate in dry farming on the plateau and irrigated farming in the canyons. Usually fields, once planted, are left for long periods without attention, but if the area is large and the crop important, some member or members of the family will stay to tend the farm.

> We have a camp in the canyon where we grow corn, squash and melons, also grapes, peaches and apples. Everyone who lives in our camp works together. Someone stays there to keep the farm from the sheep and the squirrels.

> I plant my own fields. My sons-in-law help my sons. Each camp takes care of its own fields.

> My brother and I look after the farm in Paiute Canyon.

> The sons-in-law and the one son of Old Man White Hair who lives in that camp with him work his field.

> And, of course, they share the crop with the old man.
>
> My father-in-law has a farm in Paiute Canyon. I work on that farm with him and his sons, those young boys who go to school. We help each other on the ditch and we share the crops. The ditch was washed out so now a man stays down there in the canyon to watch the water situation.
>
> This land my boys farm belonged to their father. We left the land we had cleared over at Mexican Water, when we moved back near my husband's family.

Again we found no evidence of any group larger than the extended family which regularly cooperated for farming. In the past, care of the irrigation ditches was the responsibility of each family having an adjacent farm, but at the present time, the Chapter pays for the cleaning of the ditches out of Tribal funds as one of the local work projects.

WORKING FOR WAGES

Members of the family who work for wages contribute to the household income. The employees at the school either live with their extended families or spend weekends with them whenever possible. One of the girls at the school contributes money to her orphaned brothers and sisters who are being raised by their grandmother. Temporary employment of the men and a few women on federal and tribal projects such as water development, building a Chapter house, road improvement, and emergency public works can easily be absorbed by a large sheepherding family. The wage worker is the first one to acquire a truck; the first pick-up in Navajo Mountain was purchased by a school employee. When some $80,000 came into the area for the construction of the Chapter House, a number of trucks were purchased. These are individually owned and licensed, but they serve for general family transportation on demand. Relatives (and every truck that goes to the trading post, to the Chapter House, or to Tuba City is crammed with kinfolk of all ages) may pay for the gasoline, but the principal expense of operation is borne by the titular owner.

SINGING FOR CURING CEREMONIES

Other sources of income in Navajo Mountain are divining and singing. Both men and women can be diagnosticians or diviners. There are several methods of divination: hand-trembling, crystal-gazing, and star-gazing. A diagnostician works alone and is hired for a small sum, a dollar or two or three, to diagnose an illness or to name a thief or a witch. Only one man in Navajo Mountain is a crystalgazer; there are no star-gazers; four women and eight men are hand-tremblers. Hand-trembling is not an ability acquired through training, but is a talent bestowed upon one without his knowing how it happened.

> I have been a hand-trembler for about twenty years, ever since my oldest child was born. It was then, when they were having a Sing over me, that I suddenly had this power.

Becoming a Singer is strictly a matter of memorizing the various Chants; Singers specialize in different Chants. Success in alleviating symptoms of misfortune and evil is the only criterion for assessing ritual skill, and skill alone is the determinant in choosing a particular specialist. General reputation is unimportant. For instance, one Singer at Navajo Mountain who is lauded for his curing ability is accused of being a witch, has spent time in Federal prison for the crime of incest, and is a molester of children. Another man, well liked as a practitioner, is a heavy drinker and gambler.

At Navajo Mountain there are eight Singers who are between 60 and 80 years of age, and one who is in his 50's. A Singer needs assistants, usually younger men who are learning the Chants. In other areas the aides may also be women; only men sing at Navajo Mountain. Four men in their 20's and 30's are learners. Navajo Mountain Singers have been variously taught the Chants by their fathers, their mothers' brothers, a father's brother and a mother's parallel cousin (called "uncle"). They have been given or have inherited medicine bags from these same categories of kin.

The older Singers of the communities are kept busy, but none of them earns a complete living from his specialty. In addition to sheep and money, partial payment for Sings frequently consists of cloth, baskets, and buckskins.

CRAFTSMANSHIP

The principal craft in Navajo Mountain is weaving, an occupation usually of women. One hears now and then of a man who weaves, but this is so unusual that he may be suspected of being a transvestite or latent homosexual. No men weave in Navajo Mountain, but two men relatives, living elsewhere, were mentioned as weavers. Men make the upright loom that is set up each time a new rug is begun either in the hogan if it is cold weather, or outside under a brush shade (ramada), if the weather is warm. Making rugs is a leisure-time occupation, and often weaving is begun when the household is in want of cash. Rugs are sold to the traders and the money belongs to the weaver, but as with other forms of income in a household, the payment may be used to settle family bills or buy clothes for the children.

Every woman in Navajo Mountain knows how to weave, having learned the art as a child from an older woman, her mother, her mother's sister, or her mother's mother. Most

Navajo Mountain rugs are small, rough horse blankets, but a few women know how to create fine rugs. One person alone conceives the design and controls the making of the rug, although others may help out under the weaver's direction.

> My mother and sisters weave. They use both vegetable dyes and aniline dyes. They weave in their spare time only. We never buy rugs from other Indians. Every family in Navajo Mountain has some weaver.

> There are just three good weavers in Navajo Mountain, my mother and two others.

Another craft activity for women is the making of coiled baskets, and bottle-shaped basketry containers which are covered with pitch so that they will hold water. The wide, low bowls are used in weddings and in some ceremonies and may serve as part payment to the Singer. Most of the wedding baskets today are made by Paiute women and sold to Navajos, but in Navajo Mountain not only Paiute but Paiute *Áshįįhí* and Navajo women engage in the craft. Pitch bottles are becoming rare, replaced by the army or boy-scout canteen, and the traditional vessels are sold to tourists or kept as family souvenirs.

> We sell our baskets at the Shiprock Fair for ten dollars. It's getting harder and harder to find the right kind of grasses to make them with.

> The ladies around here are giving up basket-making and weaving. It's too hard to do. It takes too much time. Basket-making is really dying out.

Men's crafts consist of dressing buckskin and making moccasins, lariats, whips, and hobbles. One man in Navajo Canyon is reported to make saddles, but most of the saddles we saw had been bought from a trading post. Four men were said to be silversmiths, but we did not see anyone working at this craft nor did we see any locally made silver articles for sale. The leather goods are bartered with other Navajos and are rarely sold to the trading post.

WELFARE INCOME

Since July 1, 1950 the States have furnished welfare aid in the categories of old-age assistance, aid to dependent children, and aid to the needy blind according to the State plans approved under the Social Security Act. These disbursements are subsidized up to 80% by the Federal government. The recipients of welfare assistance, although entitled to their checks as individuals, frequently share the cash with particularly needy children or other members of the extended family.

Maintaining the Household

Men do the heaviest work in the household maintenance. They build the hogans, fell the trees, prepare the logs, which are sometimes hauled for long distances, and cover the hogan with mud. Traditionally, all male members of the camp helped each household head to build a hogan and many still do lend aid; however, there are cases where the individual owner of the hogan is asked to pay relatives for their labor. A son will help build a hogan for his aged mother or assemble a welfare house for which the Navajo Tribe has contributed the lumber.

The cooking, care of the children, sewing of skirts and blouses and children's clothes, and hand washing is done by the women. All Navajo Mountain women make garments of bright-colored satin and plush bought from the trading post and sewn on old-style, foot-pedal Singer sewing machines. Young girls learn these tasks and help their mothers and sisters with the household chores.

The handling of machinery is frequently considered to be man's work. Men usually grind the corn in a meat grinder set up either outside in the ramada or inside in the hogan. They may run the coin-operated washing machines at the trading post. Although there were 20 trucks and cars in the area in 1962, only three women had learned to drive. Men repair their own cars out of necessity, the nearest garage being nearly a hundred miles away. Both men and women drive wagons, but men usually perform this task. Men hunt during the season in parties of men only, but because of the decrease of game what was once a basic means of subsistence has become a sport. The Navajo Tribe or the States control the issuance of hunting licenses.

Organizing of the extended-family activities is usually done by the oldest man who is still able to work, in consultation with the other adult men of the camp. The oldest able-bodied woman plans the women's work in joint household enterprises, but again a great deal of consultation is expected. During a weekend that we spent with a family in Paiute Canyon, the father organized the day's activities (the mother was working at a school in another district). At breakfast he made assignments to the children: the teenage girls were to cook and wash the dishes; the 11-year-old boy was to fetch water and carry packages. The father's task was to round up the horses; the older boy was to roll up the bedding, and he and his father were engaged to work on the Tribal project of cleaning out the irrigation ditches. One girl was assigned to take us horseback riding through the canyon. In other families, if the mother is a strong personality, she will plan all of the day's activities and distribute the chores.

Navajos are accustomed to hard work and they have no respect for a shirker. If a son or a son-in-law living elsewhere comes with his family to visit and does not contribute to the income of the camp, roundabout pressure will be put upon him either to cut short his stay or find some gainful work.

> Alexander has been visiting for several weeks with his family but I heard my father ask him the other day just when he was planning to go back to Cow Springs where his wife's people live.

> If relatives come back to Navajo Mountain their family takes them in. They don't hint about their getting a job, well, they might hint—my wife might hint about my getting a job.

Inheritance

Navajo Mountain inheritance practices follow the traditional patterns in many instances, although the old ways have been modified by the grazing-permit system and the Navajo Tribal Courts. A more comprehensive discussion can be found in our article, "Navajo Inheritance Patterns: Random or Regular?" (1966). These practices are flexible, so flexible in fact that one of our informants said, "Every family does it differently." However, there are patterns of correct procedure and norms around which each specific case is, so to speak, negotiated, and it is possible for a disgruntled heir with a "legitimate" claim to force a redistribution. Unless the assignment of a livestock permit is involved, estates in Navajo Mountain are disposed of in informal meetings of kinfolk who assemble after a death. Someone present is asked to serve as administrator. Formerly this person was a member of the matrilineage, and today this is often still true.

The burial of jewelry and personal effects with the dead is still the practice in Navajo Mountain.

> My father's jewelry, that is most of it, was buried with him.

> They buried my grandmother's jewelry along with her.

Particular rights to inheritance accrue to the following people: members of the matrilineage, the person who cared for the deceased before death, persons close to the deceased who know how to take care of the property, those most in need, a trustee for small children, those present at the distribution, and, in the case of a medicine bag, a relative who knows the appropriate Sing, particularly one who has learned from the deceased.

Living with and taking care of a person in his last days gives a preeminent right to inherit.

> The property usually goes to the children who will take care of the old ones. It goes to the closest ones, the ones who are living together.

> I didn't get anything from my mother. All her property went to that granddaughter she was living with.

> Old Man Cottonwood's livestock went to the grand-daughter and her husband who were taking care of the old couple.

Knowing how to farm and raise livestock gives a prior right to an inheritor.

> The property usually goes to the children who will take care of it, not to those who will waste it.

> Edward got his father's field. He was using it and he was living right there.

> Mom will divide her permit with Carrie and Joan. It's a question of need. My brother and I are educated and

our older sister has her own sheep permit. If Carrie
and Joan stay with Mom and help her, it's only right
for them to get Mom's sheep.

Members of the matrilineage may act as administrators or
as trustees or receive some share of the estate if only as
tokens of remembrance.

When her son was killed, Tall Woman gave his things
to his wife and children, all except his car. She kept
that for herself.

My old grandfather, that is my mother's mother's brother, decided what to do with my mother's things when
she died. My mother's sister was put in charge of the
sheep. I was only 12 years old at the time, but later my
brothers and sisters and I divided the sheep among
ourselves.

Some of my grandfather's things went to his *Lók'aa'
dine'é* grandchildren, those grandchildren of his sister's
in Kayenta.

Gerda got a necklace and Emma got a bracelet that be-
longed to their mother's brother. It was something to
remember their uncle by.

Only those persons present at the distribution share in the
estate.

I was away in Guam when my grandfather died so I
didn't get anything. I suppose I could have had something later if I had asked for it.

In Navajo Mountain the only estate cases probated in the
Navajo Tribal Courts involved the inheritance of grazing
permits, and in one case the distribution of railroad compensation paid for a worker's accidental death. Most of the
grazing permits went to the surviving spouse or to a sister.
According to the Navajo Tribal Code, in the absence of a

will, rights to a grazing permit pass to relatives in the following order: surviving spouse, surviving children, grandchildren, parents, brothers and sisters, nieces and nephews, or, failing these, escheat to the District grazing pool.

Although Navajo Tribal Courts have jurisdiction over decedents' estates, the disposal of property is not spelled out in the Code. "In the determination of heirs, the Courts shall apply the custom of the tribe as to inheritance if such custom is proved. Otherwise the courts shall apply State law in deciding what relatives of the decedent are entitled to be his heirs."

By showing the extent of flexibility of alternatives as to who shall inherit, we have suggested the range of indeterminateness that this section allows in court practice. The tendency of the Tribal Courts, aiming at modernization, is to determine heirs in the order specified for the inheritance of grazing permits, unless the judges are pressed by individuals who, traditionally, would have enjoyed a valid claim to the estate. In such cases, court procedure may approach the old process of negotiation and mediation found in the informal meetings of kinfolk.

Community Income

Our estimate of Navajo Mountain community income for 1961/1962 falls into the traditional categories of yield from livestock, agriculture, and local enterprises and into the nontraditional categories of wage work, welfare payments, and free governmental services.

LIVESTOCK

Every family, nuclear or extended, owns some sheep. In order to preserve the land from serious over-grazing, the Bureau of Indian Affairs drastically reduced the sheep herds, and particularly the numbers of goats and horses, in the 1930's and early 1940's. A grazing-permit system to limit the number of livestock which could be grazed within an arbitrary division of the Reservation, the Land Management Division, fixed individual ownership at a set level. The Navajo Tribal Council took over the formulation and administration of the grazing regulations in 1956, but so far, with federal approval, has postponed their enforcement. As a result, Navajo Mountain has been able to rebuild its sheep herds to the level of the community count before stock reduction. In 1962, Land Management District Number 2, of which Navajo Mountain forms a part, was rated by the Indian Bureau as 67 percent overgrazed.

The Division of Resources of the Bureau of Indian Affairs in 1961 estimated the annual return of a sheep at $8.25 for meat, $2.10 for wool; of a goat at $3.00 for meat, $0.80 for mohair; of a horse at $21.00; and of a head of cattle at $78.00. In 1962, Navajo Mountain, according to figures supplied by the Branch of Land Operations, had 7,083 sheep, 1,611 goats, 313 horses, and 231 head of cattle. The income in 1961–62 from livestock was, therefore, $102,405.54. (We have deducted 10 percent of the value of the wool crop as the amount retained for weaving rugs.)

AGRICULTURE

Every family has use rights to small patches of land for dry farms on the plateau or on the mesa, or for small-scale irrigated plots in the canyons. Corn, melons, and peaches are the principal crops; these products are not sold commercially, but may be bartered with neighbors and relatives. We estimate that 275 acres are cultivated, with a yield of $5,775 yearly.

LOCAL ENTERPRISES

Hand-made rugs and baskets are sold. Moccasins, leather halters, and lariats are made for family use or barter only. A few individuals occasionally rent horses to tourists. We estimate the annual value of such local enterprises at $3,335.00, bringing the total of estimated income from traditional sources to $111,515.54.

WAGE WORK

There are six full-time wage-work jobs and one part-time job held by Navajos at the Navajo Mountain School, where they are employed as cooks, janitor, and instructional aides. The payroll amounts to $27,216 annually.

Other wage work is on specific projects. Water development, under the direction of the United States Public Health Service, brought in a payroll of $5,078. Over a 3-year period, 1960, 1961, and 1962, a total of $15,233 was paid in wages. Since the scope of the projects varied considerably from year to year, we have taken an average of the 3-year period to arrive at an annual figure. In the 3 years, 138 men were so employed.

Three Chapter officers and a Grazing Committee chairman received $16 per diem for a total of $1,535. Most of the employment is provided on emergency work projects financed by the Navajo Tribal Council and planned by the local Chapter, and, on the average, brings into the community $14,815 per year. There are rules prohibiting employment of persons without dependents who have an income of over $2,000 per year, but in practice every able-bodied male in Navajo Mountain receives a job. The total work per man for a year ranges from one to six weeks. This is a highly desired form of employment that can easily be absorbed by a sheepherding family, since other members of the family can temporarily take over the working man's share of the routine chores.

Two individuals working outside, but who maintain their spouses and children on the plateau, have a combined income of $9,200. Four people harvested sugar beets in Utah for an estimated $1,200.

In 1961 the Museum of Northern Arizona employed 16 men to dig in archeological sites for a payroll of $6,725.

The total income from wage work during the year 1961 amounted to $65,769.

WELFARE

Welfare aid is furnished to 11 recipients of Old Age Assistance and 18 of Aid to Dependent Children, for a yearly total income of $38,066.30.

FREE SERVICES

Free services from the Federal government include the cost of education in boarding schools and the health program. The Navajo Tribe, in addition, has an emergency welfare program. Layettes, dentures, eyeglasses, and small one-room frame houses which are given to certain welfare recipients have come into Navajo Mountain. Robert Young estimates the combined value of these Federal and Tribal services as $124 per person per year (1961:228–229). This represents $72,044, making the total annual income from welfare $110,110.30.

SOCIAL SECURITY

One widow and her three minor children received monthly Social Security benefits amounting to $3,072 annually.

TOTAL COMMUNITY INCOME

The total annual income for Navajo Mountain in 1961–62 was estimated to be $290,466.84, hence the per capita income was $499.94.

Table 5 recapitulates the estimated community income by sources: traditional, wages, welfare and free services, and other.

Table 5.—*Estimated Community Income, 1961–62*

TRADITIONAL INCOME

Source

Livestock	$102,405.54
Agriculture	5,775.00
Local enterprises	3,335.00
Total	$111,515.54

INCOME FROM WAGES
(by employment source)

Bureau of Indian Affairs	27,216.00
U. S. Public Health Service	5,078.00
Navajo Tribal Chapter officers	1,535.00
Public works	14,815.00
Two residents working outside	9,200.00
Sugar-beet harvesters	1,200.00
Museum of Northern Arizona	6,725.00
Total	65,769.00

INCOME FROM WELFARE AND FREE SERVICES

Source

Arizona and Utah State welfare	38,066.30
BIA and Navajo Tribe (services)	72,044.00
Total	110,110.30

OTHER INCOME

Source

Social Security benefits 3,072.00   3,072.00

Grand total $290,466.84
Per capita $499.94

Rearing the Children

Navajo husbands and wives share a strong desire to have
children, and a child is usually born within the first year
of marriage. Modern birth-control techniques of any kind
being virtually unknown, most women continue having
babies until menopause. It is not at all uncommon for a
woman and her older daughters to be having babies concurrently, or, as a matter of fact, for nephews and nieces to
be older than a maternal aunt or uncle, which occurrence
is reflected in Navajo kinship terminology, as discussed in
detail elsewhere in this work under the "born-between"
phenomenon.

Children are of considerable economic value, in that
at an early age they start helping out with the chores
around the camp, and they are especially useful in the time-
consuming job of herding the sheep. At the same time, a
number of Navajo women expressed an interest in learning
why and how "you white women have fewer babies than
Navajo women do," and there were numerous indications
that attempts are sometimes made to limit the number of
pregnancies.

> Johnson's daughter was married to a man who was
> neglecting her and their children, so Johnson had a
> Sing for her to make her barren. She didn't have any

more children for 11 years; then she had two daughters by another husband.

Mom thinks that Alma is having too many babies too fast, and that is why her last two did not live. Mom has told her that she should drink some of that tea you make from the weed which causes menstruation to stop. Then you never have any more babies.

Several marriages of many years' duration between couples who are childless indicate that sterility is not considered sufficient cause for divorce. However, such a childless couple will often adopt the child of some close kin, if one can be had.

No strong preference is shown as to the sex of a baby; girls and boys seem to be equally welcome and equally loved.

All infants at Navajo Mountain are kept on a cradleboard, which custom dictates must be made from lumber from a straight pine tree. Traditionally, the father made the cradleboard; today some fathers take pride in following the old custom, but others take advantage of the power machinery and skill of the trader, who makes the cradleboard as a gesture of good-will.

Toilet training is not severe. When a mother feels that the child is ready to control his bodily functions, she takes him outside frequently, and, by example, teaches him the proper way. Toddlers are often seen, even in cold weather, running around with bare bottoms, the easier to step outside the hogan door and relieve themselves. No child was observed being punished because he had committed a nuisance at the wrong time or place.

Our informants at Navajo Mountain denied that "war" names, the traditional "secret" names, are given nowadays to either boys or girls. The first of a series of names is given when the infant is a few days old, and is usually descriptive, such as "Red Baby," "Little Baby," or "Cry Baby."

> The mother's mother is usually present at the birth of a child. When the baby is a few days old she just starts calling the child by a name which she feels fits, and then others follow.

When the child is four years old or so, the baby name is dropped and another more suitable child's name is given. Again the name is apt to be descriptive; any particularly distinguishing characteristic—tallness, a sunny disposition, prominent ears, a misshapen hand, or bulging eyes—may result in the child being called, "Tall Boy," "Laughing Boy," "Ears Sticking Out," "Girl with Ugly Hand," or, "Scared." This name may well continue on through adulthood. Or an adult of any age may acquire another name through involvement in some incident, very frequently some incident which had amusing overtones. In many cases, names in adulthood are derived from clans, such as "Salt Woman," "Towering House Woman," or "Tall Salt." Teknonymy may supply a name for a parent, as "Yazhi's Father," or a name may be derived from the sibling relationship, such as "Áshįįhí Nez Bik'is," that is, Longsalt's Brother. A person no longer living will have a suffix meaning "former" attached to his name. It is most impolite to address a Navajo by his name, or to say it within his hearing; it is properly used only as a reference term.

English names are given now within a few days of birth and are suggested by any member of the family who may know English, by the local school teacher, or by a trader. The English name will be used on birth certificates and in school, for the census record it will supplement a Tribal census number, and English-speakers may use it quite freely as a term of address.

Some names of Navajo Mountain residents suggest that there may be an element of social control at work in the choice of nicknames. One man frequently accused of pilfering is called "The Thief." An old man said to have removed a saddle from a grave was thenceforth called "Saddle." A Christian convert is called "Preacher."

Lack of regularity in naming procedures, the multiplicity of names, and the custom of changing names constitute a great handicap to ethnographers.

The socialization of the child—training which instills in the individual the ways of thinking and the habits of behavior that will make him conform to the ideals of the society to the extent that he will become an acceptable Navajo —takes place principally within the nuclear family, and secondarily within the extended family. It is in the setting of his family camp that the child learns the language, the manners, and the values of his elders.

Mother and father are responsible for nurture, economic support, and early training, and these functions are assumed by other relatives only in cases of emergency. A child eats and sleeps with his parents and siblings in one hogan. Until he is weaned, a period which sometimes continues for as long as 3 years, he is constantly in his mother's care. Nursing babies and toddlers go with their parents to meetings, to church, to the trading post, to ceremonies, and on visits to relatives. Public meetings are conducted to the accompaniment of the noise of crying babies and the patter of small feet.

An infant is allowed to cry for only a few minutes before he is picked up by someone who will dandle him until he is quiet, or the mother will offer her breast. The baby displaced by the birth of another child may be given particular attention by the father.

Both parents teach proper behavior and discipline their children, although the mother, by virtue of her being almost constantly with them, is the chief disciplinarian. An unruly child may be punished by a rough push from the mother, sometimes a paddling. Rarely are children spanked so regularly and so vigorously as they sometimes are in our society.

> Navajos don't spank their children very often, or scold them, or let them cry; if you do these things they may get wrong ideas and, maybe, when they are grown up they might want to kill themselves, or something bad like that. I wasn't spanked in my life until I went away to school.

More often, efforts are made to control a recalcitrant child through arousing his fear. Threats are made of supernatural action, of witches, of werewolves, of whippings by the Yeis or masked gods, or even the menace of kidnapping by some stranger or by one of the community scapegoats, the local idiot, or some other odd character.

> My grandfather scares my little brother by saying, 'Crooked Legs might come and cut off your ears.'

Descriptions of good and bad behavior elicited statements strikingly similar to those collected by Kluckhohn (Ladd, 1957:335). Girls told us, "They say, 'Obey your parents. Don't lie. Don't steal. Be polite to your relatives. Be generous, especially with those in need. Don't do what the naughty boys and girls do.' " One young woman said that her father and mother told her not to go to Squaw Dances, and not to fool around too much in school. She said she was spanked as a child when she and her sister stole some sugar from their hogan to make candy in a little fry pan while they were herding sheep. A youth said he was punished for being mean to his little brothers and sisters and for neglecting the sheep. A 60-year-old man said, "My father told me, 'Be good. Don't steal. Don't bother another man's wife. Don't bother another man's stock.' He told me to be generous to other people, any people who need help, not just relatives. So I never did these bad things. I never got into fights." This self-image must be sheer self-deception as his nickname is "Liar," and he has more than once been involved in drinking bouts which led to fights that resulted in serious bodily harm. When sober he has a delightful personality and is kept busy as a Singer.

Older brothers and sisters may tell younger children what to do, "but they have a hard time making them do it."

We heard no specific reference to the prescription, "Be wary of nonrelatives," cited by Kluckhohn and Leighton (1946:225). However, when a 2-year-old child began to cry violently as one of us approached, his mother said, "Nichó," or "Your Grandmother," and the crying miraculously ceased.

The origin legends and the myths were variously reported as being told by mother, father, mother's father, father's father, mother's mother, and mother's brother. Apparently choice depends on which relatives know and are interested in the legends, and, of course, who is accessible. One family told us, "We aren't interested in that old stuff. Our father went to school and he doesn't want us to hear such things."

Legends may be told only in the wintertime. During the seasons of lightning and thunderstorms and periods of activity of snakes and bears, the telling of myths concerning these elements may attract danger to the story teller and to his audience. Inasmuch as the children are away at boarding school during the winter months, they sometimes fail to acquire this knowledge which should be imparted to the young. A traditionalist lamented that "These poor children are being robbed of their heritage."

The extended family supplements the nurture and the

instruction given by the parents. A child is surrounded by a varied assortment of kin in an extended camp and some of these will oversee the child if his mother is doing chores, or if she needs help for some other reason. In the case of the death of either parent or of divorce, the extended family cushions the disruption of family life for the child.

Traditionally, the father was not expected to support his children if the nuclear family broke up for whatever reason, and many children and fathers thus became estranged, sometimes to the regret of the father, who would have been glad to claim his children.

> My wife died leaving two small children, a girl and a boy. I married her sister, but she turned out to be a mean woman and we could not get along together. She left and she took my two children with her. I never saw my son again, but they tell me that he grew up to be a fine man. My daughter comes here once in a while to visit me.

> I had children only by my first wife; we had six when she died. My wife's mother took all of the children; we had been living with her. I returned to my mother's home, but for a while I was very lonely and unhappy.

The modern Indian court tries to enforce child-support rules, but this is often difficult as the father may leave the area to return to his own matrilineal camp if he has married into Navajo Mountain, or he may marry again and acquire new rights and obligations to his new affines.

The present-day population of Navajo Mountain includes 13 sets of siblings whose mothers died when they were young children. In five instances the children were or are being brought up by their mother's mother. In one case the mother's mother was dead and the children were raised by their mother's mother's mother. Twice the father's parents took the orphans. In another, young children went to live with two older sisters who were married. In an instance of polygynous marriage of three sisters to one man, when two of the wives died their children stayed on in the camp with their father and their mothers' sister. In another case, the father of small children married his deceased wife's sister and she brought up the children. In still another, the dead mother's sister took only the very young children, and the older ones stayed with their father, who established a new camp on land that had previously been used by his own matrilineage. No man who had married into the area continued living there after the death of his wife. One Navajo Mountain man who had married into another community returned to his mother's camp when his wife died, and brought with him a small daughter. His mother, who was an elderly widow, had made a particular request that she be given his child as her companion.

Thirteen Navajo Mountain fathers of local residents died when some or all of their children were small. The widow of one of them had been living with her husband's matrilineage in another area, but when her husband died she returned to her camp of origin and brought her children with her. Likewise, three women who had married into Navajo Mountain returned to their own relatives. A fourth woman who had married into Navajo Mountain had grown children as well as young ones when her husband died, and she elected to continue living there. Six of the widows have since remarried, two of them to brothers of the dead spouses. In each of these cases the stepfather is said to treat the children "like his own." Two of the widows have never remarried; they were both living in extended-family camps when they were widowed, and the relatives "helped out" in raising the children.

Ten divorces deprived children of a father. One of the mothers had married into the area, and she and her children returned to her former home. After the nine other divorces the fathers moved away, while the children and their mothers continued living in the extended-family setting.

Illegitimate children are likewise absorbed into the extended family, although the principal responsibility for nurture and support rests with their mother. If she marries, the stepfather will bring up the child as his own, with apparently no stigma attached. The illegitimate child frequently takes the mother's English surname in school. Actual fatherhood of the child is made known and will continue to be reckoned because of the importance of the father's clan in marriage taboos.

Childless couples are eager to adopt the child of a close relative, but Navajo parents give their children to others only under hardship. This does not apply to the custom, not unrare, of a widowed mother's mother demanding one of her daughter's younger girls to live with her as a companion, to help her in the work around the hogan, and to assist in herding. The process is gradual; the grandmother will coax the child to spend more time in her hogan, to eat and sleep there, to accompany her to the trading post or on visits to relatives. Such an "adopted" child is not allowed to go to school, because the grandmother would then be deprived of the companionship and services she seeks. The child, in the status of only-child, has affection lavished upon her, but loses close relationship with siblings and must forego her childish ways and be almost constantly at her grandmother's side. Older women who had been brought up in this manner almost always exhibited some resentment in telling about it. "She made a slave of me," they said. One late-teen-ager, however, who had spent her early years with her grandmother, until the latter's death, boasted, "She chose me to stay with her."

Children given to other relatives often come from a large family and are offered for adoption as toddlers who have been displaced by another child, frequently a baby who is sickly and makes unusual demands on the mother's time and energy. When the crisis has passed, the parents may ask for the child to be returned to them, which the foster parents usually do. In one case of a legal adoption of a Navajo child by a white couple, the father came to them some two years later and said, "Things are better with us now; we want our child back. How do I go about unsigning the papers?"

At the age of 6 the Navajo Mountain child enters the government boarding school, which is his first continuous contact with the encroaching white culture. Here the 30-odd beginners who attend each year receive instruction under the lone teacher, a woman who has devoted her life to her small charges since the inception of the boarding school in 1940. Little girls exchange their satin skirts and velvet blouses for typical white-society clothing. All of the children start learning the English language. They have to learn to sleep in beds and to eat strange foods at tables; they are subjected to bathing in tubs, to using a toilet, to having regular hair cuts, to spending day and night in the company of many children not related to them, to being disciplined by women from outside the family camp, and to sitting at desks and learning to use pens, pencils, and books. Such is the beginning of the long road to white men's education.

After 2 years of schooling, in which the concentration has been on development of the use of oral English, elementary pupils are sent to boarding schools at Kayenta or Tuba City, or off-reservation schools at Flagstaff, Arizona, or Richfield, Utah.

High-school students usually go to Flagstaff or Richfield. Special programs are available for Navajo students who have not started to school at the prescribed age. Such schools are designed to offer intensive training to young Navajos who do not read or write English and most of whom speak no English. At various times young people from Navajo Mountain have attended Chemawa Indian School, Salem, Oregon; Chilocco Indian School, Chilocco, Oklahoma; Albuquerque Indian School, Albuquerque, New Mexico; Intermountain School, Brigham, Utah; Haskell Institute, Lawrence, Kansas; Santa Fe Indian School, Santa Fe, New Mexico; Phoenix Indian School, Phoenix, Arizona; and Sherman Institute, Riverside, California. In addition to these boarding schools maintained through public funds, some young Navajo students are given free education arranged for by the Navajo Mountain Mission, at the South-West Indian Mission School at Glendale, Arizona.

Missionaries of the various denominations active at Navajo Mountain visit hogans to persuade parents to grant permission for their schoolchildren to be given religious instruction. The school cooperates by releasing such pupils for one hour each week and making classrooms available to the missionaries.

Navajo Mountain children who are sent to Richfield, Utah, for elementary and high school study or to Intermountain Special Program School at Brigham, Utah, come into contact with a white population that is predominantly of the Mormon conviction. Furthermore, Mormon families have a policy of taking Indians into their homes as "adopted" children for a school term. At least one Navajo Mountain child was living in a Mormon family during the school year of 1962.

Parents of Navajo Mountain children generally accept the fact that a speaking knowledge of the English language is desirable, and most members of the grandparental generation accede. At the same time, if a child is reluctant to leave home to go to school, the elders are not apt to exert any pressure to change his mind. Frequently a child is kept out of school if the family feels that they do not wish to be deprived of his services in herding, or if an old grandmother demands a small child to keep her company, run errands, help around her hogan, and generally be useful. In 1962, 31 eligible children were not in school. Fourteen of these young Navajos had never attended school, and the remaining 17 were early drop-outs.

Since only the Navajo language is spoken at home, or when Navajos get together, an individual who has had only brief schooling will soon forget most of the English he may have learned. None of the older generation at Navajo Mountain speaks any English and less than a dozen of the middleaged are capable of communicating in English.

Up to the present time the community has produced no college graduates, and only 10 high-school graduates.

Social Control

Isolation, difficulties of communication with law-enforcement headquarters, the network of kinship ties, and the face-to-face character of relationships in the community make for strong reliance on informal social controls. Informants when questioned, insisted that "No one is running things." Sanctions are applied only in cases of extreme wrongdoing. Desire for family and community respect and the need for reciprocity in most activities are the strongest motivations for conformity to acceptable social behavior. A good father, a good mother, a hard worker, a cooperative, friendly, generous, levelheaded man or woman is a good Navajo. He, or she, will be liked and helped. No one wants to be known as a bad son or a bad son-in-law. If one is not generous or cooperative, aid and hospitality may be withheld in retaliation.

The extreme sensitivity of Navajos to the criticism of their peers was brought home to us by the abrupt change in behavior of acquaintances and informants when we met them at the trading post or at a Chapter meeting. Those who were the most outgoing and friendly when we visited them at their own camps were the most reserved and distant when we saw them in public. No one wanted to be too closely identified with outsiders, especially outsiders who were around asking so many foolish, unnecessary, and often impertinent questions.

Drunkenness, polygyny, philandering, failure to pay bills at the trading post, or quitting a job are not admired forms of behavior, but they do not incur as strong negative sanctions as they do in our society. One person told us that Navajo Mountain residents are better behaved than Indians in other parts of the Reservation, because they live in the "shadow of the sacred mountain."

Disputes, however, do arise. If these are handled through self-help, the aggrieved person acts to settle his own case without recourse to relatives and local leaders. Self-help may take the form of discussion and mutual agreement between the contending parties. For example, a thief when confronted with his delict may agree to return the stolen property. Counterwitchcraft ceremonies directed against an accused witch may satisfy the accusers. Intense gossip may shame a debtor into paying his debt and may restrain a malefactor from repeating his wrongful act. The final sanction of self-help is a beating. The community, however, does not consider the resort to violence as justified or legitimate (except possibly in self-protection), and such a beating only gives rise to a further dispute that may be taken to a traditional meeting or to the Navajo Tribal Court. For example, an argument over range rights may give rise to a case of assault and battery, or a disagreement about who should round up the horses may result in a slander case.

The informal method of handling disputes that is considered legitimate in Navajo Mountain is the calling of a meeting between adversaries and interested members of their kin groups. No official or influential local person can demand such a meeting, although he may be asked to participate. Not only important members of the matrilineages or of the camps concerned, but frequently wise mediators from the community, unrelated, but gifted with the power of persuasion—men who "talk good"—are invited to help out.

For a few years, the hearing of disputes at the request of the disputants was a regular activity of the Chapter. Recently, the Navajo Tribal Council has taken the position that this is not a proper function of the Chapters, but should fall to the jurisdiction of the Navajo Tribal Courts. In Navajo Mountain, however, Chapter officers may be asked to assist in the informal meetings. The official role does not in itself confer authority to mediate a dispute, nor is any and every officer invited to participate. The Chapter president, for example, may ask men "who are good at this sort of thing" to help him. They are not paid for their services, but are usually fed and may be given gifts later.

The meeting is held in a hogan belonging to one of the principals in the dispute or to a relative. There may have been some preliminary investigation, some tracking of a culprit, some viewing of a damaged field, or the plaintiff may have consulted a diviner if it is a case of theft by person or persons unknown. Each disputant will tell his side of the story and any witnesses or well-wishers may add information or advice. In evaluating the evidence and in attempting to ascertain which of the parties is telling the truth, our informants denied that social status carried weight. Despite the general level of equality, some people in Navajo Mountain are poorer than others and some have fewer sheep, less land, and a smaller number of relatives, but it is the personal reputation of a litigant that counts in assessing veracity or in determining guilt. The past record of the individual will influence the assemblage. If a man is known to be a thief, or a brawler, or the type that "just runs around after women," he will most probably be found guilty if accused repeatedly of this same kind of offense. Sanctions, too, will be more severe for a repeater than for a first offender.

Mediators will speak and suggest compromise solutions. Other influential persons or Singers who are respected in the community will urge harmony, reminding the litigants as one did:

> If we don't have love we better get along anyway because we are all relatives.

The adversaries will be subjected to a great deal of informal pressure to drop their charges or to compromise their grievances, and to "shake hands and forget all about it." If the consensus of the people present is that one of the parties is in the wrong, both sides may agree upon sanctions that can take the form of restitution, perhaps the promise to stay out of each other's grazing area, a decision to go back together for the sake of the children, or the payment of compensation for an offense. The threat of turning the case over to the Navajo Tribal Court, with its sanctions of fines, paid not to the injured party but to the impersonal court, and imprisonment, acts as a strong pressure for agreement. However, the traditional meeting operated successfully before there were any courts with jurisdiction over Navajos, so it is a mistake to exaggerate the influence of this kind of threat. For example, a person was accused of battering his brother-in-law. The offender was the sole able-bodied man in a camp composed of his aged parents, his wife, and ten minor children. When the victim threatened to charge him in the Navajo Tribal Courts, his parents begged for a community meeting. Should their son be fined or imprisoned the entire burden would fall on the family.

Families will tend to support their own members and will be more sympathetic to their own side. We tested this by discussing the same case with relatives of each disputant, and the story changed markedly. However, harmony has such a high value in Navajo society that both kin groups may press for settlement and compromise. Members of the extended family will take upon themselves the obligation of helping the guilty party to make restitution or pay compensation if that is the sanction agreed upon. We questioned the family of a man who has been involved in numerous brawls and violent drinking bouts, compensation for which offenses had placed a heavy drain on family resources. We asked, "What does the family do when they have to pay out money or sheep over and over again?" "They get tired," was the answer.

There is no formal mechanism for enforcing the sanction agreed upon at the meeting. If a man, for example, promises to pay a certain number of sheep in compensation for a beating, or to make restitution for a theft, the mediators take no responsibility for seeing that the decision is carried out. Only informal pressure, nagging, and shaming by the family of the successful plaintiff will constrain the guilty party to discharge his debt. The extraordinary fact, inexplicable to the ethnologist who has been socialized in a different culture, is that the defendant so often meets his obligations.

If there is no consensus at the meeting of what is "right," or if one or the other of the disputants refuses to accept a solution proposed by the group, the case is considered "too heavy" and may be dropped. If so, it may smolder for years as latent hostility between the individuals and kin groups involved and will flare up again when another cause for disagreement arises. Finally, the case may be taken to the Navajo Courts.

Our Navajo Mountain informants discussed with us some 144 cases involving 22 different bases for dispute. None of these cases was taken to the Navajo Tribal Courts. Twenty-three of them were handled through informal kin or Chapter meetings and 121 were either settled through self-help or left unsettled.

The types of cases brought before informal meetings or raised on the floor of the local Chapter included disputes involving assault and battery, domestic troubles, disorderly conduct (drinking before, after, and during a Chapter meeting), damage to property, land questions, adultery, slander, failure to help a brother at an Enemy Way ceremony, the initiation of compensation for the family of a dead man whose killer had been exonerated by a federal court, and (in an old case) the judging of an accused witch.

Quarrels over livestock, cases of trespass, and land disputes are frequently handled by the local grazing committee, an elected body. Sometimes the head of the committee will be asked to mediate the dispute. If the case is "too hard" for local settlement, it may go to the Central Grazing Committee of the Navajo Tribal Council. Neither committee nor official has coercive power, and if no formula on which both sides can agree is presented, the case may be taken to the Navajo Tribal Courts, where a judge will adjudicate and the Navajo police enforce his legal decision. Navajo Mountain residents, however, often try to settle grazing disputes in informal kin-group meetings, or in the local Chapter, rather than avail themselves of the grazing-committee apparatus.

The Courts of the Navajo Tribe have jurisdiction over misdemeanors when committed by an Indian on the Navajo Reservation as well as over domestic issues such as mar-

riage, divorce, adoption, inheritance, and religion. There
are trial courts in each of the five subagencies and a court
of appeals at Fort Defiance, staffed by six judges, a chief
justice, clerks, and bailiffs. Tuba City has a jail, a courthouse and a resident judge who has jurisdiction over Navajo Mountain. A Tribal police captain and police force are
stationed in Tuba City. Two policemen have been assigned
to Navajo Mountain, but because of lack of housing they
are not in residence. These policemen are detailed to maintain order at the major ceremonies and are on call for investigations in the community. The Navajo Tribal Council
pays all the expenses of this law-and-order system.

Despite the fact that the Navajo Tribal Court has jurisdiction over misdemeanors, and the federal courts over the
eleven major crimes (see below), if a formal court decision
is at variance with the traditional ideas of a rightful and a
wrongful solution, the community may take up the matter
at an informal meeting or at a Chapter meeting and rectify
the judicial "error."

A young man who killed his cousin at Navajo Mountain,
was exonerated by the federal court and the killing was
adjudged to be justifiable homicide. When the man returned to the community, a meeting was held in which
pressure was put on him to pay compensation to the widow
of the dead man. He and his family gave money and sheep,
although there was no formal mechanism that could have
enforced such compensation. In another case, a Navajo
Mountain man who had been hit on the head with a rock
during a drunken brawl died shortly thereafter at the Tuba
City Hospital. The cause of death was given as cirrhosis of
the liver. Nevertheless, the community, and the relatives of
his widow, who had returned to her family of origin at Oljeto, were convinced that the man had died because of the
blow from the rock and they demanded, and got, 20 sheep
from the man who had wielded the rock; this, too, in the

absence of any coercive mechanism to enforce the demand.

We collected information on 436 court cases that cover a span of over 33 years, involving 41 types of action. The largest number of complaints were for disorderly conduct, 145; liquor violations, 86; reckless driving, 20; and failure to support dependents, 20.

There are some points that bear directly on social organization. For example, many more men than women are involved in cases of liquor violation and acts of physical violence. Of 145 cases of disorderly conduct taken to the Navajo Tribal Courts, 139 concerned men and 6, women.

By far the greatest number of all offenses taken to court are for violations of Tribal regulations, that is, disorderly conduct and the use and transportation of intoxicating beverages.

Table 6 gives some indication of the frequency of disputes by kinship categories.

As can readily be seen, the largest number of disputes, both formal and informal, are between husband and wife. It should be noted that some court cases since 1948 in which the wife appears as plaintiff against her husband are inspired by modern welfare requirements. That is, a woman must first try to place financial responsibility upon her husband for the support of her children before she can receive state and federal aid. There are many fewer disputes between brothers and sisters, and still fewer quarrels between individuals of other relationship categories. This suggests that the traditional methods of social control effectively curtail the number of disagreements between kinsmen that are carried to the point of mediation or litigation.

The federal district courts in Arizona, Utah, and New Mexico handle the eleven major crimes already referred to, when committed by an Indian on the Navajo Reservation. These are murder, manslaughter, assault with intent

Table 6.—*Navajo Mountain Dispute Cases, by Relationship Categories*

Relationship of litigants	Cases brought before—		Relationship of litigants	Cases brought before—		Total cases
	Informal meeting	Tribal court		Informal meeting	Tribal court	
Hu vs. Wi	8	1	Wi vs. Hu	14	22	45
Si vs. Br	6	1	Br vs. Si	2	0	9
MoBr vs. SiSo	1	0	SiSo vs. MoBr	3	1	5
FaL vs. SoL	2	2	SoL vs. FaL	0	0	4
Si vs. Si	3	0	—	—	—	3
Fa vs. So	2	0	So vs. Fa	1	0	3
Bił 'áshéhé vs. Bił 'áshéhé	2	1	—	—	—	3
Br vs. Br	1	1	—	—	—	2
Mo vs. Da	0	1	Da vs. Mo	1	0	2
MoSiSo vs. MoSiSo ..	1	1	—	—	—	2
MoL vs. SoL	1	1	SoL vs. MoL	0	0	2
WiSi vs. SiHu	2	0	SiHu vs. WiSi	0	0	2
Parents vs. Da	1	0	Da vs. Parents	0	0	1
Parents vs. So	0	0	So vs. Parents	1	0	1
MoBr vs. SiDa	1	0	SiDa vs. MoBr	0	0	1
MoSi vs. SiDa	1	0	SiDa vs. MoSi	0	0	1
FaBr vs. BrSo	1	0	BrSo vs. FaBr	0	0	1
FaBr vs. BrDa	1	0	BrDa vs. FaBr	0	0	1
MoMoSiDa vs. MoSiDaSo	1	0	MoSiDaSo vs. MoMoSiDa	0	0	1
MoMoSiSo vs. MoSiDaSo	1	0	MoSiDaSo vs. MoMoSiSo	0	0	1
SiDaHu vs. WiMoBr .	1	0	WiMoBr vs. SiDaHu .	0	0	1
WiBrSo vs. FaSiHu ..	1	0	FaSiHu vs. WiBrSo ...	0	0	1
BrWi vs. HuBr	1	0	HuBr vs. BrWi	0	0	1
SiHu vs. WiBr	1	0	WiBr vs. SiHu	0	0	1
FaSiHu vs. WiBrSo ..	1	0	WiBrSo vs. FaSiHu ..	0	0	1
MoSiDaDaHu vs. WiMoMoSiSo	1	0	WiMoMoSiSo vs. MoSiDaDaHu	0	0	1
MoMo vs. DaDa	0	0	DaDa vs. MoMo	1	0	1
					Total......	97

to kill, assault with a dangerous weapon, burglary, robbery, larceny, rape, incest, arson, and the embezzlement of tribal funds. Crimes are investigated by the Navajo Tribal Police Department's Detective Division or by special officers of the Branch of Law and Order of the Bureau of Indian Affairs, and the cases are then turned over to the Federal Bureau of Investigation. The F.B.I. conducts another investigation and submits the evidence to the United States Attorney in Phoenix, Salt Lake City, or Albuquerque, depending on whether the crime was committed in Arizona, Utah, or New Mexico. It is within the discretion of the United States Attorney to accept for prosecution or to decline to prosecute a case so presented. If it is accepted for prosecution, the regular procedure for dealing with federal crimes will be instituted. We collected the following information on federal offenses at Navajo Mountain: sixteen were investigated by the Navajo Tribe's Detective Division and were presented to the Federal courts. Four Navajo Mountain residents served sentences for grand larceny (stealing cattle from a cattle company across the San Juan River) and three for rape. One of the rape cases involved incest between a man and his daughter.

Table 7 lists the types and numbers of cases handled through self-help, through informal meetings, in the Navajo Tribal Courts, and in the federal district courts.

Table 7.—Navajo Mountain "Law" Cases

Cases handled through self-help

Witchcraft	17
Divorce	14
Theft	13
Estate	11
Fight	9
Illegitimate child	8
Adultery	7
Assault and battery	7
Grazing dispute	6
Fraud	5
"Child labor"	4
Land dispute	3
Slander	3
Attempted rape	2
Disorderly conduct	2
Juvenile delinquency	2
Incest	2
Property	2
Debt	1
Domestic dispute	1
Murder	1
Prostitution	1
Total	**121**

Cases handled through informal meetings

Assault and battery	5
Domestic dispute	3
Damage to property	2
Estate	2
Land dispute	2
Murder	2
Disorderly conduct	1
Divorce	1
Fight	1
Fraud	1
Incest	1
Slander	1
Witchcraft	1
Total	**23**

Cases handled in Federal courts

Larceny	5
Rape	4
Arson	3
Assault and battery (white)	1
Assault with intent to kill	1

Involuntary manslaughter	1
Homicide	1
Total	16

Cases handled in Navajo Tribal courts

Disorderly conduct	145
Liquor violation	86
Assault and battery	28
Failure to support dependents	20
Reckless Driving	20
Theft	15
Driving without license	11
Estate	11
Divorce	9
Juvenile delinquency	9
Assault	7
Illicit cohabitation	7
Interference with roundup	7
Resisting arrest	7
Adultery	6
Contributing to delinquency of a minor	5
Disobedience of court order	4
Failure to comply with divorce law	4
Debt	3
Embezzlement	3
Grazing without a permit	3
Refusal to brand	3
Trespass	3
Escape	2
Violation of probation	2
Adoption	1
Bigamy	1
Carrying concealed weapon	1
Change of name	1
Contempt of court	1
Damage to private property	1
Fraud	1
Transmitting VD to another person	1
Guardianship	1
Incest	1
Damage to public property	1
Marriage validated	1
Misbranding	1
Paternity	1
Perjury	1
Threat to do bodily harm	1
Total	436
Grand total	596

WITCHCRAFT AS SOCIAL CONTROL

The complex of witchcraft belief and behavior at Navajo Mountain differs so greatly from the other mechanisms of social control just discussed that it demands separate consideration in depth.

Witchcraft as it was described to us by the residents of Navajo Mountain readily meets the definition given by Clyde Kluckhohn: "Navajo idea and action patterns concerned with the influencing of events by supernatural techniques that are socially disapproved" (1962:5). A Navajo witch, according to their description, is a human being, man or woman, who has learned the evil ritual from another human being already initiated into witchcraft lore. It is a deliberately learned, deliberately practiced ritual, aimed against a deliberately chosen victim.

The belief derives from the sacred myths. Katherine Spencer summarizes its origin as follows: "First Man and First Woman are the first and greatest witches and thus the cause of sickness and fatal diseases. First Man presents 'to each and every one' in the eighth world [before the emergence] some of his evil power, 'so that all are possessed of witchcraft' but he also designates herbal remedies and sacrifices to remove these evils. When the Navaho lived underground 'there were many witches who changed men into different animals' " (Spencer 1947:105).

Witchcraft is suspected when there is a persistent illness that fails to respond to curing ceremonies or to modern medicine. A series of calamities such as the death of sheep, combined with illness and perhaps death in a family, gives rise to fears of witchcraft activity. Witching is an alternate explanation for any death, and it is certain to be considered a probable cause of any violent death. An unexplained fire at night, strange noises, whistlings, or sounds of animals crawling on the roof of a hogan arouse suspicion of either a ghost (the evil spirit of the dead) or a witch. If a community suffers a prolonged drought, it may be ascribed to witchcraft. Kluckhohn describes Frenzy Witchcraft, a form of love magic that induces excessive sexual activity, but though our informants agreed that witches do use love magic, no cases were brought to our attention. Acute alcoholism, as another extreme form of lack of self-control, is ascribed to witchcraft, according to Frances Ferguson (1966), but again we found no examples in Navajo Mountain. However, one case of suicide and one attempted suicide were attributed to witch activity. In sum, witchcraft explains otherwise unexplainable evil.

Navajos distinguish forms of witchcraft in terms of the different techniques witches employ to work their evil, but since in all cases the intent and final effects are similar, for our purposes it does not seem necessary to make the distinction between witches, wizards, and sorcerers. Any one of the techniques can operate at a distance so long as the witch is in possession of some bit of excrement, nail parings, hairs, or clothing containing the sweat of the intended victim. This material can be buried in a grave and, through prayer or a ceremony done backwards, used to harm the person from whom the material has been taken. Sometimes the witch makes markings on a rock, or uses plants, or materials dug from graves, or sends lightning. One type of witch is a werewolf, or "skinwalker." He covers himself with the skin of a coyote, or bear and runs great distances on all fours. Climbing on top of a hogan when a family is asleep, he can drop specially treated pollen down the smoke hole or blow such pollen through a tube into the face of his victim. Or a witch can shoot a piece of bone or stone into a person to cause sickness or death.

> They cut pieces of clothes and blanket and bury it in a grave and the person dies.

He was praying witchway, making marks on rocks. All three of my family were going to die - my mother, my sister, and her daughter.

They can kill people with yucca. A bad medicine man may be a witch. He gets yucca that was used in a ceremony and puts it in a tree and says bad prayers and the person dies. Or they can cause sickness by putting a deer hoof into a corral. That may make the sheep die.

Skinwalkers are called *yeenaaldlooshii*. They walk like dogs and wear skins. They do it at night. In the daytime they sleep. I don't know why they wear a skin; maybe so they won't be recognized. A skinwalker may want to see what everyone is doing inside the hogan. They don't come just to scare people. They throw something into the hogan, pollen or something dug out of a grave. Sometimes they come to steal sheep. They make sure that the people are asleep. I don't know if there are more or fewer skinwalkers than there used to be; I don't know who they are. Skinwalkers go to special meetings where they can meet so that no one can see them. Like a Chapter meeting, by Districts. Only people who are practicing witchcraft are told about it.

There are a lot of skinwalkers in winter time. If there are a lot of skinwalkers around, then we won't have rain.

Witches originated, we were told, a long time ago. In answer to a question about the killing of witches in the old days, a woman told us the following tale:

This is a true story; I don't know where the place was and it happened a long, long time ago. There were just too many witches; people were suffering from it. Some people had a great big corn field, and they spread the news that everyone should come and help work in the field and when the work was finished they would have a big feast. And then, I guess, they killed quite a few calves. They were going to boil the meat. Some medicine men got gall bladders from tigers, deer, lizards, horny toads, rattlesnakes—witchcrafters and skinwalkers are afraid of these things. So the medicine men dried all of these gall bladders, and when they were dry they ground them up. They also got some kind of a plant that medicine men use against these witchcrafters. They ground all these together. Then they put some of this, a tablespoon, or maybe it was a teaspoonful, in with the meat that was boiling. Most of the people from all around came, everyone except the very old who were not able to work; men, women, children, and babies came. They made bread and everything, and then they told the people to line up to get something to eat. And then all the people in the crowd lined up, got their food, and started to eat. The way this food was prepared, it would hurt all the witches and skinwalkers, but not the others.

Some people started to scratch themselves as if they itched all over. Some just laughed and got up and started to walk off. Some fell dead. Others walked on and as they walked over the hill it was seen that their skins just seemed to explode and break open all over. This happened at the end of summer. I heard this story from my mother's mother.

So all the witches and skinwalkers who were there were finished off, and these were most of them. It happened, though, that among the very old people who did not go there to work and attend the feast there were some witches and skinwalkers, and it was from these that witchcraft started up again.

Victims of a witch may be an individual, man or woman, his relatives, or his livestock. One of the reasons for practicing witchcraft most often cited is jealousy, which means that the victim of a witch may be a rich person who has too many sheep, too much jewelry, or good land and water. An aggressive leader, or obvious innovator, may be singled out to be witched. The controllers of evil magic will retaliate for a slight, or an imagined slight, or as the result of a well-founded quarrel over land-use rights. A girl who refuses to marry into a "witchy" family may be killed by witchcraft in retaliation. Someone who dies under strange circumstances, particularly a young, well-liked woman, is said to have been killed by a sibling who needs to sacrifice a beloved relative to validate his acceptance into the witches' band.

> My sister died very suddenly; she was witched. A family wanted her to marry their son, but she said she did not want to. She knew the family was witchy. So they said to her, 'That's all we wanted to hear; you won't live very long.' Then she died so suddenly that my family didn't have time to have a Sing over her.

> The two wives of Greasewood died in the same year. It was their brother who did it; everyone knew that they were his best-loved sisters.

Kluckhohn states that he has never heard of witchcraft being used to prevent rain. For this reason, we were astonished to hear from various sources that the cause of the prolonged summer drought was the machinations of an old medicine man who had married into the area. Feeling spiteful against the community which "had such good grass, and so many fat sheep," he had done a rain ceremony backwards, we were told.

> Ch'ahii's son-in-law is responsible for the lack of rain. He came over here from Gap. Ever since there hasn't been enough rain. He came here, found the sheep and horses nice and fat. Then he stopped the rain. Witches are jealous when other people have it good. He is a crazy old man who came in here trying to ruin the

whole place. The ceremony he had on top of the mountain to make rain, well, it just spoiled everything. (He
did it backwards.) Just no rain at all.

He took corn pollen to the spring, put it in there where
the water comes up. I saw it and I brushed it away because I know that's wrong.

Opinions differ as to whether or not Christians can be
victims of witchcraft. Efforts are made by missionaries to
convince Navajo Christians either that there is no such
thing as witchcraft or that their new religion protects them
from evil magic. A story was told how the Christians at a
mission near Oraibi found large animal tracks, easily identified as werewolf or werecoyote prints, which went right
up to the church and then turned away. It is probable that
all Navajos in Navajo Mountain retain their belief in
witchcraft.

Persons likely to be accused of witchcraft are those who
do not conform to the Navajo value standards, or who are
repeatedly guilty of antisocial behavior. The community
does not necessarily agree on who is believed to be a witch.
Only the most recalcitrant cases, the bad actors, the mean,
and the uncooperative are considered by everyone to be
guilty. Otherwise, we found differences of opinion depending largely on each person's, or each family's, own experiences with the accused. There is no obvious avoidance
of a suspected witch at a public gathering. This was stated
to us openly, and we never observed such avoidance behavior. Kluckhohn reports that witches are frequently
reputed to come from outside areas. It is true that some informants told us that most of the skinwalkers were from
Shonto, from Inscription House, or from Kaibito, but the
majority of the specific witchcraft charges were made against
residents who were personally known to us. Although the
victims were both men and women, and even children, no

woman in Navajo Mountain, to our knowledge, was accused of being a witch.

There are several ways of dealing with witchcraft fears. A diagnostician can be called in, either a hand-trembler, a star-gazer, or a crystal-gazer. He may diagnose the symptoms as evidence of witchcraft, and in some cases name the witch. The intended victim may then confront the witch with his evil. For example, one man said to his own father who, according to the hand-trembler, was planning to kill his son, and all of his son's children, "Why don't you kill me right now!" The witch, thus exposed, was frightened off. In another case, two men at an Enemy Way ceremony publicly accused each other of witchcraft. One charge was that of committing incest with a sister, and the counter-charge was that of causing the death of his patient in a Sing.

Hopi medicine men are thought to be especially good at sucking cures which extract the intrusive objects a witch has shot into his victim.

If a counterwitchcraft ceremony, some form of *Hochǫji* or Evil Way Chant, is held in time, the evil power will be sent back against the witch and the intended victim will be saved. If possible, the witched objects should be found and burned. If the suspected witch or any of his relatives meets a violent death within a year, the family of the intended victim accepts this as confirmation that he was the guilty party. Several violent deaths in Navajo Mountain were ascribed to witchcraft being turned back upon the witch. Only the guilty witch or his relatives will be injured by a counterwitchcraft Sing. In one case, less than a year after a ceremony had been held over a youth who had attempted suicide, an old man in Kaibito was struck by lightning while riding on horseback. His sudden death validated the suspicion of his evil plot against the boy. Such deaths may be ascribed to witchcraft, or to counterwitch-craft, depending on whether the evaluators like or dislike the suffering family. For instance, a Navajo Mountain family lost three young men, one by drowning, one by suicide, and one in an automobile accident. Friends were convinced that the family was being witched by another family with whom they had quarreled over range land, but people who disliked the dead boys' parents said that the father's evil magic had turned back against him.

There is also a belief that eventually a witch will suffer supernatural punishment.

> A person going around like he knows everything. He might say he was going to kill a person's horse—might say he's going to kill that person. Might dream the wrong things. He will get sick and die. They usually sing on a person who is dying of all the bad things he has done.

In the old days a meeting of the victim's kin could be held to make the accused witch confess his guilt, and a decision reached by consensus either to free him or "execute" him, a form of self-help which would be condoned by the community. This procedure will be described more fully in the analytical section.

Social Impact of Witchcraft. Our analysis will deal with the psychological and societal functions and dysfunctions of the belief in evil magic as we observed it in Navajo Mountain. Here, witchcraft is the principal explanation of the unexplainable, of incurable illness, and of odd coincidences adding up to a series of misfortunes.

Some of our informants obviously enjoyed telling dramatic stories of the witches and werewolves they had seen or had heard, and others relished the attention they could command from worried kinsmen and neighbors when they claimed they were being witched. By placing blame on a witch, two different families of our acquaintance exonerated themselves from guilt when their sons attempted suicide following a family quarrel. This mechanism also served to relieve the would-be suicides from responsibility for their acts.

The witchcraft complex permits the release of generalized hostility against a scapegoat in a socially approved manner. Another important function of these beliefs is that they serve as a socially acceptable framework for the expression of subconscious hostility against relatives, a form of aggression that otherwise is deeply disvalued and as deeply repressed in Navajo society. Only after examining the more than 30 witchcraft cases brought to our attention in Navajo Mountain did we ascertain that a high proportion (four-fifths) of the suspicions of witching were directed against relatives. The kin categories involved such close dyads as siblings, father and son, maternal uncle and nephew, maternal uncle and niece, grandfather and grandchild. Accusations toward affinals were found in the categories of brother-in-law against brother-in-law, sister-in-law against brother-in-law, father-in-law against son-in-law. It is not surprising that most of the allegations concerned siblings, since causing the death of a sibling is diagnostic of a witch. In addition to these kin categories, we did find witchcraft charges made between unrelated individuals, unrelated families, and as a kind of community judgment upon chronic offenders and psychopaths.

It is noteworthy that the only case that came to our attention in which women were accused of witchcraft concerned two clanless Paiute women who made such charges against each other in the course of a range dispute. This is contrary to evidence found in many matrilineal societies where women are the most frequent victims of the witchcraft accusations made by men. This behavior pattern has been interpreted as the male's subconscious reaction to female dominance.

The societal functions of witchcraft beliefs are closely

related to the value system and social organization of the traditional way of life. The paramount values are harmony, equality, generosity, reciprocity, and cooperation among kin. In the interests of harmony, no one should start or prolong a quarrel or retaliate against the relatives of an adversary (the type of action viewed as obligatory in a feuding society). An injured person should accept compensation for the wrong. No Navajo should resort to physical violence against another Navajo.

The ideal of equality means that no one should strive to become too rich or allow himself to become too poor. A leader should not take too much personal initiative, but should talk things over with the People. A good Navajo should cooperate with relatives and display kindness, generosity, and friendliness to neighbors. He should conform to Navajo religious tenets, help out with Sings, and never violate taboos such as the exogamic prohibitions against incestuous sexual relations with blood and clan kin. He should not steal. He should avoid graves and other places that have been contaminated by death, and above all he should not rob the dead. In short, one can make a list of positive Navajo values and set in direct opposition a list of negative prescriptions. Any one of the latter, alone or in combination, may be ascribed to a witch. Thus, the incestuous, the ungenerous, the mean, the overly aggressive, the uncontrolled, and the violent risk being accused of witchcraft.

Kluckhohn found that the rich, the very old, and "medicine men" were frequently under suspicion of practising evil magic (1963:59). This was not the picture for Navajo Mountain. Of 20 accused witches, only 4 were old, 4 were medicine men, and none was rich. Some of the victims of witchcraft were well-to-do, but by no means all of them. Many Navajo Mountain residents fall into these categories without ever being accused of witchcraft. Necessary to trigger the accusation is an added element that arouses hostility or ill will. For example, any Chanter is open to suspicion because of his esoteric learning, but even one who loses a patient is not apt to be called a witch unless there has been some preexisting bad feeling, or unless he has an unsavory reputation in general. One Singer in Navajo Mountain has lost four wives, a brother and a sister, and several children, but because he has always been a mild, cooperative, and good man, he has never been suspected of witchcraft. In contrast, a young man, conducting a Chant for his wife's sister, was accused by his father-in-law of witchcraft when the patient died during the ceremony being given for her. Shortly thereafter, another family, related to the dead woman, accused him of killing their sheep and making their children sick. The young Singer was an outstanding leader, a delegate to the Navajo Tribal Council and a moderately well-to-do man. We must assume that his prestige and initiative had aroused a degree of jealous hostility sufficient to set off the accusations. A third Singer suspected of "witchcrafting" was a man who had married in from outside. He was old, aggressive, wore his hair cut like a Hopi, and undertook to do ceremonies that the other Navajo Mountain practitioners did not know. In short, he was an outsider who was too obviously competitive.

A man with aberrant characteristics may become the local scapegoat, used to frighten children into good behavior, and the subject of general ridicule and butt of jokes. If through some untoward incident he becomes the focus of attention of a troubled individual or family he is likely to be called a witch.

Navajo Mountain traditionally had no superordinate authority, no government in the sense of a state apparatus, no formal courts, no police force, no jail, no sanction of banishment, no insane asylum. The sole justification for the supreme use of force—execution—lay in the condoned killing of a witch.

The fear of being witched, or being accused of practicing witchcraft, serves as a strong pressure for conformity. Let us spell this out in more detail: witchcraft beliefs act as a leveller in that they inhibit competition for wealth and power. People in Navajo Mountain are reluctant to strive for leadership in the formal political organization, and usually wait until they are "drafted" before they express interest in being elected. The acquisition of wealth must be offset by generosity. The richest man in Navajo Mountain has not been accused of witchcraft, because he does his part in the Sings given for and by his relatives. Kind behavior and kind speech help to keep a person out of trouble. One young man who was run over and killed by a truck is thought to have been witched because he talked "mean" during a dispute over range land. Since incest is a diagnostic trait of a witch, the taboo against such behavior is reinforced. Repeated acts of violence and repeated thefts may incite witchcraft accusations. Fear of the dark, when werewolves prowl and ghosts are active, serves as a kind of curfew.

> If you see a fire at night where there really shouldn't be a fire, it is the fire of a ghost. You don't go to it; you run away from it. There is a song for ghost fire.

> If I go outside and see a fire which is not really a fire, but a funny kind of light, then I will tell Mom. If this happens several times Mom will wonder what's up and have a hand-trembler or a crystal-gazer [to identify the witch or ghost].

> We went out of the hogan a couple of nights ago and we heard whistling. Adelaide thought it was werewolves.

A person who digs around or steals from graves is always considered to be a witch. This mechanism protects the wealth that is traditionally buried with the dead to placate the ghost of the deceased. One old man in another community was nicknamed "Bow Guard," because he was reputed to have stolen a silver and turquoise bow guard from a grave. There was talk that he had taught his brother-in-law and his sister's son how to work evil magic.

Threats of witchcraft may be used to enhance secular power. A councilman on the western side leaked the information that he would witch his opponents if he were not reelected. In a dispute between the families of two half-siblings over farm land, one of the disputants tried to frighten off the other family by telling people that a witchy woman had flown over Cummings Mesa and had seen with her magic glasses an open grave containing the bodies of three men of the other family who had recently met violent deaths. There was room in the grave, he said, for a fourth body, that of the last remaining son.

Shared beliefs in witchcraft aid the community in implementing sanctions against social offenders. A thief who has been confronted with his theft may return the stolen goods rather than run the risk of being called a skinwalker, or of being witched. Likewise, the person found guilty by consensus at an informal meeting will pay the compensation agreed upon rather than run such risks.

In traditional Navajo society there was a procedure for directly disposing of witches. The accused would be tied up by the relatives of the victim and held without food or water for four days, during which time every effort would be made to force him to confess his heinous offense. If the people present agreed that he was guilty he could be killed, and the community would take no action against his "executioners." If he confessed, or if the assemblage agreed that the evidence was not sufficient to prove his guilt, he

was released. We were told a story, recounted below, of one
such meeting which took place some 70 years ago. The accused witch was the first husband of an old woman who is
still living.

> I heard what an old, old lady told me. A woman hit that
> lady's husband with an axe. This man was hit by his sis-
> ter [parallel cousin] across the face with an axe because
> she wanted to kill him. He was asleep when she hit him.
> She was afraid of gossip. The reason the girl and her
> family wanted to kill him was because he had stayed
> with his sister all alone. Her family tied him up and
> they had a meeting. The girl who hit him, her mother
> and her father were on one side. The man, his wife and
> her father were on the other. Her mother was there
> too but she didn't take part because she didn't want to
> get involved. Another man had been asked to come
> to the meeting. He was a headman or councilman from
> around Shonto where the quarrel took place. All there
> was in the hogan was a barrel of water. The family of
> both sides were sitting around for a couple of days with-
> out eating. They were just sitting around to see if it
> was true that he had gone to his sister's during the
> night.
>
> His wife said, "You people weren't making believe
> you were having a Sing. You were practicing witchcraft.
> You were doing things with your sister."
>
> The man who was accused said it wasn't true, that it
> must have been someone else. They were going to kill
> him. His father-in-law didn't want anything to happen
> to his son-in-law because he loved him so much. The
> councilman didn't want him killed either. His wife
> didn't know whether he was innocent or guilty because
> he wouldn't answer their questions. She left suddenly
> with her baby. After she left the whole thing just ended.
> The old, old lady's father untied his son-in-law who
> then went away to Tuba City. He never married again.

He was so badly scarred, I guess he thought he was too ugly. He lived alone for a while then went back to his parents.

Navajo Mountain, like most if not all communities in the world, has offenders who are recidivists and who cannot be reasoned with or reformed. It also has psychopaths whose uncontrolled behavior disrupts the community. By assimilating the dangerous criminal to a witch, the community made use of the traditional meeting and execution to rid the area of the hard-core criminal. This type of meeting is rare nowadays, because the killing of anyone, even an accused witch, is prosecuted as a Federal offense. We saw the mechanism in operation as it moved up to a certain point and then stopped. A psychopath, who had served time in Federal prison for incest with his own daughter and was presently molesting children and threatening to kill them if they exposed him, was feared as a witch. An habitual thief and his son, also an habitual thief, were called skinwalkers. It was said about a man who had been imprisoned for years for raping a white woman, and who soon after his release accidentally killed a friend during a drunken brawl, that he was making violent attacks on his relatives and was forcing incestuous relations on his mother, his grandmother, his aunts, and his sister. This was the first step toward an accusation of witchcraft. In all these cases, however, the community could go no further without running afoul of Federal authority. In the old days, such offenders, assimilated to witches, could have been executed with community approval.

There is no record of an overt charge of witchcraft being taken to the Navajo Tribal Court from Navajo Mountain, although such court cases have arisen elsewhere on the Reservation. However, there is evidence that the Navajo police have been called in to protect a person against threatened witchcraft and to help track a skinwalker charged with stealing. Some informants say, however, that the police are not much good in such situations.

We have examined the functions of witchcraft as social control. Dysfunctions are numerous and perhaps more obvious. An irrational explanation inhibits the search for the rational cause of illness and evil. Sheep may be dying of an easily detected, curable disease, but time and money are wasted in a counterwitchcraft Sing. Medical treatment may be delayed while Chants are held over a sick person. A diagnostician is accorded unrestricted power to persecute a personal enemy. In one case, a Navajo Mountain hand-trembler named a person, with whom her son-in-law had had a violent quarrel during a recent drinking bout, as a skinwalker and a thief. In another, a diviner named as a witch his father-in-law, who had quarreled with, and abandoned, the hand-trembler's mother-in-law. These instances could be multiplied many times.

Witchcraft accusations block the settlement of quarrels between individuals and between families who might otherwise be reconciled. They intensify hostilities by adding a frightening supernatural element to a common realistic dispute over range rights and water rights, or over refusals to accept marriage proposals, or even over the payment of debts. Because of irrational charges, forced confession, and secret accusations against a person who is not given the opportunity to defend himself, injustice, not justice, may result.

Witchcraft beliefs and practices persist into the present day despite overall legal and political authority and Christian dogma, because modern medicine is not able to effect absolute cures in all cases, Christian prayer is not always answered, and modern legal machinery has not eliminated the disrupters, recidivists, and psychopaths.

By personifying Evil as a Witch, Navajos are assured that they can cope with dire trouble through the technique of counterwitchcraft. In this manner, their faith in the traditional ceremonial system of curing is protected, since a death or continuing illness may be interpreted as a result of undiagnosed witchcraft rather than as evidence of failure of the Chant.

Decision-making and Dealing with the Surrounding Society

Dealing with the surrounding society or societies is a function that can be subsumed as the "political" or decision-making aspect of community life. Four systems of authority with specific areas of jurisdiction formulate rules, give commands, and offer services to the Navajo Mountain community. These are the informal, traditional system, the Navajo Tribal Council, the Federal government, and the States of Arizona and Utah.

Traditional Navajo society, which had no formal units of government, never developed strong authoritarian characteristics. The locus of the traditional authority system was in the kin groups, which once exercised all decision-making power. Nuclear families or households, extended families or camps, and lineages variously direct the technology, marriage choices, child-raising, ceremonial organization, and much of the informal "legal" activity.

Leadership involving the exercise of authority considered to be legitimate by the community was intermittent, that is, it was called into action as the occasion arose. The traditional headman, the respected Singer (one of the intellectual elite), the good and wise Navajo, who could mediate a dispute, speak well, and express the consensus of a gathering after consultation, was the ideal leader. He was the person who would be chosen to voice the views of the community, or important segments of the community, in unavoidable contacts with surrounding societies. Headman or traditional leader was an achieved position of latent authority, based on ability rather than birth, and the incumbent was permitted to fulfill the role only so long as his prestige endured.

Materials on leadership were collected by the Navajo Land Claims Division of the Navajo Tribal Council in connection with the Indian claims case against the Federal government. Aged informants in the western Navajo area were asked to name old leaders. The findings present a picture of widely dispersed headmen living anywhere from Oljeto to Kayenta through Black Mountain, Shonto, Inscription House, and Kaibito to Tuba City and beyond— all the various places where Navajo Mountain people had lived. Except in regard to the historically famous Hoskinini (Hashké neiní) and his son, Atene, there was no general agreement as to former leaders. Those named by the informants included Singers, heads of large extended families, policemen, one "seven-dollar-a-month judge," and one woman. Kluckhohn was of the opinion that leadership in a small Navajo community, although not strictly inherited, frequently followed family lines (personal communication, 1960). There has been some tendency in Navajo Mountain for both informal and formal leadership to pass down the line of the founding family, at least on Rainbow Plateau. For example, Whiteman Killer's son-in-law, Endishchee or Mr. Pinetree, was the informal leader until his death. Malcolm Collier has this to say of him:

> Endishchee was undoubtedly the traditional leader and the remark made about him in 1938 was 'And who will be the leader when he is gone?' There was no clear successor in view either on the basis of position or personality and endowment. And perhaps not even on the basis of ambition (personal communication, 1960).

Endishchee's son, his grandnephew, and a stepgrandson each held the position of Tribal delegate. Because of his ability, the grandnephew succeeded in exercising both formal and informal community leadership. The "reign" of Whiteman Killer's and Endishchee's descendants or affinals was interrupted by the election to the Tribal Council of a man from Oljeto who had married onto Paiute Mesa, and some years later by the election of two Paiute Salts (Áshįįhí), one after the other, who lived on Paiute Mesa and on the northeast side of the mountain respectively.

Singers do not hold positions of leadership outside of the religious sphere unless they also enjoy prestige for their levelheadedness, their forceful but considerate personalities, and their skill as mediators. One English-speaking "medicine man" held the position of delegate in the 1930's. At the present time in Navajo Mountain, the Singers do not strive for political leadership, although they participate in Chapter activities.

The most important modern decision-making group for Navajos is the Navajo Tribal Council, which exercises legitimate power to make binding decisions in directing the domestic affairs of the tribe. In 1868, the United States Government negotiated a treaty with the Navajos and thus made them a "Treaty Tribe." The status of "domestic dependent nation" was reaffirmed as late as 1959 in a Supreme Court ruling on the case of *Williams v. Lee* (358 U.S. 217). This means that all the powers that have not expressly been taken away through Acts of Congress still reside in the Navajos as a "sovereign" people. The Navajo Tribal Council legislates for the tribe through representative leaders. A councilman (formerly called delegate) is elected from each of 74 election precincts, of which Navajo Mountain is one. A chairman and vice-chairman are chosen by the reservation electorate, and they, with the Advisory Committee, which is selected from among the members of the Tribal Council, form the executive arm of the government. Councilmen are organized into committees such as those of Welfare, Health, Law and Order, Grazing, and Resources.

A large staff of paid officials administers the Tribal programs. The capital is at Window Rock, but some Tribal officials and staff are stationed in the five subagency divisions of the Bureau of Indian Affairs at Tuba City, Shiprock, Fort Defiance, Crownpoint, and Chinle. The Tribal staff in Tuba City organizes and dispenses services to the town proper and to the outlying districts of the subagency of which Navajo Mountain is a part. An extension aide assists with sheep dusting, vaccinating, branding, grain distribution, hay buying and the Tribal Council's form of "painless stock reduction," that is, the program to buy up lambs and old ewes to encourage stock owners to cull their flocks. A community worker helps the local Chapter to plan activities and to obtain such supplies as sewing and leather-working machines, sports equipment, moving-picture projectors, loud-speakers, and so forth. A Tribal Welfare Department supervises the distribution of surplus commodities donated by the Federal government, as well as various supplies furnished by the Navajo tribe—lumber for home improvement, prefabricated houses for welfare recipients, clothes for schoolchildren, layettes, dentures, eyeglasses, and hearing aids. A lawyer from the Tribe's legal department in Window Rock is available once a week in Tuba City for consultation with individual Navajos.

The first Navajo Mountain delegates were traditional, non-English-speaking tribesmen. The 1938 delegate spoke English despite the fact that he was a "medicine man." In 1951, an English-speaking Navajo, employed as an interpreter by the Bureau of Indian Affairs, was elected to the Tribal Council from Navajo Mountain. Two subsequent councilmen have been able to speak English. The present representative to the central body is the best-educated man in the community. He has spent a number of years off the Reservation in Presbyterian missionary training, and is well-equipped to act in both Navajo and non-Navajo society. He is a member of the all-important Advisory Committee, of the Tribal Trading Committee, and of the Utah State Indian Commission. As a councilman he is careful to distinguish between that function and his role in Window Rock, where he is expected by his constituents to show initiative in securing prerequisites for the community. He is expected by the Council officers and administrators to legislate in the interests of the tribe as a whole. Back in the community, he should act only as a spokesman for the desires and opinions of the precinct and only in consultation with the Chapter membership.

Finally there is the Chapter. All adult Indians of the community are members, including the Paiutes, who have been given census numbers in the Navajo tribe. They elect the Chapter officers, a president, a vice-president and a secretary. The secretary must be literate in English, since he writes up the minutes and receives and interprets the communiqués from the Council and the Bureau of Indian Affairs. In 1962, all three Chapter officers had had some formal education.

Through this organization, which meets regularly, usually once a month, the Councilman polls community opinion and communicates Tribal policy to his constituency. Here Tribal programs concerning grazing, welfare, grain distribution, water development, and elections are discussed and implemented. The building of the Chapter House in 1959 was financed by Window Rock and largely carried out with local labor. One of the principal, and doubtless most appreciated, activities of the Chapter is to plan the public-works program that employs, using Tribal funds, most of the able-bodied men of the community for 10-day periods, four times a year.

Although it is possible to distinguish two lines of authority, traditional and modern, in Navajo Mountain today, there is no such distinct separation between them as Adams depicts for Shonto (1963:68). Even as early as 1938, Malcolm Collier noted that more and more problems were being taken to the delegate for solution, despite the fact that at that time the council members were not paid and the Tribal Council itself had little authority apart from the Bureau of Indian Affairs (1966:34). Today, rather than a sharp distinction there is a blurring of the lines between formal and informal leadership by Chapter officers and councilmen, who are exercising both *de facto* and *de jure* political leadership.

The federal government interacts directly with the Navajo Reservation and its small segment, Navajo Mountain, through three principal authority systems: the Bureau of Indian Affairs, the United States Public Health Service, and the federal district courts. The federal government still retains trust responsibility for Navajo Reservation Indians, which means that many of their regulations concerning such matters as disposal of funds and disposal of land require the approval of the Secretary of the Interior. The Bureau of Indian Affairs, as part of the Department of the Interior, administers federal services and exercises federal supervision over Navajo Indians through its agency at Window Rock. The agency in turn is divided into five subagencies. Tuba City is the center for the largest of these, covering some six million acres, that is, most of the western section of the Navajo Reservation. The Reservation is further divided into 18 land-management districts for the purpose of grazing control. Navajo Mountain, Shonto, and

Inscription House form Land Management District Number 2, a division that is also used as a political district by the Navajo Tribal Council. The official center for grazing activities for Western Navajo is at Kayenta. Education, roads, welfare, advice on range management, and soil conservation are among the Indian Bureau services. More and more, the federal government is turning over the direction of, and responsibility for, activities to the Navajo Tribal Council.

The United States Public Health Service furnishes medical care for the Navajo Reservation. The hospital that serves Navajo Mountain is in Tuba City. In the early 1960's, Navajo Mountain was visited monthly by a doctor and a dentist who held a clinic at the local Chapter House. In recent years, the U.S. Public Health Service has assumed responsibility, with the cooperation of the Bureau of Indian Affairs and the Navajo Tribal Council, for the development of sanitary domestic water sources.

The states of Utah and Arizona, which halve the community of Navajo Mountain, can neither administer law nor collect taxes on the Reservation. In 1924, all Indians in the United States were made citizens, with the right to vote in general elections. Arizona, however, disfranchised the Indians as wards of the government, and suit had to be brought by an Indian in 1948 to compel the state to permit them to vote in general elections. Despite this ruling, the state's literacy clause (for Arizona) effectively disfranchises most of Navajo Mountain. The states and the federal government cooperate to furnish welfare aid to reservation Indians. Arizona maintains a state employment office in Tuba City. Utah receives 37½ percent of the oil-lease royalties derived from Indian land lying within its borders. These funds are earmarked for use on projects beneficial to Indians and are administered by the Utah Indian Commission. Navajo Mountain has requested a clinic, scholarships, and a scenic road to Oljeto as their share of the benefits.

Only a few residents of Navajo Mountain understand clearly where decisions come from or why they have been made. They accept the regulations and proposals or resist them in terms of their own, their family's, or their community's interests. They may be only vaguely aware of the fact that Navajo Mountain lies within circles of political authority which extend far beyond the canyons and rivers and mountains of the little community.

Meeting Life Crises

Birth

Childbirth is recognized by all Navajos as a period of potential danger. Generally speaking, a woman carries on with her daily routine of work, but takes some care against straining herself. During the last few weeks of pregnancy other members of the household, or of the extended family, will relieve the expectant mother of her share of herding, or bringing in firewood for the cookstove, or any other chores that might tax her strength.

By tradition, all women had Sings before the birth of a child. Today the older women who are still giving birth probably are more inclined to have a Sing as a matter of routine precaution than are the young women, just as it is the older women who more frequently have their babies at home while the younger women go to Tuba City to the Public Health Hospital. Because of the 85-mile distance to the hospital and the poor roads, which may even be closed for days at a time, many women who would prefer to give birth at the hospital are forced to do so at home.

More than one woman has been delivered at some make-shift birthplace en route to Tuba City.

At the first sign of any complications in the delivery, a "medicine man" will be called in, and a hand-trembler may be consulted to foretell the hour of birth.

> Cynthia's husband had to go away on a job soon before she was due, so he asked the missionaries to see that she got to the hospital. When the time came her parents got a hand-trembler and a medicine man, and refused to allow her to be taken. She was in hard labor and the baby was crosswise. After more than eight hours had passed the medicine man said the missionaries could take her. The hand-trembler said, 'When the Pleiades are there (pointing to a position in the sky) the baby will come.' He was about an hour off. It was snowing, only a jeep could get through; it was a rough ride, much jiggling; the baby changed position and was born in the jeep just this side of Inscription House.

In home deliveries, the expectant woman's mother, if she is available, is almost invariably the chief assistant, of-ten aided by the patient's sisters and her mother's mother. Once again, Navajo flexibility allows a wide choice, and circumstances most frequently determine who will assist.

> Who is present? Just those people who want to be there, no special people.

The father of the baby makes a point of being present if possible. A man will try to arrange his work so that he can spend time close to the hogan when his wife is due to de-liver. If his mother and sisters live near by they are often in attendance at the birth.

> When my son, Hashké, was born I was separated from

> my husband, so he wasn't there. My mother was, both
> my sisters, my father and a Singer. They are the ones
> who chased Hashké out.

The newborn infant is washed by the midwife, who then
wraps the baby in cloth. No special arrangements are made
for the disposal of the afterbirth or cord, they said, which
contradicts information from other parts of the Reservation.

Puberty

An important event in the life of a girl is the puberty
ceremony held at first menstruation. Old women when with
us proudly pointed to the place where they had had their
"coming-out" party, a four-night ceremonial. Most Navajo
Mountain girls are given this ritual. This is never the all-
tribal public affair of the Mescalero Apaches, such as Ruth
Boyer describes (1962), but a family affair given by the father and mother of the girl. Any friend of the family is welcome to attend the function, but arrangements are generally
in the hands of relatives of the young lady. Men, as well as
women, participate in the ceremony, which is actually an
announcement that the girl is considered ready for marriage. If first menstruation occurs when the girl is away at
school, the ceremony will be postponed until her next visit
home.

An analysis of the kinship connections of those participating in several puberty ceremonies showed that often
both mother's and father's relatives were there "to help
out." All of the participants lived nearby and were apt to
be those relatives who regularly engaged in interaction with
the family of the girl. If the father of the girl is a "medicine
man" he may sing over her.

Marriage

In seeking to derive meaningful conclusions from extensive data on sexual unions in Navajo Mountain, we were immediately confronted with the difficulties of defining "marriage." *Webster's Third International Dictionary* of 1965 defines "marriage" as "the state of being united to a person of the opposite sex as husband and wife: wedlock; the institution whereby men and women are joined in a special kind of social and legal dependence for the purpose of founding and maintaining a family." The *Legal Encyclopedia* (Samuel G. Kling, 1965) defines it as "the state of being legally wedded." *Notes and Queries on Anthropology*, 1954 edition, defines marriage as "a union between a man and a woman such that children borne by a woman are recognized as legitimate offspring by both partners" (1954: 71). Kathleen Gough Aberle believes that legitimizing children is the "minimum necessary criterion applicable to all those unions which anthropologists customarily label 'marriage'." She says, "Marriage is a relationship between a woman and one or more other persons which provides that a child born to a woman, under circumstances not prohibited by the rules of the relationship, shall be accorded full birth-status rights in his society or social stratum" (1961:363).

None of these definitions seems to encompass the important features of "marriage" in Navajo society. Edmund Leach felt some of the same uneasiness, and approached the institution from the point of view of the "allocation of a number of distinguishable categories of rights" (1966:107–109). He lists different rights on the basis of whether they are allocated to husband or to wife; the monopoly of sexuality; rights to the labor service of the partner;

property rights; affinity between a husband and his wife's brothers; and rights which affect the status and property of the children. James Bosch, in an analysis of the discussions regarding a definition of marriage that was held in the Navajo Tribal Council in 1940, raises some of these same problems.

We prefer to discuss the mating patterns among Navajos in terms of "significant unions," taking them up under the aspects of the preferred form of marriage, acceptable forms of marriage, other consequential unions, and unacceptable unions.

"Marriage" is a form of heterosexual mating which conforms to certain rules and allows particular indispensable societal functions to be performed in a socially acceptable manner. One of the principal functions is to regulate sexuality, that is, to provide recurrent, socially acceptable sexual satisfaction for the partners involved; in no known society is sexual activity completely uncontrolled.

A second extremely important function of "marriage" is economic cooperation and mutual responsibility, with some degree of permanency. Among the Navajos, economic cooperation concerns not only the husband and wife, but the extended family in which they reside and with whom they share work responsibility. Cooperation between the "wedded" man and woman serves to maintain their own household, to support children if there are any, and to assist individual members of the nuclear family to acquire property, particularly livestock, in their own names. Not only do husband and wife hold separate title to livestock, but child herders receive gifts of ewes and mares.

Another function which "marriage" performs is to provide companionship and emotional security. We emphasize this because one can derive a false impression of the depth and strength of the affective tie between spouses in a society such as the Navajo, where the romantic complex is missing (as Navajos themselves admit), where marriages are arranged, where extended-family life provides constant social interaction outside of the nuclear family, and where, particularly in the pre-Fort Sumner days, husbands were absent for long periods of time on trading expeditions and raids. We noted repeatedly during the course of our field work how often husbands and wives herded, made trips to the trading post, visited relatives, and attended Sings together. Even rides in search of wood and water were often made by a man in company with wife and children. Especially striking is the mutual respect and responsibility that aged couples show for each other, and the care a spouse will take of a sick husband or wife. We have recorded the story of a Navajo woman who tells of her unhappy first marriage, and the good treatment she received from her second husband. In gratitude, now that he is old and blind, she willingly does everything in her power to give him aid and comfort in his distress.

> . . . I started living with my present husband; he has never abused me, either with words or physically . . . . In this way I found out that if you begin to live with a man as his wife you regard him as a mother to you. You have to depend on him for subsistence. This man was like a mother to me until he lost his eyesight. I never thought of deserting him because of his condition. I still have a love feeling for him. I have never neglected him; I stay right by him helping along with whatever I possibly can.

A further function of marriage is the extension of kinship relations. As Paul Bohannon says, "Marriages create the type of relationship called *affinity*. A person is an affine of his spouse and of all his spouse's kinsmen save her affines" (1963:57). In Navajo society interaction with affines both within and outside of the extended family is of importance in property rights and in support for ceremonial activities.

One of the primary societal functions of "marriage" is to produce and rear children. This, however, is not the only function of an acceptable union, and, therefore, cannot be the chief criterion of marriage. Such a limited definition would deny the validity and societal functions of a union entered into by couples who for one reason or another are unable to have children. The regularization of sexual satisfaction, the economic cooperation and mutual responsibility, and the companionship and emotional security that such a union can provide suffice to justify the acceptability and social value of the mating.

Among Navajos, "marriage" does not determine the "legal" heirs to an estate, as is the case in so many societies. Any Navajo child expects to inherit from his mother or from other members of his matrilineage regardless of whether or not he has a "legal" father. Traditionally, children inherit token gifts of affection from their father, with consideration in the choice of heirs being given to persons with such further qualifications as having cared for the deceased before his death, being present at the distribution of the estate, or being adjudged capable of managing the property. Here, sociological fatherhood can play a more significant role than biological fatherhood.

In some societies of the world the sociological father (pater) can be a complete replacement for the biological father (genitor), but in Navajo society the determination of biological paternity is necessary because of the incest taboos. A child needs to know the clan of his genitor, whether or not this man recognizes paternity or assumes any responsibility for his child, since the incest taboo forbids mating between a person and a member of his father's clan, and between persons whose fathers belong to the same clan. Also, in a society that accepts stepfather/stepdaughter mar-

riage, a distinction between the sociological and the biological father is crucial.

The functions we have just described apply to what we
can call "marriage" among Navajos, that is, to those socially acceptable heterosexual unions with some element of
permanence and mutual responsibility as distinguished
from "other consequential unions" and "unacceptable
unions." At Navajo Mountain, there are 92 marital arrangements that meet this definition of marriage.

The following compilation shows the duration of the
marriages in force in Navajo Mountain as of 1961/1962:

Number of years:

1–5	6–10	11–15	16–20	21–30	31–40	41–50	51	plus

Number of couples:

21	20	16	6	18	7	1	3

PREFERRED FORM OF MARRIAGE

Arranged marriage. Marriage in traditional Navajo society is an alliance between two families of different clans;
it is a sober economic contract rather than a love match.
By preference, negotiations are carried on by the two families, and it is not infrequent for the bride and groom to
meet for the first time at the wedding. This is still the pattern for the majority of marriages that take place in Navajo
Mountain. Out of 92 marriages in force (couples living
together) as of 1962, 55 marriages were arranged, 17 were
unarranged, and on 20 marriages we lack the requisite information.

Conventionally, a spokesman for the boy will take the
initiative in asking the parents of the girl to arrange a
meeting to discuss a possible marriage. Any man or woman
who is a good worker, healthy, of a pleasant disposition,

generous and helpful, who meets the exogamic prohibitions, and is a member of a family with which the prospec-
tive partner's mother, father, and mother's mother would
like to be allied, is considered a good match. If the ages of
the chosen mates are somewhat comparable and the two
individuals are physically attractive, so much the better,
but these are not prime requisites. After the first overtures,

> a feast is held and the families talk over how to get the
> young people started. They talk about what the gifts
> will be, and what the son-in-law will be expected to do
> around his mother-in-law's place.

Modern tribal rules have imposed a provision stating
that "A person consenting to the marriage of a minor shall
be liable for the support of any children born to that minor
until the minor reaches the age of 21 if a male, or 18 if a
female" (Title 9, Section 5, *Navajo Tribal Code*). At least
some Navajo Mountain parents of young girls bear this
responsibility in mind while the negotiations are under
way.

The girl being sought is consulted and her consent is
solicited. While the maiden usually takes the advice of her
elders even if she does not know the boy, every girl we
questioned said, "They would not make me do it if I said,
'no'."

> My grandmother, who raised me, told me that the man
> I was to marry was coming tonight. I was surprised. I
> was doing something at the time, I don't remember
> what. I was asked to burn some cedar. I refused; I said
> I was tired. I had just finished hauling wood. My hands
> were cold and I didn't feel like doing anything. When
> I heard this news I began to have all kinds of thoughts.
> I thought of running away. Across the canyon from our
> home, my uncle lived and I thought of going to live
> with him. I told them this and they told me I would run

into the same situation. Someone over there would want to marry me, wherever I went. My brother then began to talk to me. 'You shouldn't plan such things; you should marry this man.' He was my favorite brother and I paid attention to what he said. In those days the young girls used to mind what their elders told them to do. . . . This is the way I was married.

The advice of other members of the girl's family is asked; our informants were positive in stating that either mother's mother of the pair involved has the authority to veto the marriage. In a survey of 26 marriages in Navajo Mountain, we found the following people acting in behalf of the groom: father, mother, mother's brother, father's father of the bride (this occurred in the marriage of a Navajo girl to a white man), mother's mother's brother (in a case where the boy's own mother was dead and his father had remarried out of the community), mother's brother's son (in the case of a young man whose mother's only brother was dead), a sister, an older brother, a mother's mother, a mother's father, children of the suitor, and a missionary.

Acting for the girl were mother, father, mother's brother, father's mother, sister and sister's husband (in a case of sibling exchange).

A brother-in-law, in one case, acted in behalf of his dead brother's widow.

Mother, father, and mother's brother were found to be active participants in marriage arrangements more frequently than any of the other relatives mentioned.

Because of the theoretical importance of the mother's brother in a matrilineal society, we went to considerable pains to investigate his part in marriage arrangements, to determine how formal and how indispensable he is in these negotiations. We found that the preferred pattern is to have a maternal uncle assist the parents and grandparents of both girl and boy in making a proper pact, but other kin, and even an unrelated headman or respected elder, can play the same role. We found some families where mothers' brothers took turns in acting for their sisters' children. When there is no mother's brother readily available, a stand-in may very well serve. A young man asking a missionary to represent him said, "Will you be my uncle?"

In the course of Navajo marriage negotiations, a customary presentation of an agreed-upon amount of money, jewelry, horses, cattle, or sheep is made by the suitor's agents to that group of people who are bargaining on the part of the bride-to-be. The girl's representatives later divide the gift among themselves according to their own terms. In no sense can this "payment" be considered a progeny price, since any children born to the couple will automatically be members of their mother's clan, will probably grow up in the camp of their mother's extended family, and, in the event of divorce or death of the parents, will usually remain with their maternal relatives.

Equally important in the transaction is the working out of a verbal contract which defines the rights and obligations of the groom in his role of son-in-law. These contractual rights and obligations cannot be viewed as "bride service," since they will be activated only if and when the couple is living matrilocally. In that situation, the son-in-law will be expected to do part of the work around the camp under the leadership of his father-in-law, or whatever relative of the girl is acknowledged as head man of the camp, for as long as he continues to be a member of that camp and shares in the economic resources common to all. If the marriage is a lasting one, the newcomer may look forward to eventually succeeding to the position of head man, or of establishing his own neolocal camp on land to which his bride's matrilineage has a use-right claim. If circumstances dictate that the couple live patrilocally, then the daughter-in-law assumes obligation to take part in the general woman's work around the camp, under the supervision of her mother-in-law.

Both the "bride price" and the labor pledge are, in our opinion, a form of prestation, the action of paying in goods and services what is due by custom. A man who makes a generous gift to his bride's negotiators, and who is a willing and hard worker, assures himself of respectful treatment and full use rights of resources in his new camp.

The particulars of marriage negotiations were variously described to us. A marriage that took place some 20 years ago carried a bride price of a cow and a horse, which went to the bride's brothers. A more recent marriage gift was $150 and a silver belt. Father, mother, and father's mother of the bride divided the money, and her sister received the belt. This gift was contributed by the groom's mother, father, and mother's sister. A silver belt and necklace were given for another girl. A mother gave money from her Old Age Assistance check for her son's bride price, but when the prospective bride's older sister and brother persuaded her to return to school instead of marrying, the money was returned. The bride price given for an elderly widow was divided among her children. In another case, an elderly man's children provided the gift for their father's fourth marriage. A group of young people, all away from their family camps while engaged in work at an archeological site, included a young man and a young woman who fell in love. The suitor sent two of his own brothers and a clan brother, who were co-workers, to ask the girl's mother for her. The mother agreed to the marriage and accepted cash in the sum of $130 and a silver-and-turquoise necklace.

The final step in marriage procedure is the wedding feast tendered by the bride's parents for the groom's family and other kin. This is the wedding proper and is solemnized by the eating of mush and pollen from a wedding basket. The bride's father acts as master of ceremonies, inviting guests to eat and presenting small gifts to the groom's family group. The mother of the bride is not present, as she has begun to avoid her son-in-law, "The one I do not see" (*doosh' iinii*).

At the wedding, speeches of good advice and good wishes are made by the father of the bride, the father of the groom, the bride's mother's mother, and respected elders and visitors. The resident missionaries are frequently invited to attend and to give counsel. Attendance at one wedding party described to us included not only members of the bride's family and the immediate family of the groom, but distant relatives of the groom's lineage and their spouses. Also present were the bride's father's father and her father's sisters.

After the wedding the couple takes up residence in, preferably, the extended family of the bride's parents. But like all preferred patterns in Navajo society, residence arrangements will vary with circumstances.

> When a man and his wife are thinking about a wife for their son, they are talking about all those different girls. And maybe there is one, and the woman likes that girl and that girl's mother. . . . Then the man goes over and talks to those people and says they want the daughter for a daughter-in-law. And all those people talk about it, and they think about that boy—if he is big and strong and a good worker. Just the way the boy's father and mother think about that girl, if she can work and take care of the sheep. And then, the girl's people want to know all about the different camps around the boy's place, and who all the people are who live there. And the man says, 'Here's some belts and bracelets. Take

what you want.' And then he asks when he should come back with that son. And maybe they say in three days, or five, or seven. And he asks what do they want, how many horses, and maybe they say, 'Three, and a cattle.' If they like the boy they say that. And if they don't like him so well, maybe they ask for seven or eight. But maybe only three, if they like him all right.

A boy's mother and father plan a marriage; they talk it over in their own hogan. They decide to ask for a woman; they have a present which they take over. These presents are to make them feel good. You pay for it. You eat and have to pay ahead of time. They set up the day for the wedding. They leave in the evening and go to an empty hogan. A lady comes in with corn mush; older people give advice. After that the parents go home and leave them alone. The couple are given bedding, dishes, food. Presents were given to the boy's family, usually food. *Ha'da zii'ziihi. Yada'jee't'ii.* Two words for presents. Boy's parents to girl's parents, *naa'liyei*—what they pay when they eat. You don't have to return the presents when there is a divorce.

ACCEPTABLE FORMS OF MARRIAGE

With typical Navajo flexibility, there are alternate forms of marriage that are acceptable, valid, and long-enduring.

Get-Together and Go Steady. Two young persons who have become acquainted may set up coresidence without consulting their families, and are regarded as respectable married folk. Nowadays, initial meetings which eventuate in marriage may take place at school, in a work situation, or at the still popular Squaw Dance (Enemy Way ceremony). Informality is by no means an exclusively modern pattern; an elderly man described his first marriage:

> We noticed each other while we were herding sheep.
> We got together, and after that we went steady.
> (The phraseology of this statement is the interpreter's.)

The marriage lasted until the death of the wife.

Some "get-together" unions are formalized with a marriage license from the Navajo Tribal Council at Window Rock when a baby is conceived. One educated young man told his story:

> I met Liz at a Squaw Dance; we really liked each other. I took her home in my car; the second and third nights of the ceremony the same thing happened. After that I went to her place every weekend. After awhile we got together, and then pretty soon Liz was expecting a baby. I took her over to Navajo Mountain to meet my mother and father. They liked Liz, so we went on to Tuba City and got a Tribal license. Now we have five children. I really respect [love] my wife and children.

The couple initially lived in the camp of the husband's parents, but are now residing with the wife's mother, where the young man's labor and cooperation are needed.

Such marriages, with no premarital arrangements, no bride-price, and no ceremony, are in no manner or degree less stable than the preferred arranged type. Nor, on the other hand, do these unions that might appear to have certain advantages as love matches show any evidence of being happier or more enduring than the family-arranged contract between two people who have never met previously.

Licensed marriage. Social benefits accruing from State and Federal sources, welfare assistance, and allotments for wives and children of Navajo men serving in the Armed Forces imposed upon the Navajo Tribe the necessity of formulating an acceptable definition of marriage. In 1944 the Tribal Council passed a resolution that also validated marriages "not contracted by church, State, or Tribal custom, wherein such members are recognized as man and wife in the community in which they live."

Following a series of amendments, and much discussion of the issue, Council Resolution, CO–54–56, passed October 29, 1956, states:

> (a) Navajo Indians may contract marriage by signing in the presence of two witnesses, who shall also sign, the marriage certificate. . . . In such cases the marriage shall be valid regardless of whether or not a ceremony is held.
>
> (b) The contracting parties may marry according to the rites of any church, in which case they, the officiating clergyman, and two witnesses shall sign . . . the marriage license. The authority to officiate at marriages of any person signing a Tribal marriage license as a clergyman shall not be questioned.

According to James Bosch, "This resolution may represent a return to something more nearly resembling aboriginal practice."

Nowadays, many of the younger couples in Navajo Mountain are obtaining marriage licenses from the Navajo Tribe.

Christian marriage. Christian marriage is accepted by Navajo Mountain, although as yet few such marriages have been performed there. The most elaborate ceremony, complete with printed invitations and wedding gifts, presented to the bride and groom instead of to their relatives, took place between a converted Navajo Mountain man, a veteran of World War II, and a young woman who had been brought up at a Christian mission.

Polygyny. Polygyny is an acceptable form of marriage.

Despite 100 years of pressure against the practice by the United States Government, the missions, and the present-day ruling of illegality in the Navajo Tribal Code of marriage regulations, it continues to occur, particularly in isolated areas. Subsequent wives, and their children, enjoy the same privileges that the first wife and her offspring are entitled to, and are subject to the same obligations. Half-siblings, in most cases, share as close a bond as do full siblings.

The arrangements for succeeding marriages are usually informal, entailing no bride price or other form of prestation, and no ceremony. A family who is pleased with a son-in-law, and wants to reinforce the tie, may offer him another daughter. A woman who had been a second wife for many years, and had borne ten children to her husband, told us:

> When my older sister was about to have her first baby, my mother and father said to me, 'We want you to go and live with that man and be a wife to him.' So I did.

An 80-year-old woman explained:

> My mother and father arranged my marriage to my sister's husband, because there weren't very many men here in those days.

The hazards of raiding and the hunt, and the tendency of men to die at an earlier age than women, probably created the imbalance.

Propinquity breeds polygyny. A man and his wife's sister, living in the same camp, seeing each other daily, perhaps herding together, will sometimes feel a mutual attraction and start engaging in sexual intercourse without asking the consent of anyone. This relationship may continue and shade into an accepted polygynous marriage, if the first wife is amenable. When the affair becomes evident, frequently because the paramour is pregnant, the first wife may accept the situation with equanimity and the attitude that "This is the way things are; members of the same family should share with each other and live in harmony."

> I was about 16 years old when I married the man . . . he liked me and desired me. About three or four years afterwards my younger sister appeared. They just happened to meet each other and got together without any ceremony and all this talking-over business that I had. My brother heard about this and right away he began to talk to me by saying that if my sister joined in marriage with me I shouldn't turn my back to her, but I should appreciate her and work with her, 'and everything will be all right with you and the man.' My sister had more children than I did; she had more grandchildren than I. My husband was a good provider for such a big family; he never neglected any of us. That's all the story.

Not every wife is calm-tempered, or readily brought to submit to sharing her husband; some wives told of their unhappiness when they initially learned what was going on. The wife may refuse to accept the situation, and attempt to drive her sister away. One toothless, wrinkled old lady nearing the age of 100—with no visible trace of having once been a *femme fatale*—told us that she had eloped with her sister's husband:

> My sister didn't want me to marry the man. He wanted me, so we ran away together.

Two adolescent informants told us between giggles about the friction which goes on in a nearby hogan that houses two sisters, their husband, and 15 children. Each woman frequently says to the other, "Why don't you leave, you are not wanted here. Get out!" Since each of the wives

regularly gives birth to a new baby every year, it appears
that this sentiment expresses the point of view of the rivals,
rather than that of the husband.

One Navajo Mountain woman secured her own position
as monogamous wife when her older sister died following a
spontaneous abortion that is said to have resulted from in-
juries received when the two women engaged in physical
combat. Some 20 years later, this determined woman was
successful in breaking up a liaison between her husband
and her sister's daughter, but only after two children had
been born to the lovers.

Stepfather/stepdaughter marriage is a socially approved
form of polygyny, numerically second only to sororal polygyny. On several occasions we were told, "She became
too old to be a wife to him, so she gave him her daughter."
One informant cited several instances known to him
wherein a man married a woman with a baby girl on the
specific understanding that when the child was old enough
she would become his wife.

Not always is the younger woman "given" to the husband; sometimes he "takes" her. In two cases in Navajo
Mountain, men married women who were already pregnant by another man. The daughters were raised by the
men as their own children, but when they reached puberty
the stepfathers made it evident that they felt the urge to
follow the traditional custom of marrying a stepdaughter.
In each of these cases the girl's mother rushed her away to
an off-reservation school, and she did not return to the
area to live until after she had married a man of her own
age.

Marriage of a man to two or more unrelated women has
been reported to be a Navajo practice. However, at Navajo
Mountain, there are no such marriages today, nor were
we able to trace any through our extensive genealogies.
Such marriages do not serve to reinforce an existing tie

between two families, but rather to weaken that tie, and for this reason alone would be looked upon with some disfavor.

There are in Navajo Mountain today six sets of polygynous marriages. Four of the sets are made up of one man married to two sisters; another set is composed of a man married to mother and daughter; the sixth set is a grouping of one man married to two sisters, plus the daughter of one of the women. One of the men presently married to two sisters was the husband in two earlier sets of polygynous marriages. He was previously married to two Paiute sisters. When his union with the first of these wives ended in a divorce, this also brought to an end his relationship with the younger wife. He then married two Navajo girls who were maternal parallel cousins; both of these wives died. Twenty-two survivors of polygynous marriages, which were dissolved through death or divorce, still live in Navajo Mountain.

In one of the sororal polygyny sets, the joint husband lives neolocally with one wife while the younger woman continues to live in the camp where she was raised. The man and his grown sons by the older wife perform services for the second family, hauling wood and water, moving the family to a summer camp, and driving them to the trading post. He does not, however, furnish economic support; part of this comes from her mother's sheep and the balance from Aid to Dependent Children. Thus, ironically, the second wife has certain advantages over the official wife in that she qualifies for Tribal welfare perquisites. This plural marriage of a rather young, educated Navajo is the source of many jokes both behind his back and to his face. In one of the other cases, the man, his co-wives, and all of their children live in one hogan. This practice is rare, according to Clyde Kluckhohn (personal communication, 1960).

Duration of the plural marriages still in force as of 1961 is shown in the following table.

Table 8.—*Duration of Navajo Mountain Plural Marriages, as of 1961*

SET	MARRIED FIRST WIFE	DURATION OF MARRIAGE (YEARS)	MARRIED SECOND WIFE	DURATION OF MARRIAGE (YEARS)	MARRIED THIRD WIFE	DURATION OF MARRIAGE (YEARS)
	circa		*circa*		*circa*	
1	1910	51	1910	51	—	—
2	1923	38	1927	34	1940	21
3	1935	26	1940	21	—	—
4	1937	24	1943	18	—	—
5	1948	13	1953	8	—	—
6	1955	6	1955	6	—	—

REPEATED MARITAL ALLIANCES BETWEEN KIN GROUPS

Efforts to compile genealogical data with reference to the long-resident matrilineages in Navajo Mountain resulted in information on certain lines which goes back to the 1880's, and which in some cases is eight generations in depth. From these genealogies we have assembled a marriage population, the criterion of selection being the fact that at least one of the partners to the matrimonial union had at some time or another been a resident of the community up to and through the year 1962. This yields a sample consisting of 350 marriages, which will be the basis for the following analysis of marriage practices among the Navajo.

Sibling Exchange. A common form of marriage in the past, as well as the present, is sibling exchange; that is, sisters of one family marry brothers of another family, or brothers and sisters marry sisters and brothers. In defining siblings we include half-brothers and half-sisters, and a polygynous family has been counted as one nuclear family.

Sibling exchange is an efficient form of marriage in that it repeatedly links two families with each succeeding match, reinforces one of the strongest kin ties, that of siblings, and binds together the grandparents, who then share an interest in more than one set of grandchildren. A second marriage into the same sibling group is often arranged, or at least initiated, by the brother or sister who first married into the unit.

There are 20 cases of sibling exchange between nuclear families, for a total of 62 marriages in our sample; this represents almost 18%. The greatest number of marriages in any one set of exchanges is eight, with two marriages to a set showing the most frequent distribution.

No. of cases	No. of marriages in each case	Total marriages
2	8	16
1	5	5
1	4	4
5	3	15
11	2	22

In the two cases where eight sibling exchanges were made, the marriages took place more than 50 years ago, when there were very few people living in the Navajo Mountain area.

Four families made sibling exchanges with more than one family. The two largest families living in the area today have contracted such reciprocal arrangements with, in one case, four families; in the other case, three families. Two families have each exchanged siblings with two families.

In four instances of sibling exchange, additional siblings

from one family have married members of the other family's matrilineage. The following tabulation indicates the relationship of the married person to the siblings of the family in which he or she is listed.

Extension of sibling exchange

Family 1		*Family A*
8 siblings	married	8 siblings
Si	"	SiSo
SiSo	"	Si

Family 2		*Family B*
5 siblings	married	5 siblings
Br	"	SiDa
MoSiSo	"	Si

Family 3		*Family C*
2 siblings	married	2 siblings
Si	"	$MoSi^1So$
Si	"	$MoSi^2So$

Family 4		*Family D*
2 siblings	married	2 siblings
Si	"	MoBr
SiDa	"	Br

What might be considered an attenuated form of sibling exchange is the marriage of siblings of one family to members of the matrilineage of another family. The relationships in each family where this extension of the sibling-exchange principle has taken place are shown below.

Attenuated sibling exchange

Family 1		*Matrilineage A*
Si	married	Ego
Br	"	SiDa

Family 2		*Matrilineage B*
Br¹	married	Ego
"	"	Si
Si¹	"	MoSiSo
Si²	"	"
Si³	"	"

Family 3		*Matrilineage C*
Si	married	Ego
Br	"	MoSiDa

Family 4		*Matrilineage D*
Br¹	married	Ego
"	"	Da¹
Br²	"	Da²

Family 5		*Matrilineage E*
Si¹	married	Ego
Si²	"	MoSiSo
Si³	"	"

Family 6		*Matrilineage F*
Si¹	married	Ego
Si²	"	"
Br	"	SiDa

Sororate. The custom whereby a deceased wife is replaced by her sister or other close relative is alleged to be a preferred form of secondary marriage among the Navajo. Our marriage population includes five such occurrences. In three instances the dead woman's place was taken by her sister; in one, the second wife was a parallel cousin; in the final instance, the replacement was a sister's daughter. All of these marriages were so recent that the husband is still living.

Levirate. The custom whereby a deceased husband is replaced by his brother or other close male relative is reported in the anthropological literature to be more a feature of patrilineal societies than of matrilineal societies. There are seven such marriages in the population being considered. Brother replaced brother in four cases; in one case a parallel cousin married the widow; in another case the second marriage was to the deceased man's mother's brother. The seventh marriage was arranged, an "old-age mating" between a widow and her husband's mother's parallel cousin. One of these marriages took place in the late 1800's, but the other six were so recent that at least one participant of each marriage is still living. Three of the secondary marriages ended in divorce.

Successive Marriages with Siblings. Two men married sisters of the first wife after a divorce dissolved the first union; two women married their divorced husband's brothers.

The Influence of Clan on Marriage Choices. All the genealogies we collected at Navajo Mountain give us information on 1,537 persons belonging to 23 clans. (In this count we have considered *Kin łichii'nii* and *Tł'izi łání* as one clan; *Naaneesht'ézhi Tábąąhá* and *Tábąąhá* as one clan; *Biįh bitoodnii* and *Tó dich'ii'nii* as one clan; *Ashįįhi* and Paiute *Ashįįhi* as one clan.)

We will first consider marriages that break the clan incest prohibitions. An analysis of 322 marriages shows two marriages into own clan, or 0.62%. These marriages are both within the *Táchii'nii* clan. On further investigation of this breach of the strongest of exogamic prohibitions, we found that the violations took place between a line of *Táchii'nii* people recently derived from intermarriage with Ute tribesmen and an older line of Navajo *Táchii'nii* clansmen.

Among the 501 spouses whose fathers' clans are known to us, we found 19 individuals marrying into father's clan, or 3.8%. Among 462 spouses where father's clan is known for both of the mates in marriage, 32 individuals married people who were born for the same clan, that is 6.9%. While these percentages are not definitive figures, they do give some indication of the relative strength of the exogamic clan prohibitions.

Older people in Navajo Mountain complain that young people nowadays no longer pay attention to clan in choosing a mate, especially within their fathers' clans or clan groups. They marry people they meet in school without consulting their elders and are "getting all mixed up." The father of one young woman reluctantly agreed to permit her to marry a young man whom she had met at school. The suitor, whose home was on the other side of the Reservation, was eligible in every respect except that his clan was the same as that of the girl's father. The marriage did not take place, and the following year the young woman set up housekeeping with a man who was her mother's father's sister's son, a genealogical position that made him her mother's brother, since all of parents' cousins are assimilated to parents' siblings. In addition, the pair were born for the same clan; in kinship terminology they were Br/Si. The marriage was a *fait accompli* before any of the parents knew about it, and they did nothing to break it up.

Some anthropologists have reported a Navajo preference for marriage into mother's father's clan, or into father's father's clan. Among 366 spouses whose mothers' fathers' clans are known to us, we found 71 individuals marrying into mother's father's clan, or 19.4%. Among 323 spouses for whom we have the necessary information, there are 58 individuals marrying into father's father's clan, or 17.9%.

A chart showing intermarriage by clans for 322 marriages is included in the appendix.

Inasmuch as we do not have a census of the population that would indicate the choices available for each marrying individual at any one time, we cannot claim that our data indicate clan preferences. A first marriage, if it is an arranged marriage, is based on the desire of two families to be allied; subsequent marriages between these two nuclear families or their lineages serve to reinforce the tie. In analyzing our genealogies, we found that successive marriages by the same individual into one clan, or by siblings of the same family into one clan, were in almost every instance based on previous genealogical, rather than on purely clan, connections. Thus, repeated marriages into the same family, or lineage, will give the false appearance of marriage preferences between clans.

OTHER CONSEQUENTIAL UNIONS

In a category we have called "other consequential unions" are those matings that have produced a child. We defined marriage as a union with some degree of permanency, mutual responsibility, and economic cooperation, the elements that are lacking in the type of union here being considered. If both partners are unmarried, the transitory mating is condoned, although it is neither welcomed nor wholly accepted. No stigma attaches to the child, who will be taken into the mother's family, and if she marries will be raised by the stepfather (sociological father) as his own. The marital status of such an offspring's progenitors will not affect his property or inheritance rights in his mother's family.

This raises the question of whether or not there is any concept of the "illegitimate child" in Navajo society. There is a word for "bastard" given variously as *"yotqa'ashki"* (Franciscan Fathers 1910:451), as *"yatashki"* (Young and Morgan 1958:7), and in the course of our field work as *"wotashki."*

Navajo origin myths deal with the concept of "illegitimacy" if we can so interpret the story of the Hero Twins born to Changing Woman through contact with the Sun.

She tries to discourage her boys from seeking their father. At first he denies the relationship saying, "I won't have children." Later after a series of severe tests he acknowledges the paternity (Spencer, 1947:40).

There are several of these kinds of consequential unions in Navajo Mountain, one in which the genitor admits paternity and takes some responsibility for the child if only through token gifts. In another type he admits paternity but takes no responsibility for the child. As we have said, there is a need to establish biological fatherhood because of clan affiliations and the incest taboos. Perhaps this is one reason why paternity is more readily acknowledged in these aberrant situations than would be the case in the wider society. Men readily admitted to us that they had fathered children in other areas many years before. Informants will volunteer the information that their parents were not married. One man told us about an experience while he was living in a camp with his parents and his siblings (the numerous offspring of three sisters by one man), when "A strange guy rode up and said he was looking for his father. My father seemed to know him all right so we sat down together for some mutton stew and a long talk. But it was kind of funny."

A young woman told us with little hesitancy that her father had sired a half-brother on the other side of the mountain. We had observed no direct interaction among the offspring of the two matings, but when we investigated marriage patterns we discovered that there were seven later marriages between relatives of the two parents of the "wotashki." The following list shows the relatives of his mother who married relatives of his father.

Relatives of mother		Relatives of father
Former sister-in-law	married	Brother
Half-brother	"	Daughter
Half-brother	"	Daughter (levirate)

Daughter	"	Son
Brother's daughter	"	Son
Daughter's daughter	"	Brother's son
Half-sister	"	Son

It is as if the original adulterous mating had initiated a series of subsequent unions between relatives of the pair, such as might have ensued after an acceptable first marriage.

Perhaps the category of "illegitimate child" should be reserved for those cases where the father is unknown because of the promiscuity of the mother. Again no stigma attaches to the child, but he is disadvantaged because he does not know his "born for" clan, and thus runs the risk of illness for an unwitting violation of the incest taboo. Even this status of "my father is unknown" is readily admitted by Navajos. It was rather startling to hear small schoolchildren in Shiprock learning to say in English, in answer to the question, "Who is your father?", "My father is unknown."

In making a count of children born in Navajo Mountain whose fathers were not joined with their mothers in any permanent relationship, we have relied on the word of informants, plus a count of those children who have retained their mother's surname rather than adopting the name of their stepfather. That is to say, the number of children born out of wedlock may actually be higher than the figures given us, which indicate that there were only eleven such people in the resident population of 1962.

In addition to the above cases, three Navajo Mountain Paiute women have borne illegitimate children to Navajo men of the 1961–62 population. The community did not look upon any of these liaisons as a marriage, even though in at least one instance the affair persisted over a long enough time to produce several children. Neither were the women in what might be called concubine status, in that, so far as we could find out, they received no help from the men involved, nor did the fathers accept responsibility for the children.

UNACCEPTABLE UNIONS

The most completely unacceptable union is an incestuous one. We have discussed this matter at some length in connection with clans, pointing out that such a union involves mating not only within the biological family but within certain tabooed categories of clan kin. Cases of incest bring strong social disapproval as well as illness. Families warn their children against this form of sexual intercourse and will try to break up unions between too close relatives. One such marriage between maternal parallel cousins in Navajo Mountain was taken to the Navajo Tribal Court by the mothers of the man and of the woman, and a judgment to dissolve the marriage was obtained. We quote the court record:

> Wherein marriage is prohibited by Navajo custom as well as by the law of the United States. These two defendants are cohabiting and did have sexual relations being related within the degrees. Mothers of both defendants are full sisters. Therefore the court gave the order that they shall not to have any sexual relations anymore or living together as man and wife hereafter.

The charge was "illicit cohabitation." The male defendant pleaded guilty and was fined $10 and sentenced to serve 10 days in jail.

The treatment of illnesses caused by incest takes the form of a Sing, Moth Way, rapidly becoming obsolescent. Frequently the need to identify the cause of the malady will bring forth a confession from the patient.

Fornication is "human sexual intercourse other than between a man and his wife" (*Webster's Third New International Dictionary*, 1966). It is condoned, understandable in view of the natural desires of mankind, and not considered to be a sin, but it is disvalued.

Promiscuity, "running from woman to woman" or "from man to man," is regarded as a sign of giddiness and irresponsibility. Part of the training of all Navajo girls is to warn them against sexual activity outside of marriage. When two families discover that a young man and a young woman have been indulging in sexual intercourse, some effort will be made, if the partners are acceptable as affinal kin, to "put them together" for the establishment of a household. Virgins are essential for certain roles in particular Sings and the statement has been made that a virgin will bring a higher bride price than a nonvirgin or even that the bride price will be returned if the bride is not a virgin (Dyk 1938:150). We have no new light to throw upon the matter.

Adultery is condemned. The origin myths are full of stories of adultery wherein the severe punishment of mutilation is inflicted on the offending ones. Infidelity of the chief's wife and her neglect of her duties precipitated the legendary separation of the sexes that caused such great suffering to the women. They quickly learned that they were not self-sufficient; many of them took to masturbating with stones, which practice engendered monsters. The hero hermaphrodite, Begochidi, after the women had wept and repented and been taken back by their men, said, "There will be a law—the male shall rule. . . ." (Spencer 1947:35, 36). Training of Navajo boys always includes the admonition not to "bother another man's wife." Such activity is presented not so much as morally reprehensible conduct but as the cause of social disruption and disharmony. Infidelity may give rise to jealousy and the breakup of a marriage. However, the stability of many Navajo marriages, despite the known adultery of one or the other of the partners, indicates that infidelity is condoned. A wife who remains with her transgressing husband or a cuckold who continues to live with an erring wife is not treated with pitying scorn as in our society. Rather they are thought to be making a sensible and realistic response to an unfortunate situation.

Polyandry is another form of unacceptable sexual behavior. Whereas concurrent unions between a man and several women (polygyny) is a valid form of marriage, concurrent unions between a woman and several men is promiscuity or adultery, "just like dogs." We asked an old man who had had five wives to tell us the reason for his various divorces. "My wives got away from me. They were whores. All whores." Our interpreter repeated the word several times to make certain that we understood its full implication. We were astonished and not a little dismayed to find these traces of the double standard in a matrilineal society.

Forcible rape is a wrongful act. The family of the girl may bring the matter to an informal meeting of kin and community, and if lack of consent is made evident, compensation can be fixed and the wrongdoer required to pay. In one case in Navajo Mountain, a man paid $25 to keep the girl's family from taking a rape charge to the Navajo Tribal Court. There seems to be no concept of statutory rape as opposed to forcible rape. There is evidence that child marriage was acceptable in the past. We learned of one case of "marriage" with an eight-year-old. A Navajo superintendent on the Western Side wrote in 1928 to the Assistant Indian Commissioner, "In two or three cases it has been necessary for us to deprive some of the young men of their girl wives between the ages of eleven and sixteen, these girls having been placed in school" (National Archives). This offense is prosecuted in the Navajo Tribal

Court as "contributing to the delinquency of a minor." It
is probable that until the new regulations of the Indian
courts, the rape of a young girl was not considered as substantially different from the rape of an adult.

Prostitution is disvalued. It is in no wise the organized
business operation found in some societies, but rather an
activity in which the individual woman lets it be known in
the community that she is willing to receive men for compensation. At least two women in Navajo Mountain were
laughingly referred to as "prostitutes," but no evidence
was offered to prove that they were having sexual relations
(and illegitimate children) for money rather than for their
own amusement. Oliver LaFarge in *Laughing Boy* presents
prostitution as an acculturation phenomenon. Clyde Kluckhohn and Father Berard Haile have labeled one of the
Navajo Sings as "Prostitution Way," which would suggest
that harlotry must be an old practice. Gladys Reichard,
however, vigorously objects to this interpretation. She says:

> The chant so oddly referred to by Kluckhohn and
> Father Berard as 'Prostitution Way' ('adjiłe) . . . seeks
> to undo the effects of any kind of recklessness. It may be
> sung to encourage success in love, trading, and gam-
> bling, and to dissipate the evil results of uncontrolled
> lust. Except for sexual indulgence, none of the things
> for which it is prescribed has even a remote relation to
> prostitution, and the name is misleading on other
> grounds; it assumes that the Navajo institutionalize
> prostitution and class all recklessness with it. Therefore
> to call the chant 'Prostitution Way' besides being inac-
> curate, is insulting to the person it is sung over, since a
> married man may need it as well as one who contem-
> plates a dangerous undertaking. 'Excess,' 'Recklessness,'
> or 'Rashness' Chant would more accurately suggest its
> meaning.
>
> If prostitution is defined as payment for women's fa-

vors, the Girls' Dance and even the betrothal should be so classed. I do not accept this definition or classification. Occasionally a girl refuses to marry, lives alone, and has many male visitors, or a girl may move about from settlement to settlement, creating jealousy among the women who say of her, 'She has no mother.' They do not mean that she is bereaved but that she is responsible to no one; such a girl is, in Navajo eyes, a prostitute (1950:140).

This brings us to the question of whether or not payment is required for sexual favors, so that sexual rights are property rights in Navajo society. Kluckhohn and Haile take this position. In the recording of "Prostitution Way" made by Father Berard, the female genital organ says, ". . . if nothing be paid me in exchange something bad will be the outcome. If he (man) do it to me without a compensation he shall fall just below it, she said. . . ." Thus is the sanction for the marriage gift stated (Spencer, 1957: 139). A case which we collected from the National Archives seems to support this position. In 1923 a man was accused of raping a fourteen-year-old girl. The victim in her testimony, to prove that the act was really *rape*, said that her grandmother had told her "not to do that without pay." Her father had said that to her too. Now she had been herding sheep with a six-year-old girl when this man came around and promised her $6 but he didn't give her the money, even after promising it. Ergo, *rape*.

However, to contend that all sexual favors in Navajo society are regarded as property transactions is an oversimplification. There are several instances in the *Son of Old Man Hat* and elsewhere in the anthropological literature that describe the seduction of young men by older women, obviously for sheer carnal pleasure since the young men owned little property and could not be expected to pay (Dyk, 1938). It is difficult to believe that any culture known to man has been able to reduce all acts of sexual intercourse to cold-blooded business transactions.

Divorce

Descriptions of divorce practices in studies of Navajo customs emphasize the ease with which the marital relation can be terminated. Traditionally there was no formal court action, and a woman had merely to "put her husband's saddle outside the hogan" to indicate that she had had enough. A man would walk away "to look for his horses and never come back," or so a recent divorce was described to us. There are, however, numerous records of informal meetings in Navajo Mountain between members of the two families concerned that were held to persuade quarreling couples to remain together, particularly if they had children or if the son-in-law was an asset to his mother-in-law's camp.

Because of the individual ownership of livestock and the use rights to land that one retains in his family of origin, divorce does not mean destitution for any of the people involved. Nowadays, the grazing-permit system makes a formal division of property necessary, and the various welfare agencies require court action to try, if possible, to force the father to support his children.

We have dealt with marital disputes in general, whether they ended in separation or not, under role relations between husband and wife, and have shown that this is an area of great strain. Of 162 unions entered into by the population of Navajo Mountain as of 1960–61, 92 marriages are still in force, 37 ended in death of a spouse, and 33 ended in divorce. Of the 33 divorces among the resident population, we have specific information concerning 28 through interviews or court records. Ten of these marriages were dissolved by order of the Navajo Tribal Courts, and 18 were dissolved informally. Among the stated reasons for the divorces were "meanness;" nagging by a wife; social difficulties of a couple who had committed clan incest; and the fact that a young man who had married into the area from Kaibito could not bear the isolation. A shotgun marriage formalized at the insistence of the missionary ended in the divorce court because the bride would not speak to the groom. In no case was sterility considered to warrant divorce; at least four childless couples in Navajo Mountain have lived together in harmony for more than 10 years.

A breakdown of the alleged causes of divorce (more than one reason may be given in any one case) is as follows:

Adultery	12
Desertion	4
Laziness	3
Assault and battery	2
Incest	2
Meanness	2
Witchcraft	1
Isolation	1
Shotgun wedding	1
In-law trouble	1
Total	29

Adultery is the most frequent cause. Navajos extend this charge to include the mother of twins as an adulteress. For example, a man deserted his wife when she bore his two sons, because one of the many beliefs about the origin of twins is that they are begotten by two different men.

Of the 21 men and 18 women now living in Navajo Mountain who have been divorced at least once, 19 men and 10 women subsequently remarried.

It has been stated that children are a strong integrating force and become some guarantee of the stability of a marriage (Leighton and Kluckhohn, 1947:83). Navajo Mountain data shows that of the 33 divorces between couples who have at one time or another been residents of the community, and where there is still at least one surviving spouse, 7 divorces were between childless couples, 14 took place after the birth of one child, 7 after two children, 2 after three children, 2 after ten children, and 1 couple was divorced after the birth of eleven children. The following table shows the duration of each of the marriages terminated by divorce.

Table 9.—*Marriages ended by divorce**

NUMBER OF COUPLES AND DURATION OF MARRIAGE

NUMBER OF CHILDREN	UNDER 2 YEARS	2–5	6–10	11–20	OVER 30
0	6	1	—	—	—
1	7	7	—	—	—
2	—	6	—	1	—
3	—	1	1	—	—
10	—	—	—	1	1
11	—	—	—	—	1

*At least one surviving spouse living in Navajo Mountain in 1960–61.

The genealogical record of inhabitants of Navajo Mountain indicates that marriages today show as much stability as those in the past, if not more. A comparison of young couples today—for example, those in the 20- to 40-year age bracket—with those of preceding generations shows that in the younger group, only one of 6.5 marriages, on the average, has resulted in divorce, whereas in the 40- to 60-year age bracket, the rate was one out of two marriages. Most of the people born 60 or more years ago had had several mates during their lifetimes.

Some of the separations that eventuated in formal or informal divorce were described as follows:

> Mostly my husband stayed with my older sister who was his older wife. He used to come to see me while my sister was living. My son-in-law, Slim Tábąąhá, used to be a medicine man. He sang for my sister's daughter when she was sick. The trouble started when my husband said that Slim Tábąąhá had killed her through witchcraft. There was no fight. He just said it. Then he didn't come around any more.

> My granddaughter's husband was lazy. I told him to go after the horses so he could herd sheep. He went after them all right, but he never came back.

> Your Honor, my wife has inflicted grievous mental suffering upon me, by bringing her relatives into any discussion and arguments that we have had and the result has been that our arguments are becoming more and more serious and unless divorce is granted there may be serious bodily injury.

Illness

Navajo fears and anxieties are primarily focused on disease and death. Almost the whole of the ceremonial system borrowed from the Pueblos has been reoriented to ways of curing illness. Of 60 different song-ceremonials, more than 50 are utilized for curing (Vogt, 1960:27).

All illness is said to result from the violation of taboos or from the deliberate action of a witch. The breaking of a taboo is not necessarily an intentional transgression, but in many cases is committed inadvertently. The list of prohibitions is almost endless; the usual informant will give an incomplete account unless he has specialized knowledge on the subject.

> It was forbidden a long time ago to eat fish. Also to cut hair. Now they cut their hair, even some who haven't been to school. The idea was that if they did these things a sister or a brother would die. This belief died with schooling. We don't eat snakes or grasshoppers. Squirrels, rabbits, prairie dogs are all right. Dogs and cats should not be eaten; it will bring bad luck. We don't eat coyotes or lizards. Chicken and eggs are all right; you can eat a blue bird, but no other bird. It is bad luck if an owl comes and sits on a tree near your hogan. If you don't do anything one of the family will die. Medicine men have a prayer for this.

The first step in the curative process is the diagnosis of the ailment, or of malaise such as bad dreams or faintness. This is the work of a diagnostician, in Navajo Mountain principally a hand-trembler. The specialist will determine the cause of the illness, will suggest the proper curing ceremony, and sometimes will recommend a particular medicine man to conduct the rite.

Although the concentration in a Navajo Sing is on an individual, the patient, the giving of a Sing is a family affair and is the contingency that requires the greatest amount of cooperation demanded in traditional Navajo society.

Death

The final crisis is death. Death in old age is accepted by Navajos as the normal end of the life cycle and there is no morbid preoccupation with this eventuality *per se*. The evil side of a person's being remains, however, to contaminate his corpse, his possessions, the place of his death, and,

above all, his grave. Ghost defilement is dangerous to the
welfare, the health, or even the lives of those who come into
contact with it. If death occurs during a Sing, the Sing
must be stopped immediately. The hogan within which the
demise has taken place will be destroyed and the whole
camp will move to a new location. Even the logs that
form the dwelling are unusable for any purpose. Nowadays,
many Navajos die in the hospital, thus freeing the family
from the necessity of quitting their camp.

Preparation of the body for burial is a family duty that
must be performed by kinsmen unless a missionary or
trader can be enlisted to take over this unpleasant obligation. The body is dressed in best clothes, decorated with
jewelry, wrapped in cloth, and sometimes buried with torn
money. Formerly a horse was killed over the grave. These
customs are largely falling into disuse, although there is
danger of affronting the ghost if one is too miserly or indicates lack of respect for the deceased by not sacrificing
enough wealth at his burial. Sometimes an individual an-
ticipating imminent death will instruct his family as to
what he wishes to have buried with him.

> Before John Roanhorse shot himself, he shot his favor-
> ite horse. We found it dead right there by the hogan.

Men more often than women are assigned to bury the
dead. Four men are selected, frequently including a son
or sons of the deceased. They must remain in mourning
for four days after the burial and undergo a ritual cleansing
at the end of the period.

> The men who take care of this must make a holy day
> for four days. Everything must stop somehow. They
> must take a sweat bath and put pollen in their mouths
> before they can eat.

As a missionary I am frequently called upon to bury the dead. There is no cemetery here; we have been going to get one for years, but no one does anything. The Navajos now want a box. I would just as soon make the box myself, although one time I didn't know how much cloth the family was going to wrap around the corpse and I made the box too small. I insist that the family of the deceased dig the hole; too many times I ran into solid rock three feet or so down.

Traders, too, have experienced difficulties when they have consented to dispose of the body. One complained about the hostility engendered toward him when word got around that he had buried an important medicine man with the body oriented in the wrong direction.

No funeral services are held, nor is any attempt made to mark the grave for remembrance. Relatives who assemble after a death have come together not to mourn the dead, but rather to distribute his property.

Avoidance of uttering the names of dead people has been reported (Kluckhohn and Leighton, 1946:41). Our experience at Navajo Mountain did not confirm this statement. True, our informants seldom initiated a conversation about those who were dead, but they evinced no reluctance to talk very freely when we brought up the subject. Their attitude might be expressed as, "He is finished, gone and forgotten."

PART THREE

KINSHIP
TERMINOLOGY

The Research Problem

A study of Navajo kinship terminology was undertaken by the authors with the purpose of collecting kin terms used at Navajo Mountain, so that these terms might be compared with those found in other areas of the Reservation. The aim of the study was (1) to explain, if possible, whether the extreme variation in kinship terminology reported by different anthropologists stems from regional differences, faulty reporting, or the flexibility of the Navajo kinship system, (2) to correlate Navajo kinship terms with expected role behavior, and (3) to assess possible changes in terminology.

Kin terms were obtained from 10 men and 15 women,

from whom we had previously acquired genealogies. They ranged from 17 to 80 years of age, and in education from high-school students to non-literate, non-English-speaking men and women.

At many points, the Navajo kinship system resembles other Apachean systems, but the closest similarity is to Western Apache kin terminology. One of the explanations for this is that both tribes have matrilineal clans, and this affects terminology in the more distant positions. Traditionally, Navajos do not address one another by name, but use kin terms, widely extended to clan relatives, and, even, out of politeness, to strangers.

A clan may be defined as "a consanguineal kin group whose members acknowledge a traditional bond of common descent in the maternal or paternal line but are unable always to trace the actual genealogical connections between individuals" (Bellah, 1952:139). A Navajo is said to be born *into* his mother's clan and born *for* his father's clan. Rules of exogamy forbid marriage into own clan, into father's clan, and between individuals whose fathers belong to the same clan. Exogamic rules extend to certain clans which are considered to be "the same as," or closely linked to the prohibited clans.

It became apparent immediately that Navajos view their kin terminology as being wholly governed by clan affiliation; they were prone to offer clan explanations even for regular terms based on traceable kin relationship. Several older Navajos queried us about our own kinship system, and were at a loss to understand how a people could possibly trace relationships when they had no clans.

Informants found it difficult to give a term for a hypothetical relative; they found it impossible to do so when it was a question of a quarternary, or more distant, position, that is, one related to Ego through three or more intermediate links. Also, young people who had been away at

school were usually unable to offer theoretical explanations
for kin-term usage, or to supply terms for many kin categories. They explained that they are not taught relationships according to a system. "We hear other people use
words for relatives and we learn that way. Someone might
say about a man, 'This is your uncle,' and then we know
to call him that." An 80-year-old woman, when questioned
about terms for her mother's cousins, said, "I did not ask
what to call people who were already dead when I was
born." This caused great hilarity among interpreters and
listeners-in.

We decided to limit our questions to individuals whose
relationships and clan affiliations could be traced through
our genealogical charts. Even here, difficulties were apparent. No informant had a full complement of kin. In
this much-intermarried community, Ego might be able to
trace kinship with a distant relative through more than
one channel. This presented a problem of multiple choice
and the need to investigate what, in such circumstances,
governed the selection of terms.

The greatest variation in Navajo Mountain, as elsewhere
on the Reservation, comes in terms used for what Murdock
calls "distant relatives," those who are more remote than
tertiary relatives (1949:95). This includes mother's and
father's cousins, the children of Ego's cousins, and their
children in turn. For children of Ego's cousins we received
terms appropriate to each one of four generations, grandparental, parental, own, and children's. A Navajo woman
in her thirties tendered a clue when she declined to guess
at the proper term to be used for the hypothetical children
of her mother's brother's son. She explained that she would
have to wait until he married in order to know his children's clan, because their clan, which would be derived
from their mother, might well determine what she would
call them. Pursuing this lead, we addressed ourselves par-

ticularly to the problem of kin terms used for distant relatives and an analysis of when, where, and how clan terminology governs such distant positions.

The discussion of Navajo kinship terms will be divided into the following sections: (1) Explanation of the Kinship Charts, (2) Distinctive Features of Navajo Kinship Terminology, (3) Extension of Kin Terms by Clan Affiliation, (4) Linked Clans, (5) Distant Relatives, (6) A Model Illustrating Non-regular Clan Affiliations between Ego and Father's and Mother's Cousins, (7) The Bases for Choice among Alternate Terms for Distant Relatives, (8) Changes and Regional Variations, (9) Criteria for Distinguishing Terms, (10) Classification of the Kinship System, and (11) Kinship Terminology and Role Behavior.

Symbols employed in charts 1, 2, 3, and 4, below, are the following:

$=$ indicates married

| "   descended from

⊓   "   sibling

△   "   male

○   "   female

Navajo Kin Terms

MAN OR WOMAN SPEAKING

-má	Mo, MoSi.
-zhé'é	Fa, FaBr.
-naai	OlBr, MoSiOlSo, FaBrOlSo, FaMoBrOlSo, FaSiSoOlSo, FaSiDaSoOlSo.
-tsili	YoBr, MoSiYoSo, FaBrYoSo, FaMoBrYoSo, FaSiSoYoSo, FaSiDaSoYoSo.

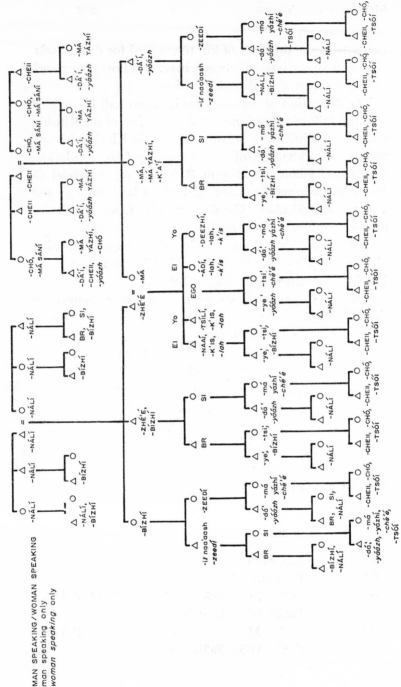

Chart 1. *Navajo Kinship Terms of Reference and Address*

MAN SPEAKING/WOMAN SPEAKING
man speaking only
woman speaking only

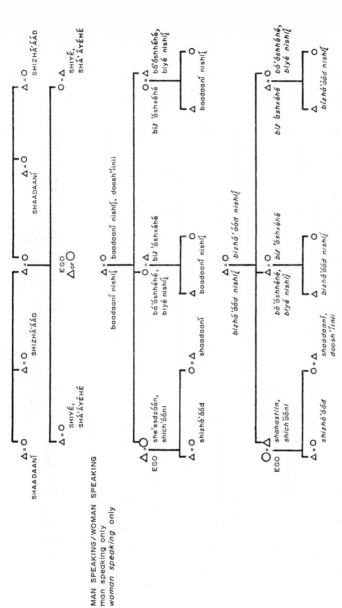

Chart 2. *Terms for Affinals*
(*reference only*)

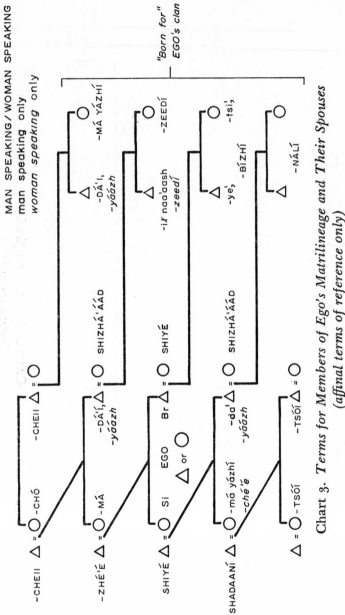

Chart 3. *Terms for Members of Ego's Matrilineage and Their Spouses*
(affinal terms of reference only)

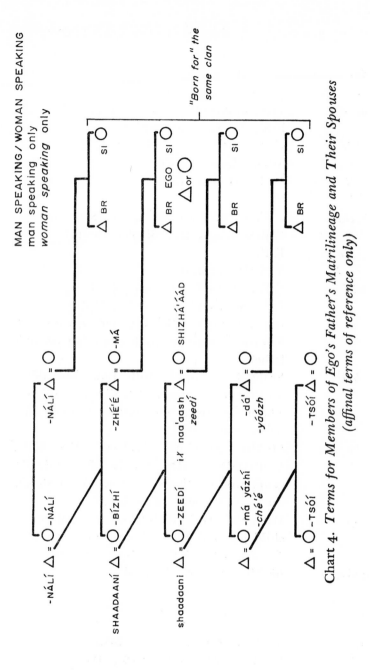

MAN SPEAKING / WOMAN SPEAKING
man speaking only
woman speaking only

"Born for" the same clan

Chart 4. *Terms for Members of Ego's Father's Matrilineage and Their Spouses*
(affinal terms of reference only)

-ádí	OlSi, MoSiOlDa, FaBrOlDa, FaMoBrOlDa, FaSiSoOlDa, FaSiDaSoOlDa.
-deezhí	YoSi, MoSiYoDa, FaBrYoDa, FaMoBrYoDa, FaSiSoYoDa, FaSiDaSoYoDa.
-k'a'í	MoSi (obsolescent) , Mo female Co.
-má yázhí	MoSi, Mo female Co.
-dá'í	MoBr, Mo male Co.
-dá'	Variant of *-dá'í.*
-bízhí	FaSi, FaBr, BrSo, BrDa, MoSiSoSo and Da, FaBrSoSo and Da, FaSiSoSoSo and Da, FaCo.
-zhé'é yázhí	**FaBr.**
-zeedí	MoBrDa, FaSiDa.
-nálí	FaFa, FaFaBr, FaFaSi, FaMo, FaMoSi, FaMoBr, FaFaSiSo and Da, MoBrSoSo and Da, person in grandchild generation to whom Ego traces relationship through that person's father.
-cheii	MoFa, MoFaBr, MoMoBr, DaSo, MoFaSiSo, MoBrDaSo, male of grandchild generation to whom Ego traces relationship through that person's mother.
-chó	MoMo, MoMoSi, MoFaSi, MoFaSiDa, MoBrDaDa, DaDa, female of grandchild generation to whom Ego traces relationship through that person's mother.
-tsói	DaSo and Da, MoBrDaCh, person of grandchild generation to whom Ego traces relationship through that person's mother.
-má sání	MoMo, MoMoSi, MoFaSi.

MAN SPEAKING

-ye'	So, BrSo, MoSiSoSo, FaBrSoSo.
-tsi'	Da, BrDa, MoSiSoDa, FaBrSoDa.
-ił naa'aash	MoBrSo, FaSiSo.

-má yázhí	SiDa, MoSiDaDa, FaBrDaDa, FaSiDaDa, FaSiSoDaDa, MoBrDaDa.
-dá'í, -dá'	SiSo, MoSiDaSo, FaBrDaSo, FaSiDaSo, FaSiSoDaSo, MoBrDaSo.
-k'is	Br, friend.
-lah	Si.

WOMAN SPEAKING

-yáázh	So, SiSo, MoBr, MoSiDaSo, FaBrDaSo, FaSiDaSo, FaSiSoDaSo, MoBrDaSo, Mo male Co.
-ché'é	Da, SiDa, MoSiDaDa, FaBrDaDa, FaSiDaDa, FaSiSoDaDa, MoBrDaDa.
-k'is	Si, Br, friend.
-lah	Br.
-zeedí	MoBrSo, FaSiSo.

AFFINAL TERMS

shizhá'ááad	FaBrWi, MoBrWi, SoWi, stepmother.
shaadaaní	FaSiHu, MoSiHu, DaHu, stepfather.
shiyé	BrWi, SiHu.
shá'áyéhé	BrWi, SiHu.
shich'óóni	spouse.

MAN SPEAKING

she'esdzáán	Wi.
sizaani	Wi.
doosh'íinii	WiMo.
baadaaní	
nishlį	WiFa, WiMo, WiBrCh, WiSiCh.
biyé nishlį	WiBr, WiSi.
bá'áshhéhé	WiBr, WiSi.
bił'áshxéhé	WiBrWi, WiSiHu.

WOMAN SPEAKING

shahastiin	Hu.
shich'óóni	Hu.
shaadaani	DaHu.
doosh'íinii	DaHu.
bizhá'ááá	
nishlį	HuFa, HuMo, HuBrCh, HuSiCh.
biyé nishlį	HuBr, HuSi.
bá'áshhéhé	HuBr, HuSi.
bił'áshxéhé	HuBrWi, HuSiHu.

Explanation of the Charts

Terms in CAPITAL LETTERS are used by both men and women speakers; terms in lower case letters are used by men only; terms in italics are used by women only. Alternate terms are separated by commas. The orthography is that of Young and Morgan (1951). Terms on Charts 1, 3, and 4 may be used for both address and reference; affinal terms on Chart 2 are used for reference only.

Chart No. 1. A Navajo kin term is always used with a possessive prefix, and cannot stand alone. Terms are shown on the charts with a hyphen, for example, -*má* (Mo). In actual use it is *shimá* (my mother), *bimá* (his or her mother), and so on.

Only regular clan-determined alternates are shown on the chart; these are given in distant positions where the clan relationship of Ego to the paired relative is fixed by the rules of descent and will invariably be the same regardless of the specific individuals and the specific clans involved. To give one example, Ego's FaMoBrCh will always be born for the same clan that Ego is born for, with the result that they may, reciprocally, call each other by the terms

Br and Si. In practice, the spread of terms in most quaternary and more distant positions is much greater, inasmuch as terms derived from specific clan affiliations may be used as alternates. This will be discussed more fully under *Extension of Kin Terms by Clan Affiliation* and *Distant Relatives*.

Chart No. 2 gives affinal terms with the possessive prefixes which are necessary to clarify the differing types of relationship. (See p. 220.)

Chart No. 3 gives kin terms for members of Ego's matrilineage and their spouses and the terms used for children of the men of Ego's matrilineage.

Chart No. 4. Kin terms for members of Ego's father's matrilineage and their spouses are given here, together with the terms used for children of the men of that matrilineage.

Distinctive Features of Navajo Kinship Terminology

Kin terms are used both for address and for reference. There are also descriptive terms that are not used in address; for example, one's mother's sister may be referred to as *shimá bideezhí,* or *shimá bádí* (MoYoSi, or MoOlSi).

Members of a clan consider themselves to be consanguineally related, and clan affiliations determine certain distant kin terms. A person, being born into his mother's clan and born for his father's clan, is related to members of both clans, and either affiliation may dictate the choice of terms.

No distinction is made between terms for the polygynous wives of one's father. Half-brothers and half-sisters are usually addressed and described by the same terms as are used for full brothers and sisters. However, in the case of a man marrying a woman and her daughter by a previous marriage, a child of the younger woman may address and refer to his father's son by the older woman as *shidá'í* (MoBr).

The term *-lah* is used for sibling of opposite sex regardless of relative age; *-k'is* is used for sibling of same sex regardless of relative age. Women may also address brothers as *-k'is*, and the same term may even be used by both sexes for men and women friends. However, we were told that to use this term to address a friend is not polite, but is rather like saying, "Hi, buddy!" A Chinle friend and informant wrote this response in answer to a question asking for the custom there, "A brother never calls his sister *sik'is*. This is very vulgar. Ditto a sister to brother. However, a brother can call another brother *sik'is* and ditto with sisters. Same goes for [parallel] cousins. As a rule *sik'is* is used almost exclusively by male to male cousins and female to female cousins. I feel that a lot of times *sik'is* is interpreted to mean friends. I may be wrong, but I do not agree with this."

There are certain very polite words, or forms of address. Our interpreter said, "If my nephew was in a polite way he would call me *shahastói* or *hadá'í*, and I, for politeness, would call my mother *hamá*." *Hastói* is a term meaning "elder male." *Sizaani* is a comparable term for "elder female." The prefix *ha-* for "one's" instead of *shi-* for "my" is the polite feature in *hamá*. One informant said that to show a greater degree of politeness to one's father, he should be addressed as *shitaa'*.

Terms of affection include the diminutives *-chó yázhí* and *-cheii yázhí* for "little grandchild," and *-dá' yázhí* for "little nephew."

Plurals are sometimes formed by adding *-ké* to the singular, such as *-bizhiké, -dá'aké* for BrCh and SiCh, man speaking. The plural of *-tsói* for grandchild is *-tsóóké*. *Sik'isóó* is the plural of *sik'is*. The term *-tsélke'é*, plural of *tsilké*, youth, is said by Young and Morgan to refer to grandsons and nephews in a group (1951:258). Our Chinle respondent says, "This is a greeting word used to address a group of young men, sometimes to flatter an older group." The term *-ch'eeke'é*, plural of *ch'iké*, maiden, is used in referring to one's granddaughters and nieces as a group, according to Young and Morgan. Again our Chinle friend differs, and describes it as the feminine counterpart of *-tséłke'é*. The term *-k'éí* refers to blood and clan relatives.

The term *-tsóí* is never used in the grandparental generation, but is a reciprocal for *-cheii* and *-chó*, which terms also serve as alternates for *-tsóí* in the grandchild generation. A son's child is *-náli*, and a daughter's child is *-tsóí*. The extension to other members of the grandchild generation is as follows: Ego will call an individual in this generation *-náli* if he is tracing the relationship through that person's father; if Ego is tracing the relationship through the individual's mother, *-tsóí* or *-cheii*/*-chó* will be used. These terms appear as regular alternates in the second descending generation even when clan terms or reciprocals may offer other choices.

Naakidi nándli (twice grandchild) is used for the children of male *-náli*, and *naakidi nacheii* and *naakidi nachó* for children of *-chó* and of female *-náli* in the grandchild generation.

Relative age affects the choice of terms in certain positions. Regular terms for siblings distinguish between older and younger brother, *-naaí* and *-tsili*, and older and younger sister, *-ádí* and *-deezhí*.

Navajos also use precise terms, "first born," "second born," and so on to "last born," to designate order of birth.

A phenomenon which reverses the generations of two individuals is explained by Navajos as "born-between," and operates in the following manner. If a mother's sister, or a mother's brother, is younger than Ego, then Ego will call this maternal aunt/uncle by a sister's daughter or sister's son term. Reciprocally, Ego will be addressed by the term used for maternal aunt/uncle. Ego will call the children of this younger-than-he (she) mother's sibling by a grand-child term, and they will answer with the reciprocal. The mother's sibling in question will call female Ego's children brother/sister, as though they were parallel cousins, and will call male Ego's children by the cross cousin terms.

For example: If Ego is *older* than his (her) mother's sibling, the following shift in generations will take place:

A. 1. Male Ego to mother's brother: "nephew" (shidá')
    2. Mother's brother to Ego: "uncle" (shidá'í)
    3. Ego to MoBr's children: "grandchildren" (shinálí)
    4. MoBr to Ego's children: "cross cousin" (female, sizeedí; male, shił naa'aash)

B. 1. Male Ego to mother's sister: "niece" (shimá yázhí)
    2. MoSi to Ego: "uncle" (shidá'í)
    3. Ego to MoSi's children: "grandchildren" (sitsói)
    4. MoSi to Ego's children: "cross cousin" (sizeedí)

C. 1. Female Ego to mother's brother: "nephew" (shiyáázh)
    2. MoBr to Ego: "aunt" (shimá yázhí)
    3. Ego to MoBr's children: "grandchildren" (shinálí)
    4. MoBr to Ego's children: "parallel cousin" (Br/Si)

D. 1. Female Ego to mother's sister: "niece" (shiché'é)
    2. MoSi to Ego: "aunt" (shimá yázhí)
    3. Ego to MoSi's children: "grandchildren" (sitsói)
    4. MoSi to Ego's children: "parallel cousin" (Br/Si)

The Navajos express such a relationship as *ata'ashish-chíín*—"I am a born-betweener," that is to say, born between one's mother and her sister, or between one's mother and her brother.

This "born-between" terminology also applies, when relative age makes it appropriate, to all of mother's cousins, who are assimilated by Ego to mother's siblings, and operates also in the extension of kin terms to clan relatives.

A peculiar difficulty in obtaining information on this subject lies in the fact that Navajos themselves are apt to be unfamiliar with the process unless circumstances were such that they or their family were directly touched by it. However, the writers, having concentrated on the accumulation of very complete genealogies, were able at Navajo Mountain to pose the question of more than a score of kin pairs where the nephew/niece was older than the uncle/aunt. In each case the answers were unequivocal in substantiating the practice.

The span of age difference is in no way a factor in determining whether the "born-between" rule is used. In three cases the mothers of small babies whose ages were positively known to us through formal records were asked what these young relatives, who were only a few months apart in age, would call each other, and what they would call each other's progeny when they would eventually have some. The answers clearly indicated that the "born-between" rule would be followed.

Inasmuch as it is generally agreed that there is some regional variation in kin-term usage among the Navajo, an attempt was made to determine whether or not the phenomenon being reported might be a local custom. Informants were found at Inscription House, Chinle, and Window Rock who confirmed that these areas do use the "born-between" terminology in a like manner.

This mechanism *does not* operate between a person and his or her father's sibling. We have instances of a shift of generation between a person's father and the father's mother's sibling who is younger than the father. The change in terminology is then followed by Ego through analogy. "I call my grandmother's brother 'cousin' because my father called him 'nephew'." In these cases it is Ego's father, not Ego, who is "born-between." We have no recorded case of a person being considered as "born-between" his or her father and a paternal aunt or uncle who is younger than Ego. It is apparent that this phenomenon occurs only within one's own matrilineage and clan and not between a member of father's matrilineage and a person who is born for that matrilineage.

Affinal terms are used only for reference. In addressing affinals, kin terms expressing blood or clan relationship will be used. If there is no other relationship, kin terms will be selected by appropriate age.

There are three principal stems, -zhá'áád, -aadaaní, and -yé ("to marry"). The term -zhá'áád is used for women, and -aadaaní for men, who have married Ego's blood kin in the first ascending and first descending generations. The term -yé (not to be confused with -ye'—"son") is used for spouses of own siblings. When Ego refers to his spouse's blood kin, Ego uses the same term and adds nishlí ("I am"). That is, while sibling's spouse is shiyé to Ego, Ego will say biyé nishlį when referring to spouse's sibling. As Aberle says, "Thus those who marry Ego's consanguines are 'his' in-laws, belonging to him. On the other hand, his wife's consanguine kin do not belong to him— he belongs to them. These usages are perfectly symmetrical for male and female speakers" (Aberle 1961:199).

The term shá'áyéhé is an alternate for shiyé, which refers to persons who have married Ego's siblings. Reciprocally, the siblings of Ego's spouse refer to Ego as bá'áshhéhé, which Young, according to Aberle, translates as "for him (her) I married." Ego and persons who have married Ego's spouse's siblings use the same, or self-reciprocal, term of reference for each other, bił 'ashxéhé, which Aberle translates as "one married into the same unit (into which I married) " (1961:199). The self-reciprocal doosh'íinii, "the one I do not see," may be used for wife's mother (man speaking) and for daughter's husband (woman speaking).

The terms for husband, *shahastiin,* and wife, *she'esdzáán,* mean "my man" and "my woman" respectively. *Shich'óóni,* an alternate, may be translated "my friend" or "my companion." It is an expression which, according to our interpreter, is "coming in lately." *Sizaani,* our informants say, is used by some old men for their wives. Other terms are *bił hinshnáanii,* which Aberle translates as "we two live together," and our informants describe as "an old term still in use," and *sha'ááá,* a vulgar term for "my wife" which is used, we were told, "by drunks." *Shiką'* is the male counterpart for "my husband," and is equally vulgar. The words mean "my female," and "my male" respectively. *Shiyé* is a "shorter form" of *shá'áyéhé. Shizhá'ááá* is used for stepmother, and *shaadaaní* for stepfather. In a letter from Chinle, we were told:

> Depends on how much love and respect you have for your stepfather, or stepmother. In case love and respect exist, they are referred to as father and/or mother. On the other hand, they may be *my mother's husband* or *my father's wife. Shaadaaní* (same as son-in-law) is also used to refer to a stepfather, and joshingly to a stepmother. If this latter term is used, the person referred to is generally further identified by name or some other recognition: viz., *Shaadaaní* Dwight; *Shaadaaní,* the councilman, etc. Clan status also becomes very important here. If stepfather is the same clan as your real father, naturally stepfather will become *shizhé'é* (my father). Same goes for stepma. If your stepfather is a member of paternal grandfather's clan he is *shináli* - it goes on and on . . . .

Our interpreter gave a list of actual terms of address which he uses for his affinals, as follows:

FaBrWi .... *shimá* .... Own clan; mother called her Si.

Wi of FaBr #2 . .*sizeedí* . . . . .She is his **MoBrDa.**

FaSiHu . . . .*shicheii* . . . . .Older member of own
clan; grandmother
called him Br.

MoBrWi . . . .*shibízhí* . . . . . . .She is **FaMoSiDa.**

Wi of MoBr #2. .*shádí* . . . . .Their fathers belong to
the same clan. Older.

WiSiHu . . . .*sitsílí* . . . . .Own clan member. A
little younger.

WiBr . . . .*shinaai* or *sik'is*. .Their fathers belong to
the same clan. Older.

WiBrWi . . . .*sizeedí* . . . . .Her father belongs to
Ego's clan. Relatively
same age.

WiBrCh . . . .*sitsóí* . . . . .Ego is tracing relationship through the
mother of these chil-
dren. Their MoFa is
a member of Ego's
clan; he is, therefore,
shicheii to them, and
they are *sitsóí* to him.

shiye' and *sitsi'*. .These are alternates
when Ego is tracing
relationship through
the children's father.
Ego calls their father
Br (see above).

WiSiCh . . . .*shiye'* and *sitsi'*. .Ego calls their father Br,
so they are BrSo and
Da.

Extension of Kin Terms by Clan Affiliation

Our interpreter explained the Navajo system of extending
kin terms to clan relatives in the following words: "If an

individual is a *Tó dích'ii'nii* [own clan] I will figure his relationship through my mother, but if he is a *Ashįįhí* like my father, then I will figure through what my father would call him. My father's father, *shinálí*, is a *Tł'izí łání* clansman; therefore, all *Tł'izí łání* are *shinálí* to me. All *Lók'aa' dine'é* [mother's father's clan] are *shicheii* and *shichó* to me. If a person is born for *Ashįįhí* as I am born for *Ashįįhí* then we always call each other Br and Si no matter what the difference in age is."

The rules for the extension of kin terms by clan and clan group are as follows:

1. Kin terms extended to members of own clan and clan group are selected, by appropriate age or by analogy, from terms used for relatives, male and female, who belong to Ego's matrilineage. (See Chart No. 3) .

2. Kin terms for members of father's clan are selected, by appropriate age or by analogy, from terms used for relatives, male and female, who belong to Ego's father's matrilineage. (See Chart No. 4).

3. Persons whose fathers belong to the same clan address each other as Br/Si regardless of age or generation.

4. Ego will address an individual who is born for his clan by the term that is appropriate with regard to relative age, chosen from those terms used for children of men of Ego's matrilineage. (See Chart No. 3). It may be noted that these terms will always be reciprocals of the terms selected under rule 2, since to the individual born for Ego's clan, Ego is a member of father's clan.

5. All members of mother's father's clan are -*cheii*/-*chó*.

6. All members of father's father's clan are -*nálí*.

Theoretically, the same rules of exogamy apply to linked clans that apply to own-clan affiliations. That is, one does not marry into clans linked with own clan, or with father's clan. (See p. 205.) Kin terms are extended to members of linked clans according to the same rules that govern the extension of consanguineal kin terms by clan affiliation. In practice, however, as was previously discussed in detail (see Part II), Navajos distinguish between two types of clans, those that are "the same," and those that are "only friendly." The rules that apply to own clan do not apply to the second type.

Distant Relatives

The term "distant relative" is given by Murdock to a kin position linked to Ego through at least three intermediate relatives (1949:95). Persons in quaternary or more distant positions among Navajos may be addressed by several alternate terms, depending on whether the term is governed by (1) generation, (2) analogy, that is, Sol Tax's principle of uniform descent (Eggan, 1955:19), (3) reciprocity, or (4) clan extension.

(1) *Generation*: Alternates in the grandchild generation are -*tsói*, or -*cheii*/-*chó*, if Ego traces his relationship to that person through the individual's mother. The term -*náli* may be used in the grandchild generation for an individual to whom Ego traces relationship through that person's father. These terms are governed by reciprocity. The term -*náli* is self-reciprocal, as are -*cheii* and -*chó*. The term -*tsói* appears only is descending generations, whereas -*cheii* and -*chó* appear in both second ascending generation and second descending generation. Father's cousins may be merged with father's siblings; mother's cousins may be merged with mother's siblings, yielding -*bizhí* on the paternal side, and -*dá'i* or -*yádzh* (woman speaking) and -*má yázhí* on the maternal side. Reichard suggests that this merging of father's and mother's cousins with father's and mother's siblings is a feature of several Southern Athabascan languages (1928:79). It appears to be true for Kiowa-Apache, and true, ex-

cept for clan-influenced positions, among the Western
Apache (Bellah 1952:50, 95). In a personal communication,
September 13, 1963, Morris E. Opler says:

> Among the Chiricahua, Mescalero, Jicarilla, and Lipan
> the same terms are generally used to ego's mother's and
> father's siblings and cousins. There are some exceptions
> to this. The Mescalero may use the "mother" term for
> mother's sister, but they are not likely to use this term to
> a mother's female cousin. They tend to use an alterna-
> tive term instead. In like manner, among the Mescalero,
> the "father" term can be used to the father's brother.
> But ordinarily an alternative "father's brother" term
> will be used to a father's male cousin. But I wouldn't
> call these practices a feature of Athabascan languages.
> To my mind it is a matter of social classification and
> usage.

(2) The principle of *analogy* gives the following alternates: children of all relatives whom Ego calls Br/Si are
called So/Da, and their children are regarded as Ego's
grandchildren.

(3) By the principle of *reciprocity*, alternate terms for
MoBrDaSo/Da are *-dá'* and *-má yázhí* (*-yáázh* and *-ché'é*,
woman speaking) which are reciprocal terms for mother's
cousins, since Ego is MoFaSiSo/Da, that is, *-dá'í* or *-má
yázhí* to the paired kin in this position. Following this line
of reasoning, MoBrSoCh may be called *-bízhí*, since Ego is
their FaFaSiSo/Da.

(4) *Clan extension*: Terms governed by clan extension
fall into two categories. The first of these comprises what
we have called "regular clan alternates," that is, clan terms
used in positions where, through the rules of matrilineal
descent, the paired relative must belong either to Ego's own
clan, to his FaFa's clan, to his MoFa's clan, or is born for the
same clan that Ego is born for. Terms in these positions

regularly follow the rules explained under (3) *Extension of Kin Terms by Clan Affiliation* (p. 222). Thus FaFaSiSo/ Da may be called *-náli* as one alternate, since they are *always* members of FaFa's clan. FaMoBrSo/Da may be called Br/Si, as may FaSiSoCh and FaSiDaSoCh, since they are *always* born for the same clan that Ego is born for.

Another set of regular clan alternates in quaternary and more distant positions is governed by both clan extension and reciprocity. It is best explained from the point of view of the kin paired with Ego. For example, MoBrSoCh call Ego *-náli* because he *always* belongs to their FaFa's clan. Reciprocally, Ego then calls MoBrSoCh *-náli*. Similarly, MoBrDaCh can call Ego *-cheii/-chó* because Ego is a member of their MoFa's clan. Reciprocally Ego calls them *-cheii/-chó* or *-tsói*.

In addition to the regular clan-determined alternates, there are those alternates based on the specific (not positionally-determined) clan relationships between the specific paired kin. Terms may be influenced by any one of four different types of paired clan relationship: own clan, father's clan, MoFa clan, and FaFa clan.

There must be added to these regular, logically restricted choices the influence of relative age and affection in the selection of some alternate kin terms—what Herbert Landar, after Bloomfield, has called "complementary fluctuation in the frequency of forms" (1962:997). In our view, the bewildering number of alternates in Navajo kinship terminology, particularly in the distant positions, which has so long baffled the ethnographer and the linguist, is the result of the operation of the multiple principles we have detailed and of the variety of clan relationships that govern these distant kin terms.

Chart No. 5 is designed to illustrate the range of clan relationships which could exist between Ego and one set of

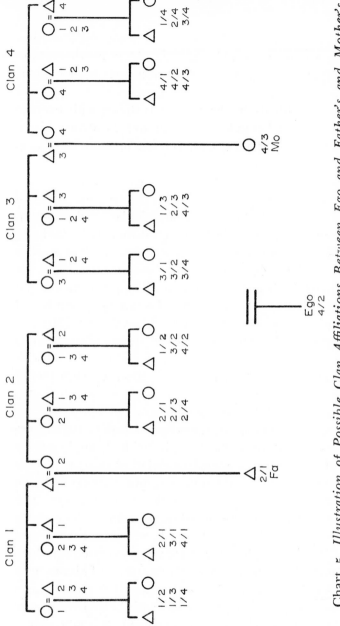

Chart 5. *Illustration of Possible Clan Affiliations Between Ego and Father's and Mother's Cousins Which Yield Alternate Kinship Terms*

(First numeral represents Ego's clan. Second numeral represents father's clan)

quaternary relatives, his father's and mother's cousins. Such relationships would yield kinship terms that would be acceptable alternates to those terms shown on Chart No. 1.

Each individual on Chart No. 5 is shown with two numerals, the first being his own clan and the second his father's clan. For instance, Ego, 4/2, is a member of Clan 4, and is born for Clan 2.

Reading from left to right on the chart, it will be seen that *Ego's father's cross cousins on the paternal side* will always belong to Ego's father's father's clan, and Ego may, therefore, call them *-náli*. However, if their father belongs to Clan 2, as does Ego's father, they may then call each other Br and Si, since they are born for the same clan. If, on the other hand, their father belongs to Clan 4, this means that they are born for Ego's clan and he can call them by an appropriate term chosen from terms used for children of the men of Ego's matrilineage. Likely terms would be *-dá'í* and *-má yázhí* if these individuals are on an age level with Ego's mother, *-cheii* and *-chó* if their ages are nearer that of Ego's mother's mother, or *-ił naa'aash* (*-zeedí*, woman speaking), and *-zeedí* if they are nearer Ego's age.

Moving to the next category—*Ego's father's paternal parallel cousins*—we note that these individuals might belong to Clan 2, the same clan that Ego's father belongs to, thus permitting Ego to call them by an appropriate term chosen from terms available in Ego's father's matrilineage. The factor of relative age would allow a spread of choice from *-náli* to *-bizhi* to *-ił naa'aash* (*-zeedí*, woman speaking) and *-zeedí*. If these people belong to Clan 3, Ego could call them *-cheii* and *-chó* since they would be members of his mother's father's clan; or they might belong to Clan 4, Ego's own clan, and be called, according to relative age, by terms selected from Ego's matrilineage, *-cheii* and *-chó*, *-dá'í* (*-yáázh*, woman speaking) and *-má yázhí*, or Br and Si.

Following the same reasoning we find that the various possibilities that may be brought about by chance clan relationships are as listed below. Regular clan-determined alternates are not included.

Father's maternal parallel cousins:

2/4—born for Ego's clan—most likely terms would be *-cheii* and *-chó*, *-dá'i and -má yázhi*, or *-ił naa'aash* (*-zeedi*, woman speaking) and *-zeedi*, terms used for the children of men of Ego's matrilineage.

Father's maternal cross cousins:

1/2—members of Ego's father's father's clan — *-náli*.

3/2—members of Ego's mother's father's clan — *-cheii/-chó*.

4/2—members of Ego's clan—any appropriate term from Ego's matrilineage.

Mother's paternal cross cousins:

3/2—born for the same clan that Ego is born for—Br and Si.

3/4—born for Ego's clan—most likely terms would be *-cheii* and *-chó*, *-dá'i* and *-má yázhi*, or *-ił naa'aash* (*-zeedi*, woman speaking) and *-zeedi*, terms used for the children of men of Ego's matrilineage.

Mother's paternal parallel cousins:

1/3—members of Ego's father's father's clan — *-náli*.

2/3—members of Ego's father's clan — *-náli*, *-bízhi*, or *-ił naa'aash* (*-zeedi*, woman speaking) and *-zeedi*.

4/3—members of Ego's clan—any appropriate term from Ego's matrilineage.

Mother's maternal parallel cousins:

4/2—born for the same clan Ego is born for—Br and Si.

Mother's maternal cross cousins:

1/4—members of Ego's father's father's clan — *-náli*.

2/4—members of Ego's father's clan—an appropriate term from Ego's father's matrilineage.

3/4—members of Ego's mother's father's clan — *-cheii* and *-chó*.

THE BASES FOR CHOICE AMONG ALTERNATES FOR
DISTANT POSITIONS

In the much-intermarried community of Navajo Mountain, many of our informants found it possible to trace distant relationships through several kinsmen, and we were faced with the problem of determining why certain alternates were chosen over others. Twenty-five cases of multiple choice in address terms were analyzed for the following components in the relationship of paired kin to Ego: (1) blood kinship, (2) own-clan membership, (3) membership in father's clan, (4) fathers belong to the same clan, (5) paired kin's father is a member of Ego's clan, (6) paired kin is a member of Ego's mother's father's clan, or (7) paired kin is a member of Ego's father's father's clan. When relationship could be traced through more than one relative, the following components were also considered: whether the choice was through (a) Ego's mother, (b) Ego's father, (c) paired kin's mother, (d) paired kin's father, (e) Ego's closest biological kin, or (f) through proximity, that is, through the relative with whom Ego interacted most.

We had expected that blood relationship would supersede clan ties, that close relatives would be more important links than the distant ones, that maternal, rather than paternal, relatives would be considered more significant channels of kinship, and that, among clan affiliations, own clan would be chosen over other clan relationships for the selection of terms. However, no one component was completely dominant. Clan affiliation sometimes overrode biological relationship. Proximity was the strongest component in indicating the kinsman through whom relationship would be traced. Of clan affiliations, the "born for" relationship was the strongest. Membership in own clan was next in frequency, and membership in mother's father's or even father's father's clan appeared more important than distant biological relationship. Sex of the connecting kin was irrelevant. Evidence from a study of multiple choices, then, tends to substantiate the claim, made by Navajos in their theoretical explanations, that distant positions are regarded as clan, rather than traceable consanguineal relationships.

Changes and Regional Variations

Unfortunately, not enough data have been assembled through the use of genealogies and specific clan affiliations to make possible a definitive assessment of the changes and regional variations in Navajo kinship terminology today. William T. Ross has collected schedules for Fruitland (1955), Herbert Landar has sampled opinions for Shiprock, Many Farms, and Fort Defiance (1962), and David Aberle gives a few variants for other communities (1961). However, unless kin terms are collected from a number of different individuals in each region, it is difficult to see the regularities within the great variety of specific relationships.

Several changes appear to be widespread. For example, the use of -taa' for Fa which is found in the origin myths is becoming obsolescent. Only one person gave us the term in Navajo Mountain. The use of -k'a'i as an alternate for MoSi is also infrequent. A 17-year-old boy told us there was no such word. Several older Navajos gave us the word as an alternate, but our interpreter explained, "They are getting out of that around here." If so, this indicates a trend away from collaterality (see p. 234).

The term -bizhi, although used extensively at Navajo Mountain for FaSi, may also be on the way to obsolescence.

A Shiprock informant said that -*bizhí* was "old-fashioned"
and the -*má yázhí* is preferable for FaSi. There is some evidence elsewhere that -*tsi'* and -*yé* are preferred to -*bizhí* for
BrDa/So, man speaking. Also, five people gave -*yáázh* and
-*ché'é* as alternates for -*bizhí* when a woman is speaking of,
or to, a BrSo/Da. This suggests a trend away from bifurcation (see p. 234).

We did not hear of any tendency to call cross cousins Br
and Si and parallel cousins So/Da or to use cross cousin
terms for FaBrCh, as Aberle reports in *Trial Run* (1955).

The disagreement about whether or not women can call
their brothers or nonrelated men -*k'is* may be based on
regional differences. A Chinle informant characterizes this
usage as "very vulgar." However, our interpreter and his
niece, while assisting Shepardson to write a postcard to her
professors at the University of Chicago, advised her to address them as *sik'isóó*. (There is always the possibility that
the interpreters were having a Navajo joke at an ethnographer's expense.)

Further differences of opinion may spring from regional
variations. Navajo friends from Lukachukai, Fort Defiance,
and Chinle say that -*chó* is used only for MoMoMo while
-*má sání* must be used for MoMo. In Navajo Mountain we
were told that they used -*chó* for MoMo, "because it is
shorter." The informants who came from the central and
eastern parts of the Reservation said that even when one of
the two wives in a polygynous marriage is the daughter of
the older wife, the children of these women by the same
father would call each other Br/Si rather than MoBr/MoSi
to SiSo/SiDa, as Reichard reports (1928:81) and as we
found to be true in the only case we could verify in Navajo
Mountain. The sibling relationship is considered to override in importance the mother-daughter tie of the respec-
tive mothers in the more acculturated areas mentioned.

Criteria for Distinguishing Terms

George Peter Murdock, following Robert Lowie and Alfred Kroeber, gives six major criteria for distinguishing kinship terms: (1) generation, (2) sex, (3) affinity, (4) collaterality—belonging to the same ancestral stock but not in a direct line of descent as opposed to lineal, (5) bifurcation (forking) —applying one term to a kinsman if the relative linking him to Ego is male and quite another term if the connecting relative is female (Murdock, 1949:104), and (6) polarity —a kin relationship involves two people and when each member of that dyad denotes the other by a different term, the criterion of polarity is being used; if polarity is ignored and both members of the dyad use the same term to denote each other the term is called a self-reciprocal. Three subsidiary criteria are (7) relative age, (8) speaker's sex, and (9) decedence—this criterion applies when a distinction of kin term is made on the basis of whether or not the connecting relative is alive or dead. These nine criteria severally and in combination include all the principles employed in the linguistic classification and differentiation of kinsmen (Murdock, 1949:101).

(1) The Navajo kinship terminology recognizes *generation,* but this is a weak principle because it is overridden by the many self-reciprocals, by the extension of kin terms through clan relationship, and by the phenomenon which Navajos call "born between," which reverses the generations.

(2) *Sex differentiation* is a criterion but is ignored in at least one set of terms, or alternates, in each of the four generations, first and second ascending and first and second descending. In own generation it is ignored in only one term, *cross cousin,* woman speaking.

(3) The criterion of *affinity* does not affect terms of address. Affinals are addressed by kin terms based on consanguineal relationship, on the extension of consanguineal terms by clan relationship, or on blood-kin terms chosen by appropriate age even if no actual blood relationship exists.

(4) *Collaterality* is a weak principle. That is, Navajos do not distinguish sharply between lineal and collateral relatives. There is no term in the nuclear family which is not extended to a collateral line. The terms for cross cousins, *-ił naa'aash* (*-zeedi*, woman speaking) and *-zeedi*, and for maternal aunt and uncle, *-k'a'i* and *-dá'i*, and paternal aunt and uncle, *-bizhi*, appear only in collateral lines. Occasionally, terms will merge in collateral lines, but will not merge with lineal terms.

(5) *Bifurcation* is an important principle, inasmuch as many terms depend on the sex of the last or, viewed reciprocally, the first connecting relative. For example, *-náli* as opposed to *-tsói* depends on whether or not the connection to Ego is made through the "grandchild's" father or through the mother. Terms in secondary positions depend on whether or not the link to Ego is through father or through mother. However, because of the frequent use of self-reciprocals, Ego-based charts have an asymmetrical appearance, because terms associated with the paternal side appear on the maternal side and vice versa.

(6) *Polarity* gives linguistic recognition to two terms for paired relations. This is overridden in many cases in the Navajo kinship system by the use of self-reciprocals.

(7) The criterion of *relative age* is important. It is expressed in sibling terms for older and younger brother, older and younger sister. It is, however, overridden by alternates *-k'is* and *-lah*. The use of *-dá'i* and *-dá'*, the first to express older, and the second to express younger, uncle-nephew relationships is controversial. Some informants

claim that the use is optional. The term -yáázh may be used
by a woman for a man of any age. Some Navajos claim there
is no distinction by age for -má and -má yázhí, and for -zhé'é
and -zhé'é yázhí. However, the use of -yázhí in such expres-
sions as -zhé'é yázhí, -chó yázhí, -cheii yázhí gives an affectionate quality to the relationship terms. The selection of
kin terms by affect, or emotional tone, is important in
Navajo.

(8) *Speaker's sex* differentiates principally terms used for
own children which are then extended to other positions.
A woman uses different words for son and daughter; a
man for cross cousin; and the use of terms -k'is and -lah,
since they are used for sibling of the same sex, and sibling
of the opposite sex, differs for man and woman speaking.

(9) *Decedence* is not a criterion in Navajo. A dead relative will be given a kin term as referent with 'ádin, "no
more," or ńt'ę́'ę́ę, "former," added.

Classification of the kinship system

Murdock classifies the Navajo kinship system as Iroquois,
because female cross cousins are called by the same term,
-zeedí, but distinguished from female parallel cousins, who
are merged with sister. It belongs to the Normal Iroquois
type, he says, because the system is characterized by matri-
liny, matrilocal residence, monogamy or sororal polygyny,
matriclans, matrilineal extension of the incest taboos, and
aunt and niece terms of the bifurcate merging type, with
alternate use of aunt/niece terms of the bifurcate collateral
type (1949:244).

We found aunt terms of the bifurcate merging type (one
term for mother and mother's sister, and another term for
father's sister) with alternate use of a mother's sister term
which yields a bifurcate collateral type (separate terms for

mother, mother's sister, and father's sister). Niece terms are of the bifurcate merging type for both man and woman speaker (one term for daughter and sister's daughter, and a different term for brother's daughter, woman speaking; one term for daughter and brother's daughter, and a separate term for sister's daughter, man speaking). There is an alternate term for brother's daughter, man speaking, which yields a bifurcate collateral type (separate terms for daughter, brother's daughter, and sister's daughter). There is no alternate for sister's daughter, woman speaking.

Kinship terminology, social groups, and role behavior

The nuclear family is not emphasized in Navajo terminology. All primary terms are extended to collateral lines, suggesting the existence of a wider kin group as the principal social unit. The extended family is, in fact, the preferred form of cooperative residential group and is more frequently encountered than is the nuclear family.

The unity of the lineage group is one of the structural principles by which a society organizes its kinship system. Radcliffe-Brown defines a lineage as a man [woman] and all his [her] descendants through males [females] for a determinate number of generations. "A lineage group consists of all the members of a lineage who are alive at a particular time . . . Lineages, both patrilineal and matrilineal, exist implicitly in any kinship system, but it is only in some systems that the solidarity of the lineage group is an important feature in the social structure" (1952:70).

Among the Navajo, the lineage principle can be seen through the extension of one kinship term, -nálí, to all members of FaFa matrilineage (and clan) and the extension of one set of terms, -cheii/-chó, to all members of MoFa matrilineage (and clan). All persons whose fathers belong to the same clan are equated with the close position of sibling, a usage that emphasizes the importance of Fa matrilineage (and clan) as a unit. Bellah says, "There seems to be some tendency to call women in own clan Mo (-*má*) or a variation thereof, regardless of generation" (1952:119). This is true for first, second, and third ascending generations: -*má* (Mo); -*má* or -*má yázhí* (MoSi); -*má sání* (**MoMo**) and (MoMoMo). It is also true for first descending generation, man speaking: -*má yázhí* (SiDa). But it does not hold for own generation either for Si or for MoSiDa (parallel cousin) or for the second descending generation (SiDaDa). Also, there are alternates for the -*má* term for MoSi (-*k'a'í*) and MoMo (-*chó*).

Although the lineage principle is to be found in Navajo terminology, it does not appear to be as strong as it is in the kinship terminology of some societies. There are no alternates for maternal cross cousin to suggest a change toward a Crow system, the extreme example of emphasis on matrilineage. Perhaps the use of one set of terms as alternates for members of MoFa matrilineage and for FaFa matrilineage shows only a tendency to simplify the classifications of the more distant relatives.

The similarity of terms for both maternal and paternal cousins and the many self-reciprocals that obscure the distinction between paternal and maternal relatives in distant positions suggest the importance of both father's and mother's kin in interaction. The extension of kin terms by clan indicates the importance of father's as well as mother's lineage and clan affiliations since they provide a wide network of potentially useful relationships in a society where kinship is the principal mode of integration.

Relative age is stressed in the four sibling terms and in the meticulous manner in which each child is designated by a reference term specifying order of birth. In a personal communication, Morris E. Opler writes:

The Chiricahua and Mescalero have no special terms for older or younger sibling. There are no special statuses or privileges for older sibling either. But the Jicarilla and the Lipan do have terms for older and younger sibling and have associated practices and expectations, too. This is especially true of the Jicarilla, where the older sibling has considerable authority over the younger. Thus Apache usage in this respect is not uniform and it is obvious that it is not an Athabascan linguistic feature that is operating.

But Harry Hoijer, in reconstructing Proto-Athabascan from terms in cognate sets for 32 Athabascan languages (14 substocks), gives at least six terms for brother and sister that express relative age. One would be forced to conclude, then, that this is an Athabascan linguistic feature appearing in Navajo whether or not the distinctions are stressed in action. We did not find the importance of relative age in sibling terminology to be correlated with behavior.

David M. Schneider distinguishes between kin terms that classify kinsmen in genealogical positions and those that express socially defined roles (1956:17). Both are found among terms for close relatives in Navajo. The extension of some terms from lineal to collateral lines and across generations indicates that some roles are equated socially rather than by genealogical position. One can infer, however, from the fact that clan membership offers alternate terms only in distant positions, that genealogical relationship is of importance for close relatives. The many self-reciprocals and the classification of lineal and collateral relatives in several cases under a single term suggest that there is a similarity of behavior and emotional affect in these paired positions. The classificatory term that equates Mo with MoSi is a reflection of the tendency of mother's sister to assume the mother role in emergencies. The equation of Fa with FaBr reflects a real obligation on the part of the paternal uncle toward his brother's children, however secondary in importance to the duties expected of the maternal relatives.

The large number of alternates in the kin terms correctly mirrors the Navajo flexibility that assigns the performance of a specific act to a preferred kin role but also permits such assignment to an alternate kin role.

Differences in emotional quality of kin relationships are indicated in various ways, as Herbert Landar pointed out in an article. His conclusions confirmed our generalizations. He says, "Investigation shows that it is possible to resolve some . . . putative contradictions by recognizing that clan membership of Ego's kinsmen, and in some cases Ego's attitude toward his kinsmen, are determinative factors in the selection of a kinship term . . . ." (1962:3). The use of variants with the diminutive *yázhí* to give an affectionate tinge to a kin term illustrates this (*-má yázhí*; *-zhé'é yázhí*). The several terms for spouse exemplify choices that express degrees of affection, respect, or even joking. Insistence upon the quality of the relationship by affect rather than by genealogical position appears to be correlated with the lack of stratification in Navajo society.

Terms that highlight generation carry overtones of superordination-subordination, whereas those that override generation tend to obscure this. Thus the choice of generation terms may indicate the type of affect expected in the paired relationship. Except in the nuclear family there is an overriding of generations. This indicates the tendency to keep a superordinate-subordinate relationship more clearly defined in role behavior within the nuclear family than elsewhere.

The fact that affinal terms for reference are segregated from genealogical kin terms suggests that affinal relations are regarded as different in quality, with different rights and obligations, from consanguineal relationships. There is a distinct set of reference terms for affinals, and members of the lineage of one's spouse are treated as a group in reference terminology. A man or a woman refers to the siblings of his or her spouse as *ba'áshhéhé*, "for him (her, them) I married," and to the spouses of wife's or husband's siblings as *bił 'áshxéhé*, "one who married into the same unit I married into." The difference in the quality of relationship between affinals and blood relationships is shown in avoidance behavior and in the joking patterns. However, the practice of extending genealogical terms to affinals in *address* may show that Navajos strive to overcome the difference.

We may conclude, as Schneider does for the Zuni, that Navajos are more interested in actual interpersonal relations than in their genealogical position. Kroeber says of the Zuni, "Their primary impulse is to have some designation of kinship for everyone possible, but [they] normally are far more interested in the person as such, and in his actual status toward themselves, than in the logical consistency or exactness of his designation" (1917:77).

Navajo society does not have a network of complex interlocking corporate groups, but it does possess a network of extended kinship ties through lineages, clans, and clan groups. This is a far-flung web of latent relationships, ready at hand to be activated in kin terminology and kin behavior whenever this is expedient, desirable, or urgent.

PART FOUR

CONCLUSION

In the course of a search for the key to the Navajo social system a title suggested itself: *It's Up to Him: a Study in Navajo Social Organization.* Just as this is a Navajo informant's regular response to questions about expected behavior, so it is his view of the society's patterned relations. For a short time, this phrase seemed also to sum up our view of Navajo social structure. Interrelations in Navajo society as exemplified by the Navajo Mountain community are so fluid and so flexible that we almost despaired of finding any patterned regularities, any "musts," with the exception of clan exogamy. The society we were contemplating, it seemed, was a model for pure philosophical anarchy.

The second problem that we encountered was finding the proper form in which to summarize our raw data on patterns of cooperation, concrete groups, and component roles.

They could not be subsumed completely under property relations, stratification, status symbols, structured groups, or determined roles in life crises. We could not meaningfully characterize Navajo social structure by interaction frequency, by quantifying the relative power weights of paired roles, by order of closeness and distance, or exclusively by any one of the many methods that have been used with varying success to analyze social relations in such societies as the Hopi, the Trukese, the Nuer, and others.

Certain basic societal functions must be performed: earning a living, regulating sexual activity, rearing the children, controlling social behavior, dealing with the surrounding society, and meeting the life crises of birth, puberty, marriage, illness, and death. We have directed the analysis to what must be done, who is expected to do it, and for whom and with whom it can be done.

Persistence in Navajo Mountain is perhaps even more striking than change when we consider that this small traditional community is surrounded by the most highly industrialized country in the world. The explanation may lie principally in the fact that orientation to the old pastoral economy and small-scale agriculture, although modified, is still basically intact. Nor are there any plans for large-scale development of alternate ways of making a living in the community. Not only the traditional social interaction patterns, rules of residence, types of groups, forms of marriage and preferred roles, but the whole value system is integrated about the sheep herds. Vogt has called Navajo an "incorporative" society (1961:328). Certainly the Navajo Mountain community has ingested outside patterns of sporadic wage work, welfare payments, and migratory labor; but these serve to subsidize rather than to disrupt the pastoral economy, and thus permit the persistence of old values and behavior patterns which obviously still offer much satisfaction to a people who have been socialized in this way of life.

Navajo society is accomplishment- or performance-oriented. The basic philosophy is pragmatic and utilitarian; the content of the Navajo moral code reflects a practical preoccupation with practical problems (Ladd, 1957:208). Navajos are more concerned with accomplishment than with the preservation of the vested interests, or the sanctioned forms, of any particular social role or any concrete unit in their society. It is more important to Navajos to get a job done, plant a field, herd a flock, bring a child into the world, marry off a son or a daughter, or cure a relative than it is to protect special rights and obligations of a role or the form of a particular concrete group.

There emerged from our analysis the evidence that Navajo society is by no means unstructured, chaotic, or anarchistic. There are preferred patterns of cooperation and preferred roles in each social event. With the exception of the basic biological limitations imposed by age, sex, and health, and the social rules governing incest, almost every interaction rule, every form of structural group, every role in the role system has alternates, and most of the decision-making is by negotiation. For each activity there is a preferred pattern of interaction, and preferred role players are assigned to regular tasks, but if the proper group is not constituted, or the proper role incumbent is unavailable, then other groups and other categories of kin will be acceptable for the desired purpose.

Causes of the extreme flexibility and the large numbers of alternates in behavior patterns may very well lie in the rapid increase and dispersal of Navajo family groups over a large area, as Aberle so cogently explains (1961:130). Changing from a hunting and gathering society of small wandering bands into a pastoral economy that required transhumance for the flocks reinforced scattered residence patterns. The extended family with a network of lineages and clans to integrate a wider circle is consistent with this basic economy. In turn, scattered residence patterns, moving about, and a high death rate often meant that a full complement of relatives was not present to play the socially proper roles at the crucial times, hence alternates were needed.

Flexibility is consistent with the demands of the situation and with a value system that emphasizes pragmatism, rationalism, and the nonauthoritarian, harmonious interrelation of kinsmen. The variations are not regional. They are not random. In all of Navajo society, decisions as to who is to do what are negotiated around a series of principles and preferred patterns, *ad hoc.*

APPENDIX

Table A.—*Size of Camps and Hogans, 1961*

Camp	Number of Persons	House-hold	Number of Persons	Camp	Number of Persons	House-hold	Number of Persons
1	22	a	1	21	14	a	2
		b	8			b	12
		c	4	22	15	a	1
		d	3			b	12
		e	6			c	2
2	10	a	1	23	2	a	2
		b	2				
		c	5	24	11	a	1
		d	2			b	4
3	23	a	7			c	2
		b	10			d	4
		c	6	25	13	a	13
4	15	a	1	26	11	a	3
		b	5			b	3
		c	7			c	2
		d	2			d	3
5	18	a	18	27	2	a	2
6	22	a	1	28	10	a	10
		b	8				
		c	4	29	12	a	12
		d	5	30	11	a	11
		e	4	31	25	a	7
7	21	a	5			b	7
		b	11			c	8
		c	5			d	3
8	14	a	7	32	11	a	1
		b	3			b	5
		c	4			c	5
9	33	a	1	33	24	a	2
		b	6			b	10
		c	5			c	7

Table A—(cont.)

Camp	Number of Persons	House-hold	Number of Persons	Camp	Number of Persons	House-hold	Number of Persons
		d	3			d	5
		e	5	34	6	a	5
		f	6			b	1
		g	3	35	3	a	1
		h	4			b	2
10	13	a	13	36	5	a	1
11	2	a	2			b	4
12	6	a	1	37	5	a	5
		b	2	38	13	a	2
		c	3			b	6
13	13	a	4			c	2
		b	9			d	3
14	12	a	12	39	9	a	9
15	11	a	11	40	20	a	11
16	17	a	8			b	6
		b	5			c	3
		c	4	41	6	a	6
17	16	a	6	42	14	a	2
		b	8			b	6
		c	2			c	6
18	11	a	3	43	13	a	11
		b	8			b	2
19	6	a	1	44	11	a	11
		b	5	45	1	a	1
20	24	a	9	46	2	a	2
		b	8	School Com-pound	3		
		c	7				

Table B.—*Composition of Camps, 1960-61*

CAMP	RESIDENCE-TYPE[1]	HOGAN	RESIDENCE-TYPE[2]	ADULTS		CHILDREN[3]
				MEN	WOMEN	
1	Bilocal	a	Head-of-camp	[*T'izí táni*, b. circa 1857, d. 1941]	= *Ashįįhí*, b. 1875.	0
		b	Patrilocal	*Ashįįhí*, So of Wi in *a* by previous marriage to a *T'izí táni*, b. 1895.	= *Táchii'nii*, from Kaibito b. 1911.	6
		c	Matrilocal	*T'izí táni*, from Oraibi, b. 1936.	= *Táchii'nii*, Da couple in *b*; b. 1937.	2
		d	Patrilocal	*Táchii'nii*, So of Hu in *b* by earlier Wi - present wife's Si, divorced, b. 1930.	= *T'izí táni*, from Tuba City, b. circa 1935.	1
		e	Matrilocal	[*Tó dích'íi'nii*, lives with Wi in 10*a*, sororal polygyny]	= *Ashįįhí*, Wi in *a*.'s deceased sister's Da. Adopted by *a*; b. 1921.	5
2	Mixed	a	Head-of-camp	[Same as Camp 1*a*, sororal polygyny]	= *Ashįįhí*, Si of Wi in 1*a*; b. 1870.	0
		b	Consanguineolocal	*Tábąąhá*, from Kaibito, b. 1923.	= *Ashįįhí*, DaDa of couple in *a*, b. 1925.	0
		c	do.	*Ashįįhí*, DaSo of couple in *a*; b. 1923.	= *Tábąąhá*, Da of couple in 44*a*; b. 1939.	3
		d	do.		*Ashįįhí*, DaDa couple in *a*; b. 1940. Fa and Mo deceased.	0
					Ashįįhí, DaDaDa couple in *a*; b. 1939. Fa and Mo deceased.	0
3	Matrilocal	a	Head-of-camp	[*T'izí táni*, b. 1893, d. 1950]	= *Ashįįhí*, Da man in 4*a* and woman in 12*a*; b. 1907.	6

No.	Residence	Husband / Person	= Wife / Spouse
8	b .... matrilocal	*Tó dich'ii'nii* from Shonto b. 1925.	= *Ashįįhí*, Da couple in *a*; b. 1930.
4	c ..... do.	*Táchii'nii* from Inscription House, b. 1931.	= *Ashįįhí*, Da couple in *a*; b. 1927.
0	4 Bilocal .... a ....Head-of-camp	*Tábąąhá*, from Inscription House; b. 1861.	= [*Ashįįhí*, b. circa 1888, d. 1955.] = [Divorced from woman in 12a. Sororal polygyny.]
3	b .... Matrilocal	*Tó dich'ii'nii*, from Kaibito; b. 1928.	= *Ashįįhí*, Da of couple *a*; b. 1928.
5	c ..... do.	*Tł'izí láni*, from Oljeto; b. 1921.	= *Ashįįhí*, Da of couple *a*; b. 1925.
0	d ...Patrilocal	*Ashįįhí*, So of couple *a*; b. 1930.	= *Lók'aa' diné'é*, from Shonto; b. 1935.
10	5 Neolocal ...... a ....Neolocal	*Tó dich'ii'nii*, from Shonto; b. 1924.	= *Tł'izí láni*, Da of Hu in 7b and his first wife, now deceased; b. 1927.
5	Neolocal polygynous.........		= *Tł'izí láni*, Si of above, sororal polygyny; b. 1929.
6	6 Mixed .... a ....Consanguineolocal		= *Tó dich'ii'nii*, Unmarried. Si of Wi in *b*, Wi in *c*, and men in *e*; b. 1921.
2	b.... do.	*Bił'ahnii*, from Oljeto; b. 1915.	= *Tó dich'ii'nii*. Si of woman in *a*, Wi in *c*, men in *e*; b. 1918.
3	c ..... do.	*Mą'ii deeshgiizhnii*, from Pinon, b. circa 1930.	= *Tó dich'ii'nii*, Si of woman in *a*, Wi in *b*, men in *e*; b. circa 1931.
	d ...Patrilocal	*Tó dich'ii'nii*, So of couple in *b*; b. 1932.	= *Táchii'nii*, Da of couple in 1*b*; b. 1939.

Table B—(cont.)

CAMP	RESIDENCE-TYPE¹	HOGAN	RESIDENCE-TYPE²	MEN	ADULTS WOMEN		CHILDREN³

CAMP	RESIDENCE-TYPE[1]	HOGAN	RESIDENCE-TYPE[2]	MEN	WOMEN	CHILDREN[3]
		e	Consanguineolocal	*Tó dich'ii'nii*, b. 1935. b. 1933. " b. 1938. " b. 1941. (These men are unmarried, brothers of women in *a*, wives in *b* and *c*.)		
7	Matrilocal..........	*a*	Head-of-camp	*Táchii'nii*, from Kaibito; b. 1895.	= *Tó dich'ii'nii*, half-sister of Hu in 8*a* and Hu in 17*a*; b. 1910.	3
		b	Matrilocal	*Ashįįhí*, So of 4*a*; b. 1904. (Four of the children in *b* are by the first wife of the Hu; the mother, deceased, was from Shonto, a *Tł'izí łąní*, sister of Hu in 15 and Wi in 16*a*.)	= *Tó dich'ii'nii*, Da of couple in *a*; b. 1926.	9
		c	Matrilocal	*Tł'izí łąní*, from Tall Mountain; b. 1937. (The three children in *c* are by a first husband, now deceased, who was a brother of the present husband)	= *Tó dich'ii'nii*, Da of couple in *a*; b. 1927.	3
8	Matrilocal..........	*a*	Head-of-camp	*Tó dich'ii'nii*, half-brother of Wi in 7*a*; b. 1891. (Three of the children in *a* are the "adopted" children of a deceased daughter; father of children is a *Tł'izí łąní* now living outside)	= *Ashįįhí*, Da of 4*a*; b. 1908.	5
		b	Matrilocal	*Lók'aa' dine'é*, So of couple in 27 *a*; b. 1929.	= *Ashįįhí*, Da of couple in *a*; b. 1932.	1
		c	do.	*Tłááschʼí*, from Tuba City; b. circa 1900.	= *Ashįįhí*, Da of couple in *a*; b. 1923.	2
9	Bilocal..........	*a*	Head-of-camp	[*Lók'aa' dine'é*, b. circa 1860; d. 1954]	= *Tó dich'ii'nii*, b. 1871.	0

	b .... Matrilocal	Ashįįhí, So of 2a; b. 1887.	= Tó dich'ii'nii, Da of a; b. 1903.	4
	c .... do.	T'iizí łání, from Nakai Canyon; b. 1930.	= Tó dich'ii'nii, Da of man in b; b. 1921.	3
	d .... do.	[T'iizí łání, from Oljeto, b. 1925, d. 1947]	= Tó dich'ii'nii, Da of man in b; b. 1925.	2
	e .... do.	T'iizí łání, from Inscription House, b. 1931.	= Tó dich'ii'nii, Da of man in b; b. 1931.	3
	f .... do.	Tábąąhá, from Cow Springs, b. 1923.	= Tó dich'ii'nii, Da of man in b; b. 1933.	4
	g .... Patrilocal	Tó dich'ii'nii, So of couple in b; b. 1928.	= Táchii'nii, Da of 45a; b. 1941.	1
	h .... do.	Tó dich'ii'nii, So of couple in b; b. 1934.	= Łók'aa' dine'é, from Shonto, b. 1941.	2

(First 3 women shown as daughters of man in b are by his first wife and the fourth is by his third wife, both deceased, sisters of present wife; sororal polygyny)

10 Neolocal	a .... Neolocal	Tó dich'ii'nii, So of 9a; b. 1914.	= Ashįįhí, "adopted" Da of 1a; b. 1916.	11
11 Neolocal	a .... do.	Ashįįhí, DaSo of 2a; b. 1918.	= Honágháahnii, from Kaibito, b. 1920.	0
12 Bilocal	a .... Head-of-camp	[Tábąąhá (4a) Divorced]	= Ashįįhí, Si of Wi 4a and Hu 13a; b. 1891.	0
	b .... Matrilocal	Táchii'nii, from Tall Mountain, b. 1925.	= Ashįįhí, Da of a; b. 1926.	0
	c .... Patrilocal	Ashįįhí, So of a; b. 1936.	= Táchii'nii, Si of Hu in b; b. 1934.	1
13 Matrilocal	a .... Head-of-camp	Ashįįhí, Brof 12a; b. 1880.	= Kįyaa'áanii, Da of woman in 19a; b. 1911.	2
	b .... Matrilocal	Ashįįhí, So of 12a woman and 4a man; b. 1920.	= Kįyaa'áanii, Da of Wi in a by an earlier husband; b. 1933.	7

Table B—(cont.)

| CAMP | RESIDENCE-TYPE¹ | HOGAN RESIDENCE-TYPE² | ADULTS | | CHILDREN³ |
			MEN	WOMEN	
14	Neolocal	a....Neolocal	Ashįhi, So of woman in 12a and man in 4a; b. 1919.	= Tł'izí łání, Da of man in 20a by deceased wife. Raised by MoSi in Tall Mountain, b. 1922.	10
15	Neolocal	a.... do.	Tł'izí łání, from Shonto, Br of Wi 16a; b. 1916.	= Ashįhi, Da of 4a; b. 1922.	9
16	Matrilocal	a.... Head-of-camp	Ashįhi, So of 4a; b. 1906.	= Tł'izí łání, from Shonto, Si of Hu 15a; b. 1918.	6
		b.... Matrilocal	Tó dich'ii'nii, from Shonto, b. 1933.	= Tł'izí łání, Da of couple a; b. 1933.	3
		c.... do.	Tó dich'ii'nii, from Inscription House, b. 1934.	= Tł'izí łání, Da of couple a; b. 1935.	2
17	Matrilocal	a.... Head-of-camp	Tó dich'ii'nii, ½ Br Wi 7a; b. 1907.	= Ashįhi, Da of couple 4a. Si of deceased first wife, sororate; b. 1920.	4
		b... Matrilocal	Tł'izí łání, from Inscription House, b. 1919.	= Ashįhi, Da of Hu in a and first wife; b. 1929.	6
		c.... do.	[Táchii'nii, from Kaibito, divorced; b. 1935.	= Ashįhi, Da of couple in a; b. 1937.	1
18	Matrilocal	a.... Head-of-camp	Táchii'nii, from Inscription House, b. 1899.	= Tó dich'ii'nii, Si of siblings in Camp 6; b. 1919.	1
		b.... Matrilocal	Hashk'ąą hadzohó, from Oljeto, SiHuSiSo to man in 4c; b. 1931.	= Tó dich'ii'nii, Da of Wi in a; b. 1937.	6
19	Matrilocal	a.... Head-of-camp	[Tó dich'ii'nii, So of couple 9a; b. circa 1890; d. 1946] Ashįhi, So of 12a; b. 1933.	= Kiyaa'áanii, from Rock Point, b. circa 1895.	0
		b.... Matrilocal	Ashįhi, So of 12a; b. 1933.	= Kiyaa'áanii, Da of a; b. 1934.	3

20	Matrilocal..........a...Head-of-camp	*Tó dich'ii'nii*, So of couple 9a; b. 1897.	= *Tábąąhá*, Da of couple 21a; b. 1916.	7
	b....Matrilocal	*Ashįįhí*, So of couple 8a; b. 1927.	= *Tábąąhá*, Da of Wi in a and first husband, man in 39a; b. 1934.	6
	c..... do.	*Ashįįhí*, So of deceased Da of 12a; b. 1930.	= *Tábąąhá*, Da of couple in a; b. 1937.	5
21	Patrilocal..........a....Head-of-camp	Paiute *Ashįįhí*, b. 1882.	= *Tábąąhá*, from Mexican Springs, b. circa 1895.	0
	b....Patrilocal	*Tábąąhá*, So couple in a; b. 1921.	= *Tó dich'ii'nii*, from Inscription House, b. 1922.	10
22	Matrilocal..........a....Head-of-camp	[*Tó dich'ii'nii*. Divorced, now in 38a; b. 1882.]	= Paiute *Ashįįhí*, Mo of Wi in 38a, Mo-Da polygyny; b. 1873.	0
	b...Matrilocal	*Tⱱizí táni*, from Inscription House, b. 1906.	= Paiute *Ashįįhí*, Da of couple a; b. 1916.	10
	c..... do.	[*Tó dich'ii'nii*, So of couple 7a; deceased; b. 1929; d. 1958.]	= Paiute *Ashįįhí*, Da of couple a; b. 1941.	1
23	Neolocal..........a...Neolocal	*Tⱱizí táni*, from Oljeto, b. 1903.	= Paiute *Ashįįhí*, Da of couple 22a; b. 1906.	0
24	Patrilocal..........a....Head-of-camp	[*Tó dich'ii'nii*, b. circa 1866; d. circa 1940]	= *Tábąąhá*, from Kaibito, b. 1881.	0
	b....Patrilocal	*Tábąąhá*, So of couple a; b. 1895.	= *Lók'aa' diné'é*, Si of Wi in c; Mo of Wi in d. Sororal and Mo-Da polygyny; b. 1900.	2
	c..... do.	Man shown in b.	= *Lók'aa' diné'é*, Si of Wife in b; b. 1904.	1
	d.... do.	" " "	= *Lók'aa' diné'é*, Da of Wi in b; b. circa 1920.	3

[The 3 children in d are "adopted." Mother, deceased, was sister to Wi in d. Father is So of couple in 46a. Remarried and living outside.]

Table B—*(cont.)*

CAMP	RESIDENCE-TYPE[1]	HOGAN	RESIDENCE-TYPE[2]	MEN	ADULTS WOMEN	CHILDREN[3]
25	Neolocal	a	Neolocal	Paiute *Ashįįhi*, So of couple 22a; b. 1916.	= *Lók'aa' dine'é*, Da of couple 24b; b. 1926.	11
26	Bilocal	a	Head-of-camp	[*T'ízi tání*, b. 1867; d. 1945]	= *Lók'aa' dine'é*, Si of women in 24b and c; b. 1908.	2
		b	Matrilocal	Paiute *Ashįįhi*, So of 22a; b. circa 1915.	= *Lók'aa' dine'é*, Da of couple a; b. 1936.	1
		c	do.	*Táchii'nii*, from Tall Mt., parallel cousin of *Táchii'nii* man and woman in Camp 12; b. 1934.	= *Lók'aa' dine'é*, Da of couple a; b. 1940.	0
		d	Patrilocal	*Lók'aa' dine'é*, So of couple a; b. 1938.	= Paiute *Ashįįhi*, Da of couple 22b; b. 1944.	1
27	Neolocal	a	Neolocal	*Tábąąhá*, b. 1905.	= *Lók'aa' dine'é*, Si of women 24b and c; b. 1910.	0
28	Neolocal	a	do.	*Bit'ahnii*, Br of Wi in 33a and Hu 39a; Fa of Wi in 40c; b. 1902.	= *Tó dich'ii'nii*, from Oljeto, b. 1938.	8
29	Neolocal	a	do.	*Bit'ahnii*, So of Hu 19a and Wi in 33a; b. 1917.	= Paiute *Ashįįhi*, Si of Wi in 30a; b. circa 1917.	10
30	Neolocal	a	do.	*Lók'aa' dine'é*, from Shonto, So of Hu 26b and divorced wife; b. 1923.	= Paiute *Ashįįhi*, Si of Wi in 29a; b. 1918.	9
31	Bilocal	a	Head-of-camp	Paiute *Ashįįhi*, MoBr to Wi in 30a and Wi in 40c; b. 1905.	= *Táchii'nii*, from Oljeto; b. 1906.	5
		b	Patrilocal	*Táchii'nii*, So of a; b. 1926.	= *Bit'ahnii*, Da of 33a; b. 1918.	5

No.	Category		Residence	Individual	Spouse (=)	Children
		c	Matrilocal	Lók'aa' dine'é, So of 26a; b. 1930.	= Táchii'nii, Da of a; b. 1930.	6
		d	do.	Bit'ahnii, So of deceased Si of woman in 33a; b. 1916.	= Táchii'nii, Da of a; b. 1929.	1
32	Mixed..........	a	Head-of-camp	[Tʾízi tání, FaBr to man in 6b; b. 1866; d. 1956]	= Paiute Ashįįhí, Si of Hu 33a; ½ Si of Wi in 22a and Hu in 21a; b. 1889.	0
		b	Matrilocal	Kiyaa'áanii, So of 19a; b. 1931.	= Paiute Ashįįhí, Da of a; b. 1934.	3
		c	Consanguineolocal	[Táchii'nii, divorced]	= Táchii'nii, MoSiSoDa of Wi in a; Da of 45a; b. 1931.	4
33	Matrilocal.......	a	Head-of-camp	[Paiute Ashįįhí, b. 1896; d. 1952.]	= Bit'ahnii, Si of Hu in 28a; Hu in 39a; Mo of Hu in 29a; b. 1900.	1
		b	Matrilocal	[Paiute Ashįįhí, So of couple 28a; b. 1923. Divorced.]	= Bit'ahnii, Da of a; b. 1919.	9
		c	do.	Tʾízi tání, from Tall Mountain, b. 1929.	= Bit'ahnii, Da of a; b. 1933.	5
		d	do.	Tábąąhá, So of couple in 20a; b. 1939.	= Bit'ahnii, Da of b; b. 1940.	3
34	Mixed..........	a	Consanguineolocal	[Ashįįhí, now Hu 13a. Divorced]	= Paiute, b. 1880.	0
		b	do.	Paiute, b. 1928, So of woman in 35.	= Paiute, b. 1934.	3
35	Mixed..........	a	do.	Paiute, b. 1912. Br of woman in b.	= [Divorced; now deceased, Da of 34a.]	0
		b	do.	Paiute, never married, but mother of 6 children.		1
36	Matrilocal.......	a	Head-of-camp	Fa of Wi in b; b. 1890.	= [Paiute, deceased]	0
		b	Matrilocal	Paiute, So of woman in 35b; b. 1934.	= Paiute, b. 1924.	2
				(The two children in b are by divorced first husband, the present Hu in 40c)		

Table B—*(cont.)*

CAMP	RESIDENCE-TYPE[1]	HOGAN RESIDENCE-TYPE[2]	ADULTS — MEN	WOMEN	CHILDREN[3]
37	Neolocal	*a*....Neolocal	Paiute *Ashįįhí*, b. 1871. (The three children are "adopted." Children of son)	= Paiute, b. 1894.	3
38	Mixed	*a*....Head-of-camp	*Tó dich'ii'nii*, b. 1882.	= Paiute *Ashįįhí*, Da of 22*a*.	0
		b....Patrilocal	So of couple in *a*; b. 1911.	= *Lók'aa diné'é*, from Oljeto, Si of Wi in *c*	4
		c.... do.	Same as *b*. Polygyny	= *Lók'aa diné'é*, from Oljeto, Si of Wi in *b*	1
		d....Consanguineolocal	Paiute *Ashįįhí*, b. 1924.	= *Tó dich'ii'nii*, b. 1933.	1
39	Neolocal	*a*....Neolocal	*Bit'ahnii*, parallel Co of man in 6*b*; b. 1895.	= Paiute *Ashįįhí*, Da of man in 46*a*; b. 1926.	7
40	Mixed	*a*....Head-of-camp	Paiute *Ashįįhí*, So of 32*a*; b. 1925.	= *Kiyaa'áanii*, Da of 19*a*; b. 1920.	9
		b....Matrilocal	*T'izí tání*, from Tall Mountain, b. 1924.	= *Kiyaa'áanii*, Da of Wi in *a* and first Hu, Br of present husband. Levirate; b. 1938.	4
		c....Consanguineolocal	*Kiyaa'áanii*, So of 19*a*; Br woman in *a*; b. 1926.	= Paiute *Ashįįhí*, Da of Hu in 28*a*; b. 1937.	1
41	Neolocal	*a*....Neolocal	*Tábąąhá*, half-brother of Hu in 27*a*; b. 1930.	= *Bit'ahnii*, Da of 33*a*; b. 1930.	4
42	Mixed	*a*....Head-of-camp	*T'izí tání*, Fa to Hu 8*a* by early marriage to a woman now deceased; Fa to wives in 1*e* and 10*a* by another woman now deceased. B. 1879.	= *Tó dich'ii'nii*, from Shonto; b. 1883.	0

b . . . . Matrilocal and patrilocal	Ashįįhí, So of man in *a*; Br of women 1*e* and 10*a*; b. 1910.	= Tó dích'íi'nii, Da of Wi in *a* by a former husband, a Tábąąhá; b. 1920.	4
c . . . . Consanguineolocal	Tó dích'íi'nii, DaSo of Wi in *a*; b. 1928.	= T'ízí tání, Da of Hu in 7*b*; b. circa 1928.	4
43 Matrilocal . . . . a . . . . Head-of-camp	Naakaii dine'é, from Inscription House, b. 1902. Tábąąhá	= Ashįįhí, Da of Hu in 42*a*.	9
b . . . . Matrilocal		= Ashįįhí, Da of couple in *a*.	0
44 Neolocal . . . . . . a . . . Neolocal	T'ízí tání, b. 1906.	= Tábąąhá, b. 1921.	9
45 Neolocal . . . . . . a . . . . . . do.	Paiute Ashįįhí, Fa of woman in 32*c*; b. 1889.	= [Táchii'nii, divorced, now living in Kayenta.]	0
46 Neolocal . . . . . . a . . . . . . do.	Táchii'nii, Fa of Wi in 39*a* by deceased wife who was the daughter of present wife by a former husband, a Naakaii dine'é (Mo-Da polygyny); b. 1879.	= Paiute Ashįįhí, b. 1891.	0
School compound	Lok'aa' dine'é woman, half-sister of Hu in 12*b* and Wi in 12*c*; unmarried; b. 1940.		1
	Lok'aa' dine'é woman, sister of children in 24*d*; b. 1940.		0

1 *Residence-type camps:*

Matrilocal—when the camp is made up of households of senior kinsmen and those of married daughters.

Patrilocal—when the camp is made up of households of senior kinsmen and those of married sons.

Bilocal—when the camp is made up of households of senior kinsmen and those of both married daughters and married sons.

Neolocal—when the camp consists of one independent household.

Mixed—when the residence unit contains households of couples or individuals who are not the children of head-of-camp.

2 *Residence-type hogans:*

Head-of-camp—senior kinsman or senior couple.

Matrilocal—when a hogan is attached to the camp of the wife's parents.

Patrilocal—when a hogan is attached to the camp of the husband's parents.

Neolocal—when the hogan is an independent family household.

Consanguineolocal—when the hogan is attached to a camp through other types of kin relationship.

3 Unmarried offspring, not necessarily minor children.

(Individuals shown within brackets are not present.)

Table C.—*Translation of Navajo Clan Names*

Adoo'tsosni	The Narrow Gorge People
Áshįįhi	The Salt People
Bįįh bitoodnii	The Deer Spring People
Bit'ahnii	The Within-His-Cover People
Chishi dine'é	The Apache People
Deeshchii'nii	The Start-of-the-Red-Streak People
Dibé łizhini	The Black Sheep People
Dzaanééz łáni	The Many Burros People
Dziłtł'ahnii	The Mountain Recess People
Haltsooi dine'é	The Meadow People
Hashk'ąą hadzohó	The Yucca-Fruit-Strung-Out-in-a-Line People
Hashtł'ishnii	The Mud People
Honágháahnii	The He-Walks-Around People
Kin łichii'nii	The Red House People
Kiyaa'áanii	The Towering House People
Lók'aa' dine'é	The Reed People
Mą'ii deeshgiizhnii	The Coyote Pass People
Naakaii dine'é	The Mexican People
Naaneesht'ézhi táchii'nii	The Charcoal-Streaked *Táchii'ni* People
Nát'oh dine'é	The Tobacco People
Nihoobáanii	The Grey-Streak-Ends People
Shash dine'é	The Bear People
T'aadii dine'é	The Slow-Talking People
Tábąąhá	The Water's Edge People
Táchii'nii	The Red-Running-Into-the-Water People
Ta'neeszahnii	The Tangle People
Tł'ááshchí'i	The Red Streak People
Tł'izi łáni	The Many Goats People
Tó'áháni	The Near-to-Water People
Tó'aheedliinii	The Water-Flows-Together People
Tó dích'ii'nii	The Bitter Water People
Tódokǫzhí	The Alkaline Water People
Tótsohnii	The Big Water People
Ts'ah yisk'idnii	The Sage Brush Hill People
Tsé deeshgizhnii	The Rock Gap People
Tséikeehé	The Two-Rocks-Sit People
Tsé kinaake'é	
Tsé ńjikini	The Honeycombed Rock People
Tsi'naajinii	The Black Rock People
Tsin sikaadnii	The Clumped Tree People
Yé'ii dine'é	The Monster People
Yoo'ó dine'é	The Bead People

Table D.—*Localized Lineages**

CLAN AND LINEAGE	PROVENIENCE	DATE OF SETTLEMENT
	Rainbow Plateau	
Tł'ízí łání		
1.	Navajo Canyon via Tuba City	1860 (circa)
2.	Tuba City	1960
Áshįįhí		
1.	Black Mesa	1890
Tó dích'íinii		
1.	Shonto via Black Mesa	1904
2.	Kayenta	1910
3.	Inscription House	1940
Táchii'nii		
1.	Kaibito	1920
2.	Tall Mountain via Oljeto	1960
Tábąąhá		
1.	Mexican Springs	1920 (circa)
2.	Navajo Canyon via Shonto	1930 (circa)
Kiyaa'danii		
1.	Rock Point	1921
Honághahnii		
1.	Shonto	1939
Lókaa' dine'é		
1.	Shonto	1960
2.	Tall Mountain	1961
	Northeastern Section	
Paiute *Áshįįhí*		
1.	Indigenous	
Bit'ahnii		
1.	Oljeto	1907
Táchii'nii		
3.	Kayenta	1910
4.	?	1920 (circa)
Tó dích'íinii		
4.	Oljeto	1948
Kiyaa'danii		
1.	Rainbow Plateau via Rock Point	1935
	Paiute Mesa	
Paiute *Áshįįhí*		
1.	Indigenous, Paiute Canyon	
Lókaa' dine'é		
3.	Oljeto	1930
4.	Kayenta	1950 (circa)
Tábąąhá		
3.	Kaibito	1893
Tó dích'íinii		
5.	Inscription House	1953
	Navajo Canyon	
Áshįįhí		
1.	Rainbow Plateau via Black Mesa	1927
Tábąąhá		
2.	Shonto	1930 (circa)
Tó dích'íinii	Shonto	1940 (circa)

* *Localized matrilineages* are based on descent through females that can be traced to the living residents of Navajo Mountain as of 1960–61.

Founding lineages were cited on p. 40 to give historical depth to Navajo occupancy of the area but may or may not have left any living descendants through females.

Chart A. *Frequency of Intermarriage Between Clans in 322 Marriages*

	Anglo	Apache	Áshįįhí	Áshįįhí (Paiute)	Bit'ahnii	Dibé łizhiní	Hashk'ǫǫ hadzohó	Honágháahnii	Hopi	Kiyaa'áanii	Lók'aa' dine'é	Mǫ'ii deeshgiizhnii	Mexican	Naakaii dine'é	Paiute	Shash dine'é	Tábąąhá	Táchii'nii	Ta'neeszahnii	Tł'ááshchí'í	Tł'ízí łání	Tó dích'íi'nii	Tsi'naajinii	Ute Táchii'nii	Yé'ii dine'é
Anglo		1																				1			
Apache																						1			
Áshįįhí					2		1			6	4			1	2		10	11	1		22	25	2		1
Áshįįhí (Paiute)					15					6	11			5	1	1	8				11	15	1		
Bit'ahnii						1			1								3	3			8	10			
Dibé łizhiní																									
Hashk'ǫǫ hadzohó																						1			
Honágháahnii											2						2	1							
Hopi																						1			
Kiyaa'áanii												1		1			2	3							
Lók'aa' dine'é														5	5		3	7							
Mǫ'ii deeshgiizhnii																						2			
Mexican																						1			
Naakaii dine'é															3						1	1			
Paiute																						2			
Shash dine'é																									
Tábąąhá																			1		10	9			
Táchii'nii																					9	18		2	
Ta'neeszahnii																						1			
Tł'ááshchí'í																									
Tł'ízí łání																						36			
Tó dích'íi'nii																							1		
Tsi'naajinii																									
Ute Táchii'nii																									
Yé'ii dine'é																									

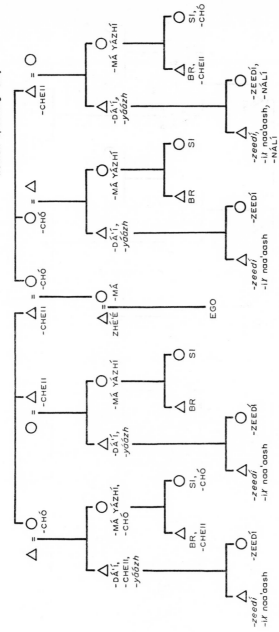

MAN SPEAKING / WOMAN SPEAKING
man speaking only
woman speaking only

Chart B. *Terminology for Children of Mother's Cousins*

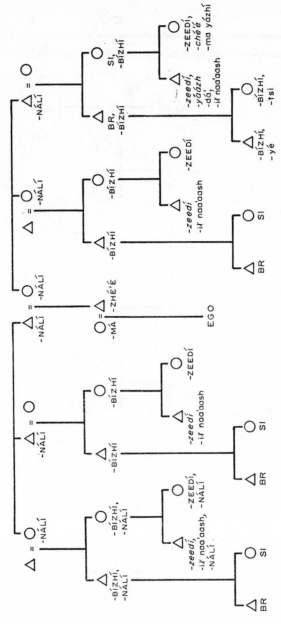

MAN SPEAKING / WOMAN SPEAKING
man speaking only
woman speaking only

Chart C. *Terminology for Children of Father's Cousins*

BIBLIOGRAPHY

A Committee of the Royal Anthropological Institution of Great
Britain and Ireland
1954 *Notes and Queries on Anthropology*. London, Rout-
ledge and Kegan Paul, Ltd.
Aberle, David F.
1955 *Navaho Kinship: A Trial Run*. Unpublished MS.
1961 "Navaho." In *Matrilineal Kinship*. David M. Schneider and Kathleen Gough, (eds.) Berkeley, University
of California Press.
1963 "Some Sources of Flexibility in Navaho Social Organization." *Southwestern Journal of Anthropology*, 19:
1–8.
Aberle, D. F., A. K. Cohen, A. K. Davis, M. J. Levy, Jr., F. X.
Sutton
1950 "The Functional Prerequisites of a Society." *Ethics*,
60: 100–111.
Adams, William Y.
1963 *Shonto: A Study of the Role of the Trader in a Modern
Navaho Community*. Washington, D. C., Smithsonian
Institution. Bureau of American Ethnology Bulletin
188.
Bailey, L. R.
1964 *The Long Walk*. Los Angeles, Westernlore Press.
Barnes, J. A.
1960 "Marriage and Residential Continuity." *American
Anthropologist*, 64:850–866.

Beals, Ralph L., George W. Brainerd, and Watson Smith
1945 *Archaeological Studies in Northeast Arizona: A Report on the Archaeological Work of the Rainbow Bridge-Monument Valley Expedition.* Berkeley and Los Angeles, University of California Press.

Bellah, Robert N.
1952 *Apache Kinship Systems.* Cambridge, Mass., Harvard University Press.

Bohannon, Paul
1963 *Social Anthropology.* New York, Holt, Rinehart and Winston.

Bolton, Herbert E.
1950 *Pageant in the Wilderness.* Salt Lake City, Utah Historical Society.

Bosch, James
n.d. *Navajo Marriage.* Unpublished MS.

Boyer, Ruth McDonald
1962 *Social Structure and Socialization among the Apaches of the Mescalero Reservation.* Unpublished Ph.D. dissertation, University of California at Berkeley.

Brugge, David M.
1964 "Vizcarra's Navajo Campaign of 1823." *Arizona and the West.* Tucson, University of Arizona Press.

Collier, Malcolm Carr
1966 *Local Organization among the Navaho.* New Haven, Connecticut, Human Relations Area Files, Inc.

Cleland, Robert Glass and Juanita Brooks
1955 (eds.) *A Mormon Chronicle: the Diaries of John D. Lee.* The Huntington Library.

Crampton, C. Gregory
1964 *Standing Up Country.* New York, Alfred A. Knopf.

Dyk, Walter
1938 *Son of Old Man Hat.* New York, Harcourt, Brace and Co.

1947 *A Navaho Autobiography.* Viking Fund Publications in Anthropology, No. 8. New York, Johnson Reprint Corporation.

Eggan, Fred

   1950   *Social Organization of the Western Pueblos.* Chicago, University of Chicago Press.

   1955   (ed.) *Social Anthropology of North American Tribes.* Chicago, University of Chicago Press.

Ferguson, Frances

   1966   *The Peer Group and Navaho Problem Drinking.* Unpublished MS.

Fischer, J. L.

   1958   "The Classification of Residence in Censuses." *American Anthropologist,* 60:508–517.

Franciscan Fathers

   1910   *An Ethnologic Dictionary of the Navaho Language.* Saint Michaels, Arizona.

Gillmor, Frances and Louisa Wade Wetherill

   1952   *Traders to the Navajos.* Albuquerque, University of New Mexico Press.

Goodenough, Ward H.

   1956   "Residence Rules." *Southwestern Journal of Anthropology,* 12:22–37.

Gough, Kathleen

   1961   "Nayar: Central Kerala." In *Matrilineal Kinship.* David M. Schneider and Kathleen Gough (eds.), Berkeley, University of California Press.

Gross, Neal, Ward S. Mason, and Alexander W. McEachern

   1958   *Explorations in Role Analysis.* New York, John Wiley and Sons.

Hammond, Blodwen and Mary Shepardson

   1965   "The 'Born-Between' Phenomenon among the Navajo." *American Anthropologist,* 67:1516–1517.

Kaut, Charles R.

   1957   *The Western Apache Clan System: Its Origins and Development.* Albuquerque, University of New Mexico Press.

Kelly, Charles

   1941   "Hoskaninnii." *Desert Magazine,* July.

   1953   "Chief Hoskaninni." *Utah Historical Quarterly,* July.

Kildare, Maurice
    1965 "Chief Scarbreast, Master Killer." *The West*, November, pp. 20–23.
    1966 "Builders to the Rainbow." *Frontier Times*, July, pp. 14–17.
Kimball, Solon T. and John H. Provinse
    1942 "Navajo Social Organization in Land Use Planning." *Applied Anthropology*, 1:18–25.
Kling, Samuel G.
    1965 *The Legal Encyclopedia for Home and Business*. New York, Pocket Books, Inc.
Kluckhohn, Clyde
    1933 *Beyond the Rainbow*. Boston, The Christopher Publishing House.
    1962 *Navaho Witchcraft*. Boston, Beacon Press.
Kluckhohn, Clyde and Dorothea Leighton
    1946 *The Navaho*. Cambridge, Mass., Harvard University Press.
Kroeber, Alfred
    1917 "Zuni Kin and Clan." In *American Museum of Natural History, Anthropological Papers*, v. 18, pt. 2.
Ladd, John
    1957 *The Structure of a Moral Code*. Cambridge, Mass., Harvard University Press.
LaFarge, Oliver
    1929 *Laughing Boy*. Cambridge, Mass., The Riverside Press.
Landar, Herbert
    1962 "Fluctuation of Forms in Navaho Kinship Terminology." *American Anthropologist*, 64:985–1000.
Leach, E. R.
    1966 *Rethinking Anthropology*. London School of Economics, Monographs on Social Anthropology No. 22. New York, Humanities Press, Inc.
Levy, Jerrold E.
    1962 "Community Organization of the Western Navajo." *American Anthropologist*, 64:781–802.
Little, James A.
    1881 "Jacob Hamblin." In *Three Mormon Classics*, com-

piled by Preston Nibley, 1944. Salt Lake City, Stevens and Wallis, Inc.

Murdock, George Peter

1949   *Social Structure*. New York, The Macmillan Co.

Radcliffe-Brown, A. R.

1952   *Structure and Function in Primitive Society*. Glencoe, Illinois, The Free Press.

1956   "Introduction." In *African Systems of Kinship and Marriage*, (eds.) A. R. Radcliffe-Brown and Daryll Forde, New York, Oxford University Press.

Reichard, Gladys A.

1928   *Social Life of the Navajo Indians*. New York, Columbia University Press.

1950   *Navaho Religion*. New York, Bollingen Series 18, Pantheon Books.

Ross, William T.

1955   *Navaho Kinship and Social Organization*. Ph.D. dissertation, University of Chicago. Microfilm.

Schneider, David M. and John M. Roberts

1956   *Zuni Kin Terms*. Laboratory of Anthropology Notebook No. 3, University of Nebraska.

Shepardson, Mary and Blodwen Hammond

1964   "Change and Persistence in an Isolated Navajo Community." *American Anthropologist*, 66:1029–1049.

1966   "Navajo Inheritance Patterns: Random or Regular?" *Ethnology*, 5:87–96.

Spencer, Katherine

1947   *Reflection of Social Life in the Navaho Origin Myth*. Albuquerque, The University of New Mexico Press.

1957   *Mythology and Values: An Analysis of Navaho Chantway Myths*. Philadelphia, American Folklore Society, vol. 48.

Stokes, M. A. and T. L. Smiley

1964   "Tree-Ring Dates from the Navajo Land Claim." *Tree-Ring Bulletin*, Vol. 26, No. 1–4, pp. 13–27.

Vogt, Evon Z.

1960   "On the Concepts of Structure and Process in Cultural

Anthropology." *American Anthropologist*, 62:18—34.

Young, Robert W.

1961 *The Navajo Yearbook, Report No. VIII.* Window
Rock, Arizona, The Navajo Agency.

Young, Robert W. and William Morgan

1951 *A Vocabulary of Colloquial Navaho.* Washington,
D. C., United States Indian Service.

1954 *Navajo Historical Selections.* Navajo Historical Series,
No. 3. Washington, D. C., Bureau of Indian Affairs.

1958 *The Navaho Language.* United States Indian Service.
Salt Lake City, Deseret Press edition.

DOCUMENTS

Museum of Northern Arizona

1961 Payroll, Glen Canyon Archaeological Survey, Flagstaff, Arizona.

Navajo Tribal Council

1962 *Navajo Tribal Code.* Orford, N. H., Equity Publishing
Co. Files, Land Claims Division. Window Rock,
Arizona. Navajo Mountain Chapter Reports. Window
Rock, Arizona.

1961, 1962 Payroll, Public Works Projects. Window Rock,
Arizona.

Navajo Tribal Courts

Case Records. Window Rock, Arizona.

State of Arizona

Department of Welfare Reports, Phoenix, Arizona.

State of Utah

Department of Welfare Reports, Monticello, Utah.

United States Government

Letterbooks of Navajo Agents. National Archives,
Washington, D. C.

Navajo Agency

1961, 1962 Grazing Reports. Window Rock, Arizona.

1961 Payroll, Navajo Mountain School.
Tuba City, Arizona.

U.S. Federal District Courts
  Case Records. Phoenix, Arizona.
  Case Records. Salt Lake City, Utah.
U.S. Public Health Service
  1960, 1961, 1962 Payroll for Navajo Mountain
                    Water Development. Window
                    Rock, Arizona.
U.S. Supreme Court
  1959 Williams v. Lee (358 U.S. 217)

INDEX